ALFRED'S Group Piano
FOR ADULTS

BOOK 1
SECOND EDITION

An Innovative Method Enhanced with
Audio and MIDI Files for Practice and Performance*

E. L. Lancaster • Kenon D. Renfrow

*The MIDI accompaniments were created using the sound set from the
Yamaha Clavinova CVP 407. These files were then converted to audio using
the USB Audio Recorder function on the CVP 407.

Second Edition
Copyright © MMIV by Alfred Publishing Co., Inc.
All rights reserved.   Printed in USA.

Alfred Publishing Co., Inc.
16320 Roscoe Blvd., Suite 100
P. O. Box 10003
Van Nuys, CA 91410-0003
alfred.com

Lancaster, E. L.
        Alfred's group piano for adults : an innovative method
    enhanced with audio and MIDI files for practice and performance
    / E. L. Lancaster, Kenon D. Renfrow.
        v. of music.
        Includes index.
        ISBN-10: 0-7390-5301-9
        ISBN-13: 978-0-7390-5301-0 (v. 1)
        1. Piano—Methods—Group instruction.   I. Renfrow,
    Kenon D.   II. Title.
    Library of Congress Control Number: 94-43951

Cover art: *Composition rythme. 1955.*
            Sonia Delaunay
            © L&M Services B. V. Amsterdam 20040102

Foreword

Alfred's Group Piano for Adults, Book 1, is designed for non-keyboard music majors with little or no keyboard experience. It also may be used successfully by independent teachers seeking creative ways to develop functional skills in their adult students. Upon completion of this book, students will have a strong grasp of functional skills, keyboard technique and musical styles, and will be ready to begin *Alfred's Group Piano for Adults, Book 2.*

Importance of Piano Study: Most music educators agree that the piano is indispensable for all musicians. Piano study helps students gain a better understanding of music theory as theoretical concepts are applied to the keyboard. Many music majors who have had no previous piano experience find the first piano classes challenging. Experience has proven that with the proper approach and consistent practice, anyone can grasp the skills necessary to function and perform at the keyboard.

General Features: The text is easy to use. It contains 26 units, each designed to be covered in one week, thus filling two semesters or three quarters of study. Schools that have longer semesters or quarters can use additional weeks for reinforcement, review and testing. Theory, technique, sight reading, repertoire, harmonization, improvisation and ensemble activities are taught thoroughly and consistently throughout the text. Descriptions of other general features follow:

- Each unit contains a balance of new information with materials that reinforce concepts presented in previous units.

- The title page of each unit contains the objectives for the unit and a space to record assignments for the week.

- Measures are numbered in all examples (repertoire, reading, harmonization, improvisation) to promote ease of use in the classroom.

- Written review worksheets, designed to be submitted to the teacher for feedback, appear periodically throughout the text.

Reading Approach: The reading approach is eclectic, combining the best elements of intervallic and multi-key reading. Reading exercises are designed to promote movement over the entire keyboard while maintaining the advantages of playing in familiar positions. Reading examples are a mixture of standard repertoire and newly composed pieces.

Rhythm Approach: Suggestions for counting are given, but the approach used is left to the discretion of the teacher. Rhythms and note values are introduced systematically, and specially designed rhythm-reading exercises promote rhythmic security.

Technical Approach: Technique is developed in a systematic way throughout the entire book. Repertoire, harmonization melodies, technical exercises and sight-reading examples are carefully fingered to aid the student in developing good technique.

Repertoire: The student begins to play music immediately. Each unit has at least one repertoire piece that may be used for performance or study. A section of supplementary repertoire is contained in the back of the book for those students who need additional music or for teachers who like a wider choice of music for students. The supplementary repertoire was chosen to represent a variety of levels and can be used throughout the book.

Harmonization: Harmonization skills are developed using single tones, open fifths, full chords and various accompaniment styles. Harmonization examples use a mixture of Roman numerals, letter symbols and melodies with no symbols given.

Accompaniments and Score Reading: Two-hand accompaniments and multiple-line ensembles help students develop beginning skills in accompanying and score reading.

Ensembles: Duets and ensembles for multiple pianos are included throughout. In addition, four-part ensembles are created from analysis of repertoire.

Features of the Second Edition: The authors wish to thank the numerous individuals who offered suggestions for the second edition. Due to recommendations by these people, the following changes were made:

- Additional reading examples were added to the earlier units and easier sight-reading examples were added to subsequent units.

- The units were reduced from 30 to 26 to allow more time for review and testing.

- Some new repertoire was chosen to more carefully reinforce chapter concepts.

- Scales and arpeggios are introduced in groups that use similar fingerings.

- Many improvisation exercises include optional suggestions for rhythm, and sections for playing by ear are given.

- More harmonization examples are included.

- The two chapters on modes from the first edition have been consolidated into one chapter.

CD-ROM: Included with each textbook is a CD-ROM that contains both audio and MIDI file accompaniments for more than 500 examples in the book. Accompaniments range from simple rhythm patterns to full orchestrations. These accompaniments add musical interest and motivate students to complete assignments both in the classroom and the practice room. Anyone who has purchased the book has permission to download the audio files to an MP3 player or burn a CD for personal use. Likewise, MIDI files can be downloaded to play back using a computer or digital keyboard. The files may not be posted online or distributed over the Internet without written consent from the publisher.

Each example in the text that contains an accompaniment is identified by an icon that shows the title number and track number for the example: 🔊 **1-1** The first number after the icon denotes the audio or MIDI file disk number. The second number is the track number within that disk.

The MIDI accompaniments were created using the sound set from the Yamaha Clavinova CVP 407. These files were then converted to audio using the USB Audio Recorder function on the CVP 407.

Teacher's Handbook: A Teacher's Handbook (22164) for the text serves as an aid in curriculum development and daily lesson planning. The handbook contains suggested daily lesson plans for the entire year, suggested assignments following each lesson plan, teaching tips for each unit, suggested examinations for the entire year and answer keys for all harmonization exercises and review worksheets. It also suggests ways to successfully integrate keyboard and computer technology into the curriculum.

The authors wish you continued success in your piano study.

E. L. Lancaster

Kenon D. Renfrow

Table of Contents

Objectives

Upon completion of this unit the student will be able to:

1. Name, find and play all keys on the keyboard.
2. Improvise black-key melodies as the teacher plays an accompaniment.
3. Apply basic musical concepts of rhythm, notation, terminology and symbols to performance at the keyboard.
4. Read and perform melodies written on the grand staff.
5. Identify and play whole steps, half steps and the chromatic scale on the keyboard.

Assignments

Week of 8/24

Write your assignments for the week in the space below.

Summer Night video

pg 27

How to Sit at the Keyboard

Before you sit, adjust the bench so that it is:
- centered in the middle of the keyboard.
- facing the piano squarely (not crooked).

When you sit, adjust the bench so that you:
- sit on the front half.
- place your knees slightly under the keyboard.
- place your feet flat on the floor with right foot slightly forward.

As you prepare to play, adjust your posture so that you:
- sit tall with relaxed shoulders.
- lean slightly forward.
- feel the arms hanging loosely from the shoulders.
- see the elbows level with or slightly higher than the keys.

Hand Position

Curve your fingers when you play, as though you have a bubble in your hand.

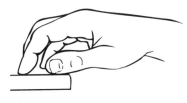

Curved fingers bring the thumb into the proper playing position and provide an arch that allows the thumb to pass under the fingers or the fingers to cross over the thumb. Play on the outside of the thumb and on the fingertip pads of the fingers.

Finger Numbers

The fingers of the left hand (LH) and the right hand (RH) are numbered as shown. The thumb is the first finger of each hand.

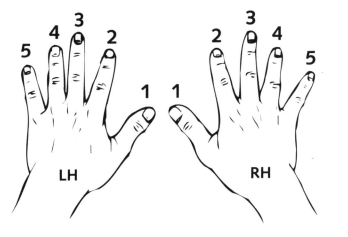

Basic Note and Rest Values

Quarter note   = 1 count

Half note   = 2 counts

Dotted half note   = 3 counts

Whole note   = 4 counts

Rests are signs for silence.

Quarter rest   = 1 count (rest for the value of ♩)

Half rest   = 2 counts (rest for the value of ♩)

Whole rest   = 4 counts (rest for the value of o or any whole measure)

Tap the following rhythm. Tap once for each note, counting aloud. Notice how the bar lines divide the music into measures of equal duration.

Rhythm Reading

Tap the following rhythms with the indicated hands and finger numbers.

◀))) 1-1

Track number within the disk
Audio or MIDI file disk number

Hands separately:

◀))) 1-1

1. RH

◀))) 1-2

2. LH

◀))) 1-3

3. RH

◀))) 1-4

4. LH

Hands together:

◀))) 1-5

5. RH
   LH

◀))) 1-6

6. RH
   LH

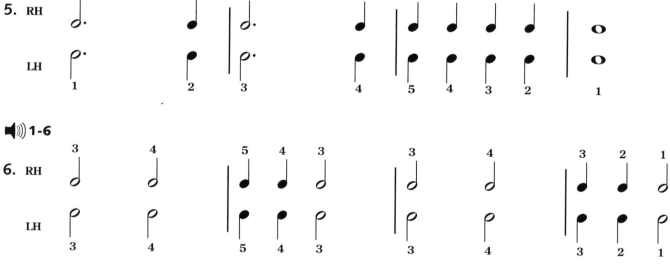

The Keyboard

The keyboard has white keys and black keys. The black keys are in groups of twos and threes. On the keyboard, down is to the left, and up is to the right. As you move left, the tones sound lower. As you move right, the tones sound higher.

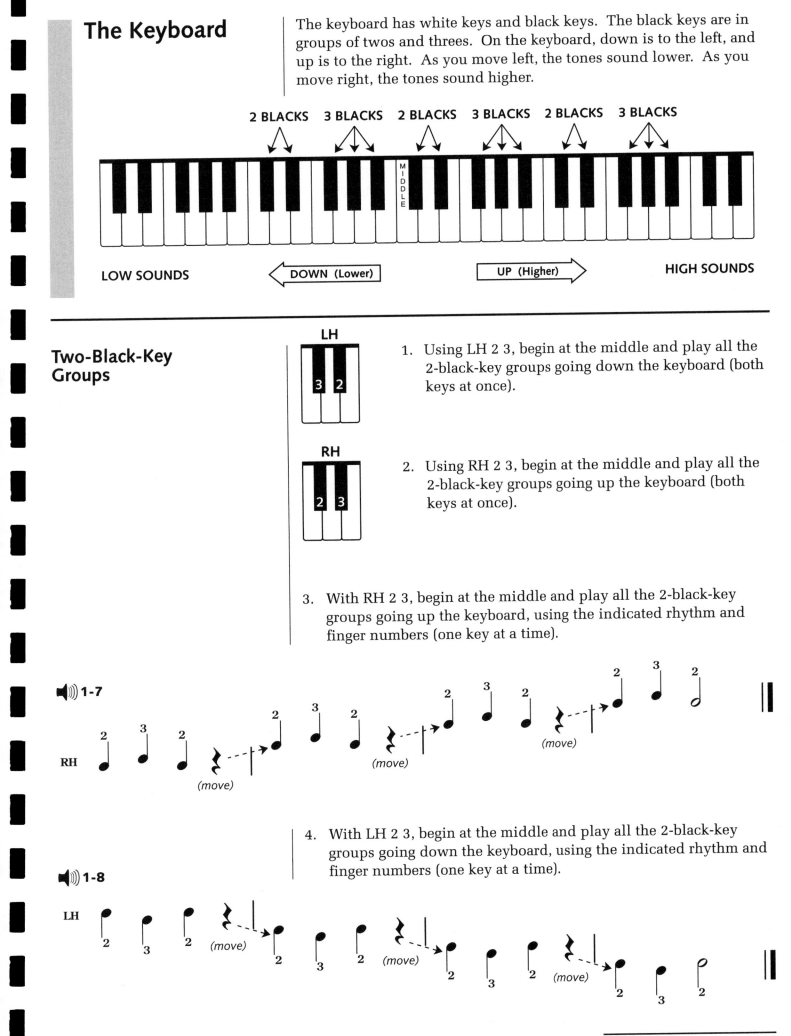

2 BLACKS **3 BLACKS** **2 BLACKS** **3 BLACKS** **2 BLACKS** **3 BLACKS**

LOW SOUNDS   DOWN (Lower)   UP (Higher)   HIGH SOUNDS

Two-Black-Key Groups

LH

RH

1. Using LH 2 3, begin at the middle and play all the 2-black-key groups going down the keyboard (both keys at once).

2. Using RH 2 3, begin at the middle and play all the 2-black-key groups going up the keyboard (both keys at once).

3. With RH 2 3, begin at the middle and play all the 2-black-key groups going up the keyboard, using the indicated rhythm and finger numbers (one key at a time).

🔊 1-7

RH

4. With LH 2 3, begin at the middle and play all the 2-black-key groups going down the keyboard, using the indicated rhythm and finger numbers (one key at a time).

🔊 1-8

LH

Three-Black-Key Groups

1. Using LH 2 3 4, begin at the middle and play all the 3-black-key groups going down the keyboard (all 3 keys at once).

2. Using RH 2 3 4, begin at the middle and play all the 3-black-key groups going up the keyboard (all 3 keys at once).

3. With RH 2 3 4, begin at the middle and play all the 3-black-key groups going up the keyboard, using the indicated rhythm and finger numbers (one key at a time).

🔊 1-9

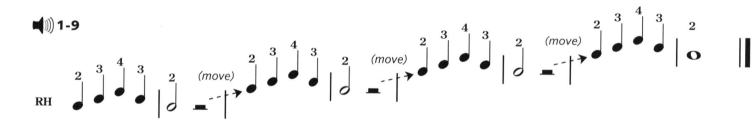

4. With LH 2 3 4, begin at the middle and play all the 3-black-key groups going down the keyboard, using the indicated rhythm and finger numbers (one key at a time).

🔊 1-10

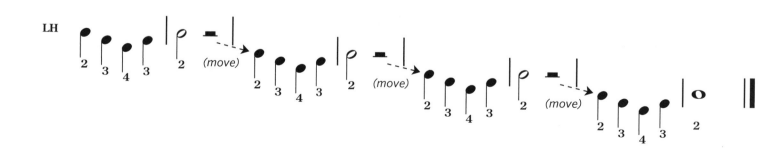

Black-Key Improvisation

Improvise an 8-measure melody using the given black-key position as the teacher plays each accompaniment. Listen to the 4-measure introduction to establish the tempo, mood and style before beginning the melody. You can use the suggested rhythm for your improvisation or create your own rhythm to complement the accompaniment.

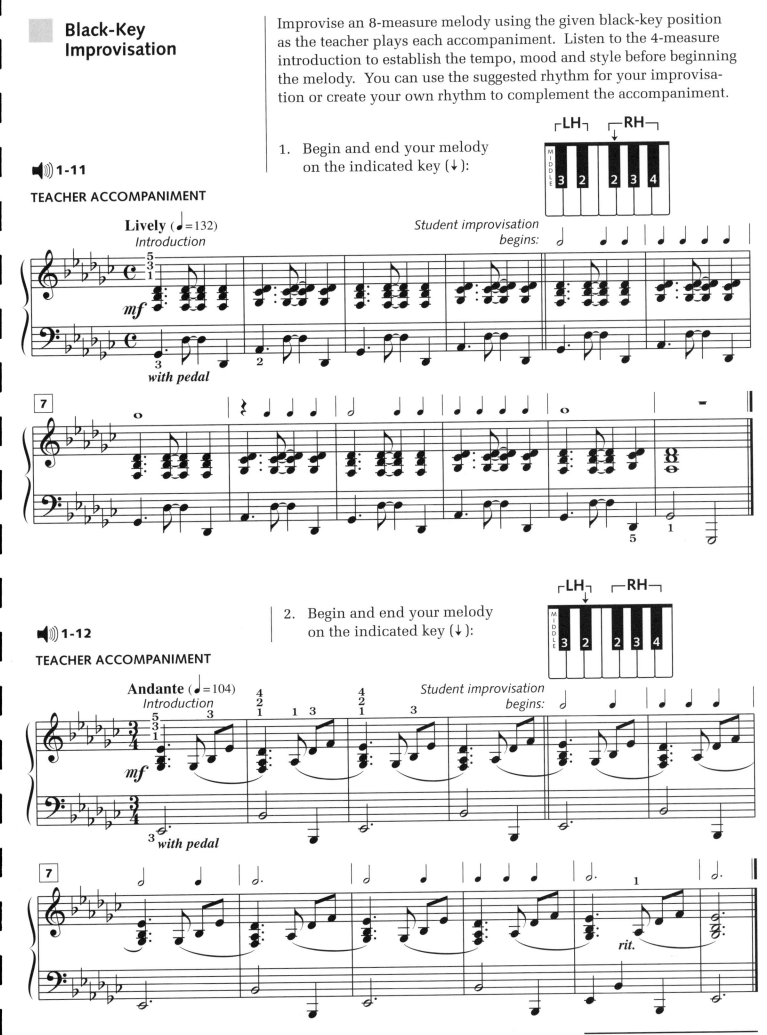

Naming White Keys

- Piano keys are named for the first seven letters of the alphabet. The key names are A B C D E F G, used over and over!
- The lowest key on the piano is A. The C nearest the middle of the piano is called middle C. The highest key on the piano is C.
- Going up the keyboard, the notes sound higher and higher.
- While most acoustic pianos have 88 keys, some digital keyboards may have fewer.

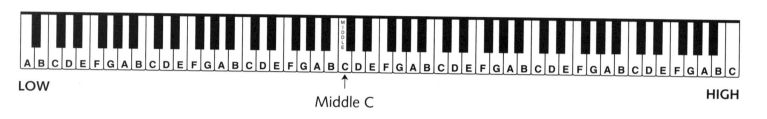

LOW   Middle C   HIGH

Beginning at the low end and moving *up* the keyboard, play and name every white key beginning with the bottom **A,** using the indicated rhythm. Use LH 3 for keys below the middle of the keyboard. Use RH 3 for keys above the middle of the keyboard.

🔊 1-13

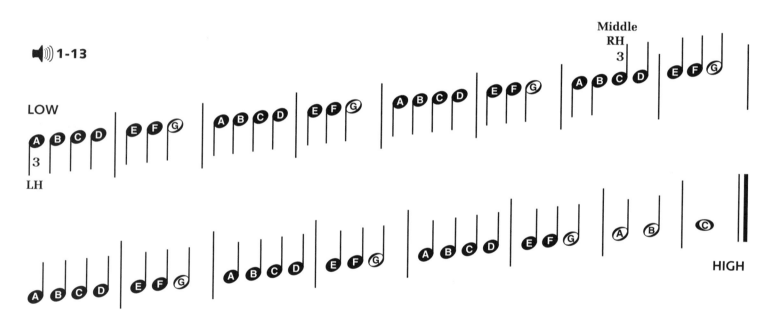

Octave

An **octave** is the distance from one key on the keyboard to the next key (lower or higher) with the same letter name.

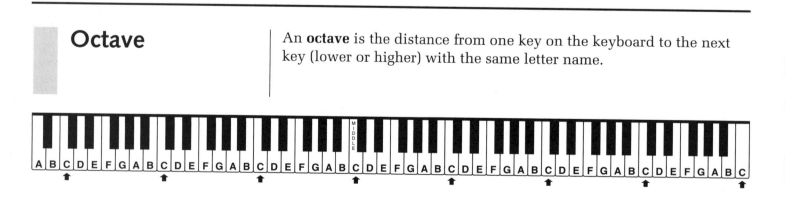

Finding White Keys

1. Beginning at the low end and moving *up* the keyboard, play every **D**.
   - Say the name of the key aloud as you play.
   - Use the following rhythm:

   ♩ 𝄽 𝄽 𝄽 | ♩ 𝄽 𝄽 𝄽 | *etc.*

   - Use LH 3 for keys below **middle C** on the keyboard.
   - Use RH 3 for keys above **middle C** on the keyboard.

Middle of
2 black keys

2. Repeat exercise 1 for **C**. (Use RH 3 for middle C.)

3. Repeat exercise 1 for **E**.

Left of
2 black keys   Right of
2 black keys

4. Beginning at the low end and moving *up* the keyboard, play every **G** and **A**, one note at a time.
   - Say the name of the key aloud as you play.
   - Use the following rhythm:

   ♩ ♩ ♩ 𝄽 | ♩ ♩ ♩ 𝄽 | *etc.*
   G A G   G A G

   - Use LH 2 1 2 for keys below **middle C** on the keyboard.
   - Use RH 1 2 1 for keys above **middle C** on the keyboard.

Middle of
3 black keys

5. Repeat exercise 1 for **F**.

6. Repeat exercise 1 for **B**.

Left of
3 black keys   Right of
3 black keys

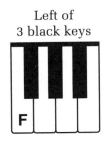

C-D-E Groups

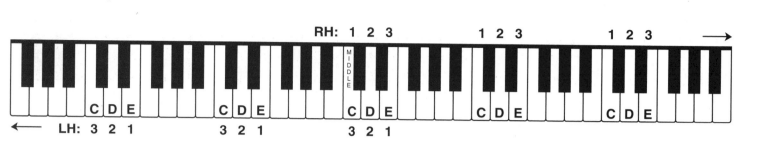

With RH 1 2 3, begin on middle **C** and play all of the **C-D-E** groups going *up* the keyboard, using the indicated rhythm and finger numbers.

🔊 1-14

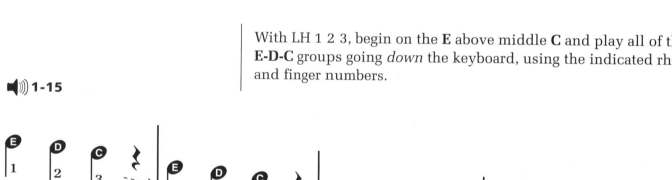

With LH 1 2 3, begin on the **E** above middle **C** and play all of the **E-D-C** groups going *down* the keyboard, using the indicated rhythm and finger numbers.

🔊 1-15

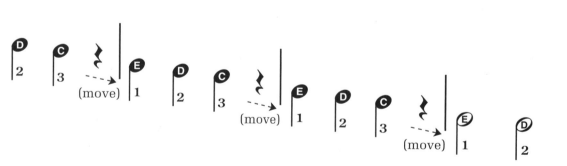

F-G-A-B Groups

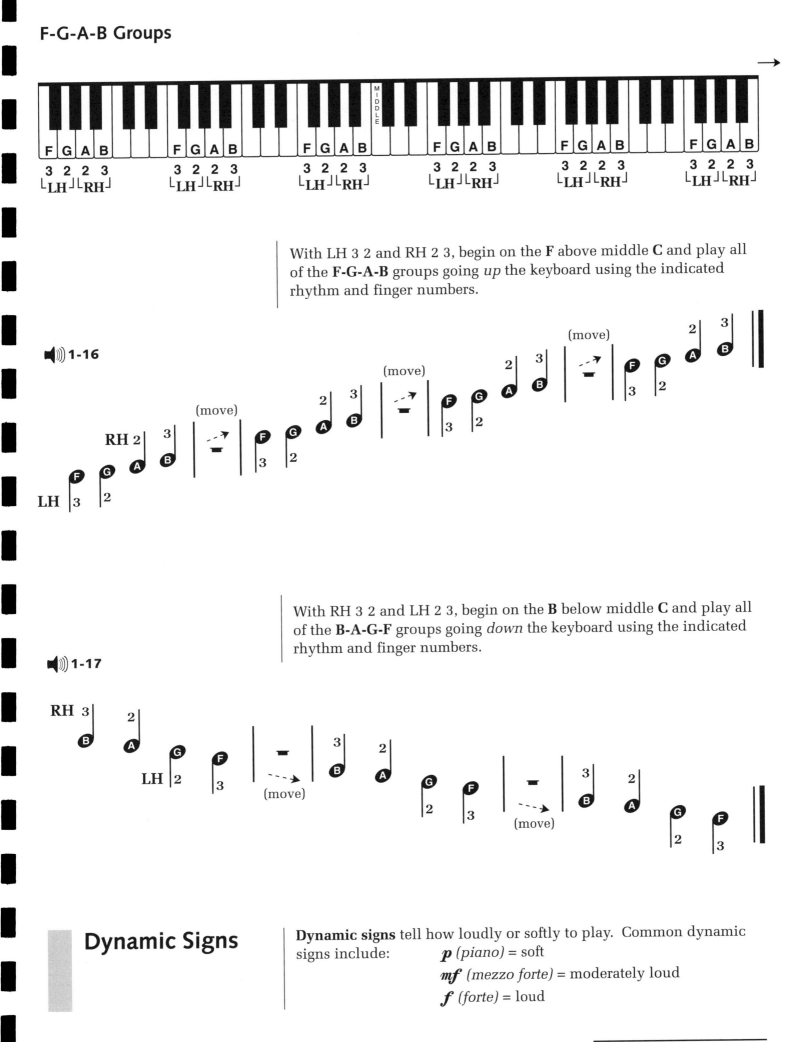

With LH 3 2 and RH 2 3, begin on the **F** above middle **C** and play all of the **F-G-A-B** groups going *up* the keyboard using the indicated rhythm and finger numbers.

🔊 1-16

With RH 3 2 and LH 2 3, begin on the **B** below middle **C** and play all of the **B-A-G-F** groups going *down* the keyboard using the indicated rhythm and finger numbers.

🔊 1-17

Dynamic Signs

Dynamic signs tell how loudly or softly to play. Common dynamic signs include:

p *(piano)* = soft

mf *(mezzo forte)* = moderately loud

f *(forte)* = loud

♪olo Repertoire

First ending (⌐1._____): play first time only.

Second ending (⌐2._____): play second time only.

Repeat sign (:‖): repeat from the beginning.

Before playing:

- Map the piece using the first ending, repeat sign and second ending.
- Find measures that are alike and similar.
- Tap the rhythm of the piece with the correct fingers.

While playing:

- Keep a steady beat.
- Observe the dynamic markings and fingerings.

starting key: **RH**

SUMMER NIGHT

🔊 1-18

Kenon D. Renfrow

TEACHER ACCOMPANIMENT

Sharp, Flat and Natural Signs

The **sharp sign** (♯) before a note means play the next key to the *right*, whether black or white.

The **flat sign** (♭) before a note means play the next key to the *left*, whether black or white.

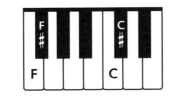

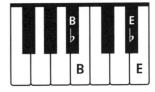

When a sharp or a flat appears before a note, it applies to that note for the rest of the measure. The **natural sign** (♮) cancels a sharp or flat. A note after a natural sign is always a white key!

Half Steps

A **half step** is the distance from any key to the very next key above or below it (black or white)—there is no key between.

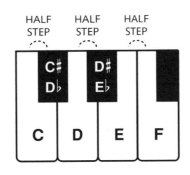

Whole Steps

A **whole step** is equal to two half steps. Skip one key (black or white).

Playing by Ear

Using black keys only, play the following melodies. If you are unfamiliar with a melody, learn it by listening to the audio file or MIDI file.

🔊 1-19   **Amazing Grace** (start on D♭)

🔊 1-20   **Auld Lang Syne** (start on D♭)

🔊 1-21   **Merrily We Roll Along** (start on B♭)

Building Whole-Step Patterns

Begin on the given key and build an ascending three-note pattern using only whole steps. Write the names of the keys in the blanks. Do not skip any letters.

1. __C__   __D__   __E__

2. __G__   __A__   __B__

3. __F__   __G__   __A__

4. __F♯__   __G♯__   __A♯__

5. __D♭__   __E♭__   __F__

6. __B♭__   __C__   __D__

Using the rhythm 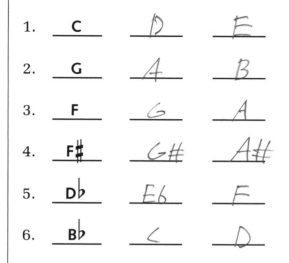 play each pattern up and down with:

   a. RH fingers 1 2 3
   b. LH fingers 3 2 1
   c. Hands together (an octave apart)

The Chromatic Scale

The **chromatic scale** is made up entirely of half steps. It goes up and down, using every key, black and white. It may begin on any key.

The fingering rules are:

- Use 3 on each black key.
- Use 1 on each white key, except when two white keys are together (no black key between), then use 1 2 or 2 1.

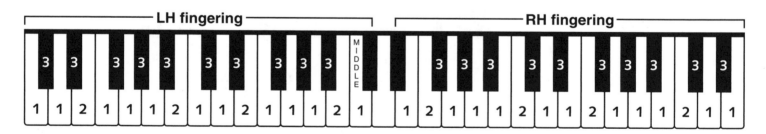

Playing the Chromatic Scale

1. Looking at the keyboard above, play the chromatic scale with the LH. Begin on middle C and go down for two octaves; then go up again.

2. Looking at the keyboard above, play the chromatic scale with the RH. Begin on E above middle C and go up for two octaves; then go down again.

3. By combining steps 1 and 2 above, play the chromatic scale hands together in contrary motion. Notice that each hand plays the same finger at the same time.

The Staff

Music is written on a **staff** of 5 lines and 4 spaces. Some notes are written *on* lines and some are written *in* spaces.

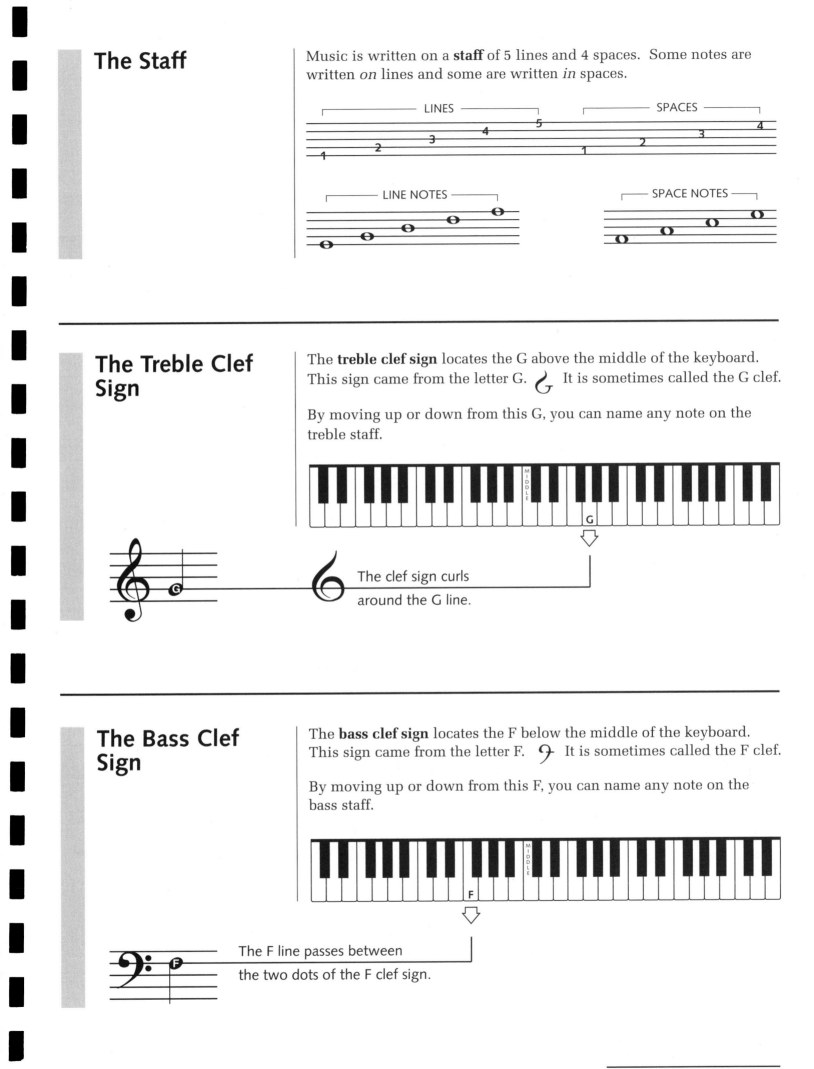

The Treble Clef Sign

The **treble clef sign** locates the G above the middle of the keyboard. This sign came from the letter G. It is sometimes called the G clef.

By moving up or down from this G, you can name any note on the treble staff.

The clef sign curls around the G line.

The Bass Clef Sign

The **bass clef sign** locates the F below the middle of the keyboard. This sign came from the letter F. It is sometimes called the F clef.

By moving up or down from this F, you can name any note on the bass staff.

The F line passes between the two dots of the F clef sign.

The Grand Staff

The bass staff and the treble staff are joined together by a **brace** to make the **grand staff.** A **ledger line** is used between the two staves for middle C. Ledger lines are also used above and below the grand staff to extend its range.

The notes with arrows are landmarks or guideposts. Learn to identify and find them quickly on the keyboard, as they assist in reading the notes surrounding them.

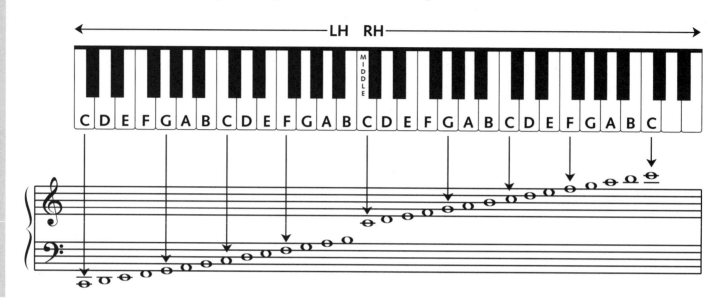

Time Signatures

Music has numbers at the beginning called a **time signature.**

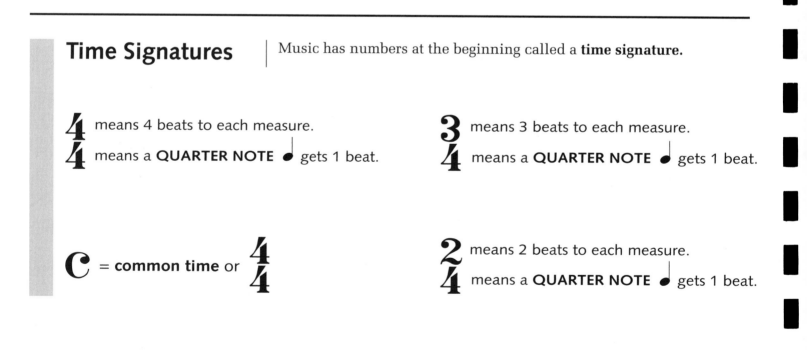

Naming Notes and Playing Melodic Patterns

In the first column, write the name of the note on the line below it. Then play and say the note names for the patterns in the other columns.

1.  *C*      

2.  *G*      

3.  *C*      

4.  *E*      

5.  *C*      

6.  *E*      

7.  *C*      

8.   *G*      

Tempo Marks

Tempo is an Italian word that means "rate of speed." Words that indicate the tempo used in playing music are called **tempo marks.**

Some of the most important tempo marks are:

Allegro	=	Quickly, happily
Moderato	=	Moderately
Andante	=	Moving along (The word actually means "walking.")
Adagio	=	Slowly

English words such as *lively, happily* and *flowing* are also used as tempo marks.

Articulation

Articulation refers to the manner in which notes are connected or separated.

A **slur** is a curved line over or under notes on *different* lines or spaces. Slurs mean play **legato** (smoothly connected).

Slurs often divide the music into phrases. A **phrase** is a musical thought or sentence.

A dot over or under the notes indicates **staccato** touch. Play these notes short!

When there are no articulation marks over or under notes, they are generally played **non legato** (disconnected but not staccato).

Reading Melodies

The melodies that follow utilize the musical concepts presented in this unit. Use the indicated tempos, dynamics and articulation as you play these exercises.

Use the following practice directions:
1. Tap and count aloud.
2. Play and count aloud.
3. Play and say note names.

🔊 1-22

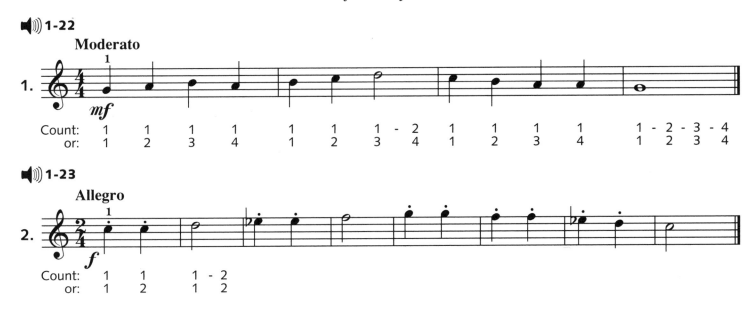

🔊 1-23

🔊 1-24

🔊 1-25

🔊 1-26

🔊 1-27

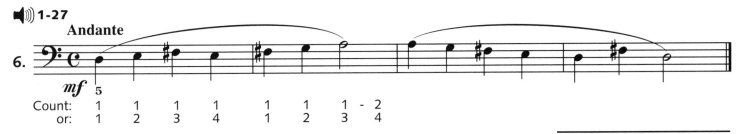

Reading on the Grand Staff

Use the indicated tempos, dynamics and articulation as you play these exercises.

Use the following practice directions:
1. Tap and count aloud.
2. Play and count aloud.
3. Play and say note names.

Review Worksheet

Name _Jacob Nick_   Date _8/27/20_

1. Write the letter name on each key marked X.

2. Write the name of each treble-clef note on the line below it.

3. Write the name of each bass-clef note on the line below it.

4. Write the numbers from column A in the appropriate blanks
   in column B to match each item with its best description.

Column A

1. Quarter note ♩

2. Half note ♩

3. Dotted half note ♩.

4. Whole note o

5. Piano *p*

6. Mezzo forte *mf*

7. Forte *f*

8. Sharp sign ♯

9. Flat sign ♭

10. Natural sign ♮

11. Half step

12. Whole step

13. Treble clef sign 𝄞

14. Bass clef sign 𝄢

15. Ledger line

16. $\frac{2}{4}$

17. $\frac{3}{4}$

18. $\frac{4}{4}$

19. 𝄴

20. Legato

21. Staccato

22. Quarter rest

23. Half rest

24. Whole rest

Column B

_____ Moderately loud

_____ Play next key to the right

_____ Distance from any key to the very next key

_____ Smoothly connected

_____ Short

_____ Locates the G above the middle of the keyboard

_____ ▬

_____ Locates the F below the middle of the keyboard

_____ 2 beats in a measure, quarter note gets 1 beat

_____ Loud

_____ 3 beats in a measure, quarter note gets 1 beat

_____ Note receiving 3 counts

_____ Note receiving 4 counts

_____ Play next key to the left

_____ 𝄽

_____ Note receiving 1 count

_____ ▬

_____ Note receiving 2 counts

_____ Equals two half steps

_____ Soft

_____ Cancels a sharp or flat

_____ Common time

_____ Used to extend the range of the Grand Staff

_____ 4 beats in a measure, quarter note gets 1 beat

Intervals and Other Keyboard Basics

Objectives

Upon completion of this unit the student will be able to:

1. Perform solo repertoire from Grand Staff notation.
2. Apply intervals and other musical concepts to performance at the keyboard.
3. Identify key signatures in major keys.
4. Harmonize melodies with fifths as an accompaniment.

Assignments

Week of 8/31/20

Write your assignments for the week in the space below.

Miniature Waltz pg 33

Intervals

Distances between tones are measured in **intervals,** called 2nds, 3rds, 4ths, 5ths, etc.

- The distance from any white key to the next white key, up or down, is called a 2nd.
- When you skip a white key, the interval is a 3rd.
- When you skip two white keys, the interval is a 4th.
- When you skip three white keys, the interval is a 5th.

Melodic Intervals

Notes played separately make a melody. The intervals between these notes are called **melodic intervals.**

Listen to the sound of each interval as you play these melodic 2nds, 3rds, 4ths and 5ths.

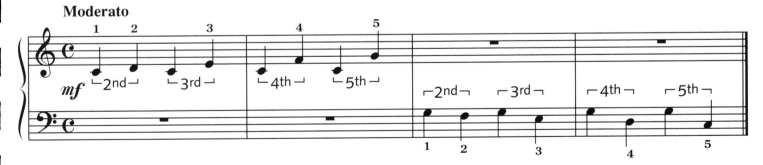

► Now play these intervals beginning on G in the RH and beginning on D in the LH. Playing music in a different key from the original is called **transposition.**

Harmonic Intervals

Notes played together make harmony. The intervals between these notes are called **harmonic intervals.**

Listen to the sound of each interval as you play these harmonic 2nds, 3rds, 4ths and 5ths.

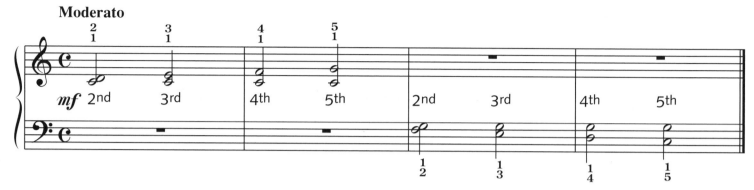

► Now play these intervals beginning on G in the RH and beginning on D in the LH.

Naming and Playing Intervals

In the first column, write the name of the note on the line below it. In the other columns, write the names of the intervals (2nd, 3rd, 4th or 5th) on the lines. Circle each harmonic interval. Then, play and say the interval names.

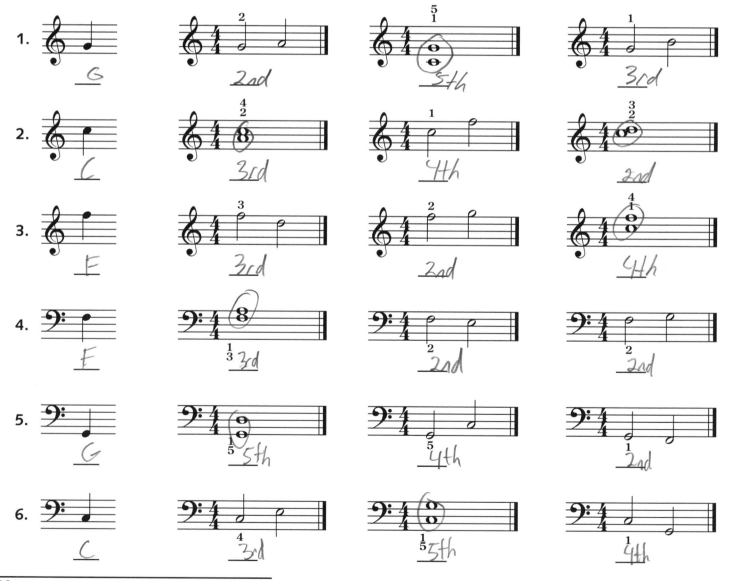

Eighth Notes, Eighth Rests, and Dotted Quarter Notes

Two **eighth notes** (♪♪) are played in the time of one quarter note.

When eighth notes appear singly, they look like this: ♪ or ♪

Single eighth notes are often used with **eighth rests.** ♪ ʼ

A dot increases the length of a note by one half its value.

A **dotted quarter note** is equal to a quarter note plus an eighth note.

$$♩ \ + \ ♪ \ = \ ♩.$$

1 count   1/2 count   1-1/2 counts

In ²₄, ³₄, or ⁴₄ time, the dotted quarter note is almost always followed by an eighth note. ♩. ♪

New Time Signature

⁶₈ beats to each measure.
eighth note gets 1 beat.

♪ eighth note
    or   } = 1 count
ʼ eighth rest

♩ quarter note
    or   } = 2 counts
𝄽 quarter rest

♩. dotted quarter note
    or   } = 3 counts
𝄽 ʼ rests

𝅗𝅥. dotted half note = 6 counts

For a whole measure of silence, a whole rest (𝄼) is used.

In ⁶₈ time, the ♩. is often felt as the pulse, with two large beats per measure.

New Dynamic Signs

mp (mezzo piano)   =   moderately soft

pp (pianissimo)   =   very soft

ff (fortissimo)   =   very loud

crescendo (cresc.)
(gradually louder)

diminuendo (dim.) or **decrescendo (decresc.)**
(gradually softer)

Key Signatures

Sharps or flats that follow the clef signs are called the **key signature**. The key signature indicates the notes that are to be sharped or flatted throughout the piece and aids in identifying the key in which the piece is written.

Sharps appear in the following order in the key signature:

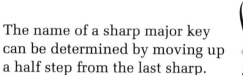

F♯ C♯ G♯ D♯ A♯ E♯ B♯

The name of a sharp major key can be determined by moving up a half step from the last sharp.

This is the key signature for the **key of B major.** A half step up from A♯ is B.

Flats appear in the following order in the key signature:

The order of flats is reversed from the order of sharps in key signatures.

B♭ E♭ A♭ D♭ G♭ C♭ F♭

The name of a flat major key can be determined by the name of the next-to-last flat.

This is the key signature for the **key of A♭ major.** The next-to-last flat is A♭.

Two major key signatures cannot be determined using the above rules:

- C major—no sharps or flats
- F major—one flat (B♭)

♪olo Repertoire

Ritardando (rit. or ritard.) means gradually slowing.

Before playing:

- Write the name of each LH interval on the line.
- Are lines 1 and 3 in the RH alike or similar? Lines 2 and 4?
- Tap the rhythm of the piece with the correct fingers, hands separately.

While playing:

- Keep the LH softer than the RH.
- Be aware of the *crescendo, diminuendos* and *ritardando.*

MINIATURE WALTZ

🔊 **1-31**

E. L. Lancaster
Kenon D. Renfrow

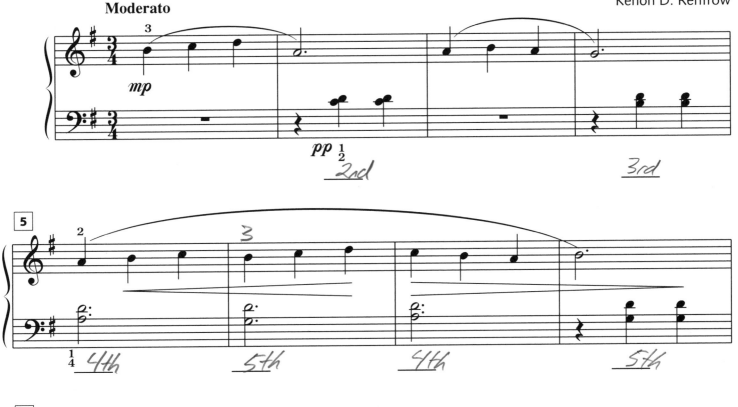

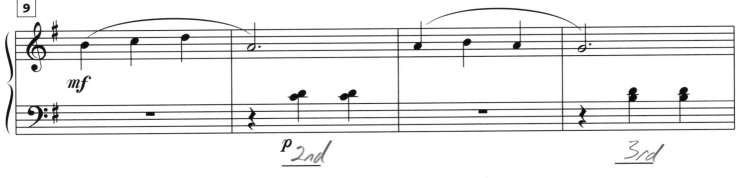

Solo Repertoire

Before playing:

- Tap the rhythm hands together, with the correct fingers.

While playing:

- To create the rhythmic feel of a minuet, slightly emphasize the downbeat of each measure.

MINUET

🔊 1-32

Alexander Reinagle
(1756–1809)

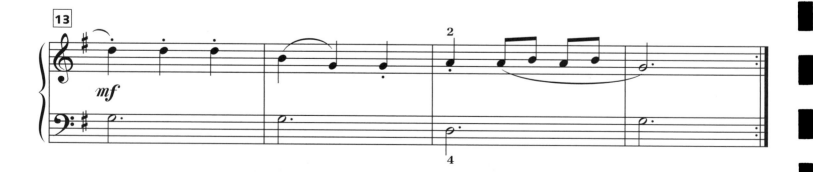

Rhythm Reading

Tap the following rhythm patterns using RH for notes with stems going up and LH for notes with stems going down. For examples using both hands, tap hands separately first, and then hands together, always counting aloud.

Reading

Identify the key of each example. Use the indicated tempo, dynamics and articulation as you play these exercises.

Use the following practice directions:

1. Tap and count aloud.
2. Play and count aloud.
3. Play and say note names.

A **fermata** sign (𝄐) means to hold the note under the sign longer than its value.

Circle four 3rds in this example.

THE CAN-CAN
(ORPHEUS IN THE UNDERWORLD)

1-41

Jacques Offenbach
(1819–1880)

Allegro

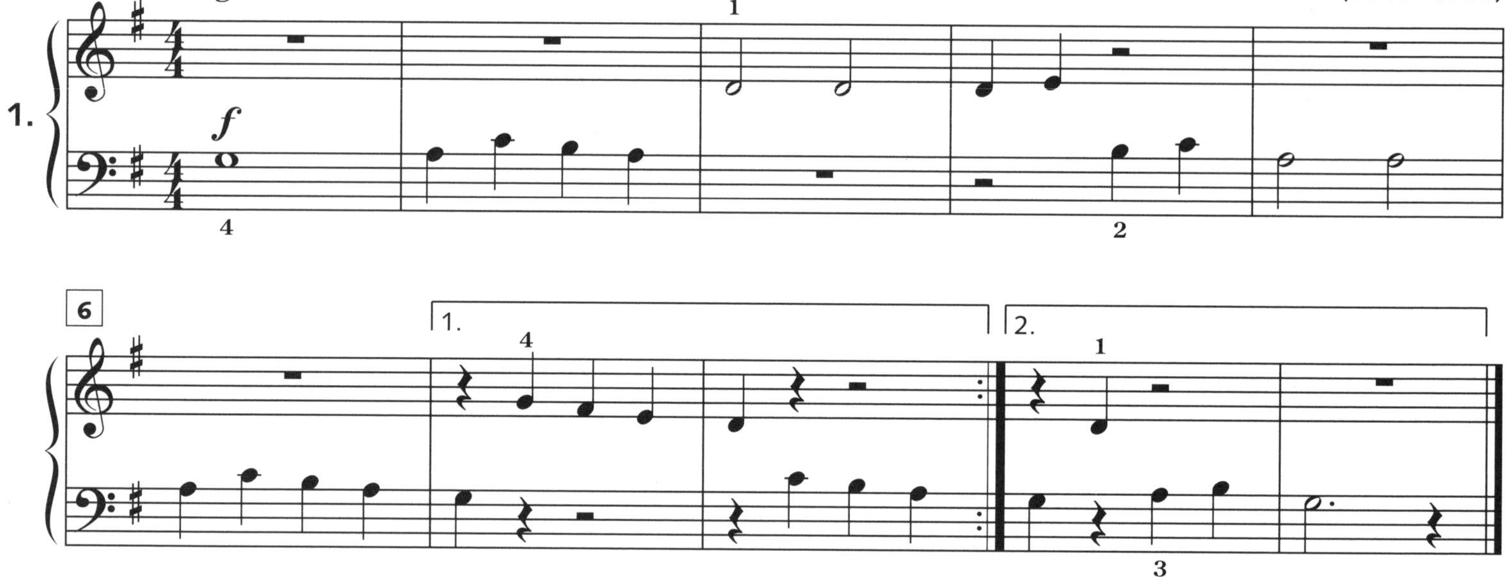

Circle a 3rd, 4th and 5th in this example.

1-42

Maestoso *(majestically)*

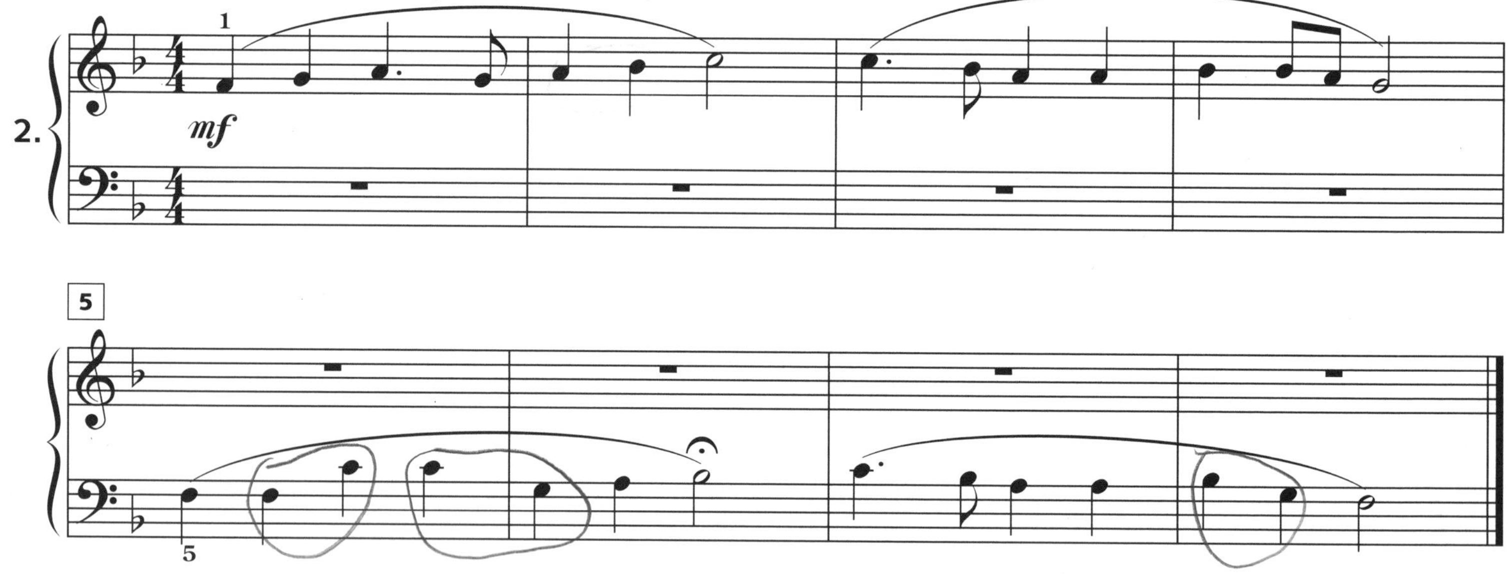

🔊 1-43

Circle one 3rd and two 4ths in this example.

🔊 1-44

Circle three 3rds and one 4th in this example.

🔊 1-45

Harmonization

Harmonize each of the melodies below by playing the harmonic 5th (used in measure 1) on the first beat of every measure.

🔊 1-46

🔊 1-47

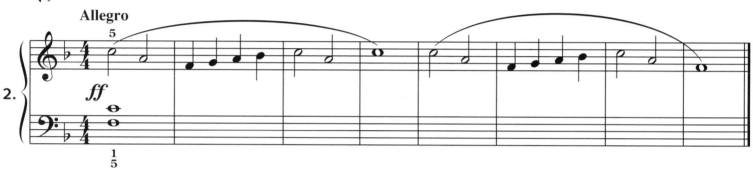

Technique

Play the following exercises that increase finger dexterity and aid in moving up and down the keyboard.

🔊 1-48

🔊 1-49

🔊 1-50

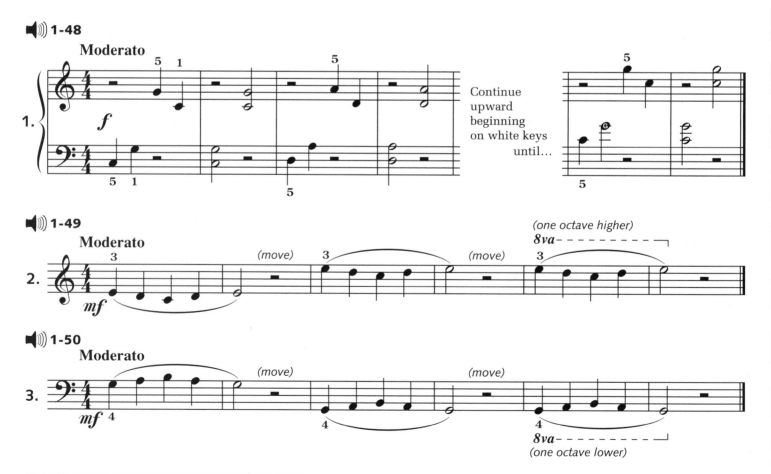

Review Worksheet

Name *Jacob Mick*   Date *9/7/20*

1. Write a half note below the given note to make the indicated *melodic* interval. Notes *on* or *above* the middle line have stems pointing down.

   Notes *below* the middle line have stems pointing up. Write the name of each note in the square below it.

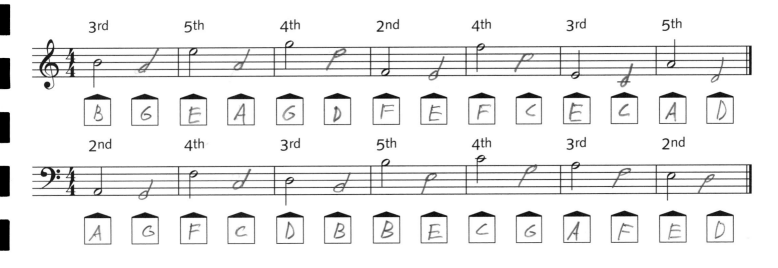

2. Identify each major sharp key signature by writing its name on the line.

   E   C#   D   A   G   F#   B

3. Identify each major flat key signature by writing its name on the line.

   Ab   Gb   Bb   Db   Eb   Cb   F

4. Write the numbers from column A in the appropriate blanks
    in column B to match each item with its best description.

Column A   ## Column B

1. ♫   _____ Moderately fast

2. Eighth rest   _____ Quarter note plus an eighth note

3. $\frac{6}{8}$ _____ One octave lower

4. Dotted quarter note ♩.   _____ Two eighth notes

5. Mezzo piano *mp*   _____ Majestically

6. Pianissimo *pp*   _____ Slowly

7. Fortissimo *ff*   _____ Gradually louder

8. Crescendo (⟨)   _____ Moving along (walking)

9. Diminuendo (⟩)   _____ Very loud
    or Decrescendo

10. rit.   _____ 6 beats in a measure, eighth note gets 1 beat

11. *8va- - - - -*⌐   _____ ⁊

12. Repeat sign   _____ In a singing style

13. *8va- - - - -*⌐   _____ Moderately soft

14. Maestoso   _____ Hold the note longer than its value

15. Allegretto   _____ Gradually softer

16. Andante   _____ Very slow

17. Fermata ⌒   _____ :‖

18. Adagio   _____ One octave higher

19. Cantabile   _____ Very soft

20. Largo   _____ Gradually slowing

Major Five-Finger Patterns

Objectives

Upon completion of this unit the student will be able to:

1. Play major five-finger patterns and major triads beginning on any key.
2. Perform solo repertoire that utilizes major five-finger patterns.
3. Sight-read and transpose melodies in major five-finger patterns.
4. Harmonize major melodies with tonic and dominant tones as an accompaniment.
5. Perform duet repertoire with a partner.
6. Create four-part ensembles from chord symbols.
7. Improvise melodies in major five-finger patterns as the teacher plays an accompaniment.

Assignments

Week of _9/7_

Write your assignments for the week in the space below.

- be at a piano on Friday

- C, D, E, F, G, A, B ← be able to play these for Friday

rep piece - due Friday

Sight read Turkish March (pg 50) - due Friday

learn Waltz pg 55 (♩= 88) by Fri

Barcarolle pg 56, pt 4 (♩=120) by Monday

Major Five-Finger Patterns

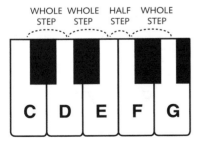

A major five-finger pattern is a series of five notes having the pattern: *whole step, whole step, half step, whole step.*

The first note of the pattern is the tonic (**I**). The fifth note of the pattern is the dominant (**V**).

LH five-finger patterns are fingered 5 4 3 2 1.
RH five-finger patterns are fingered 1 2 3 4 5.

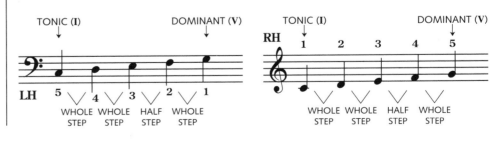

■ Written Exercise:

Write letter names on the correct keys to form each major five-finger pattern.

Example:

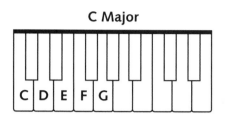

C Major

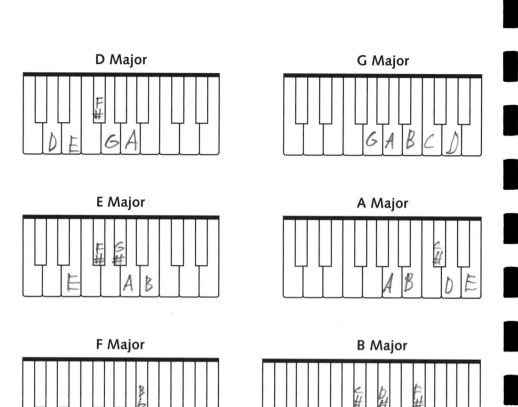

D Major

G Major

E Major

A Major

F Major

B Major

Playing Major Five-Finger Patterns

Play the following exercise that uses major five-finger patterns.

🔊 2-1

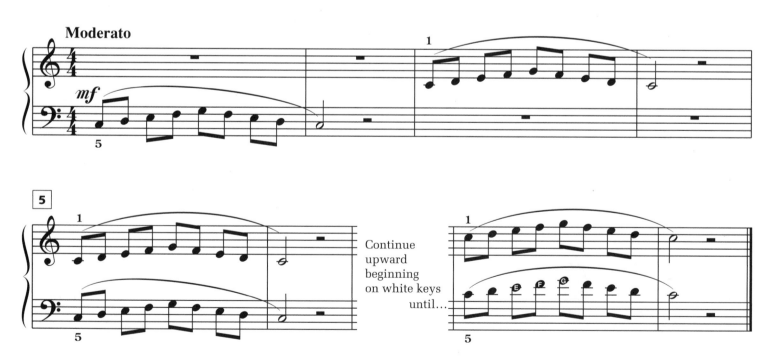

Moderato

mf

Continue upward beginning on white keys until…

Major Triads (Chords)

A **triad** is a three-note chord. The three notes of a triad are the root (1), the third (3), and the fifth (5). The **root** is the note from which the triad gets its name. The root of a C triad is C. Triads in root position (with the root at the bottom) always look like this:

LINE ——— 5th	or	SPACE ——— 5th
LINE ——— 3rd		SPACE ——— 3rd
LINE ——— ROOT		SPACE ——— ROOT

LH chords are fingered 5 3 1. RH chords are fingered 1 3 5.

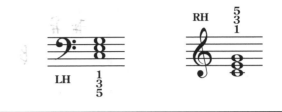

Playing Major Five-Finger Patterns and Chords

Play the following exercises that use major five-finger patterns and chords.

◀))) 2-2

Moderato

1. *mf* └ Major five-finger pattern ┘ └ Broken Chord ┘ Block Chord   Continue upward beginning on white keys until...

◀))) 2-3

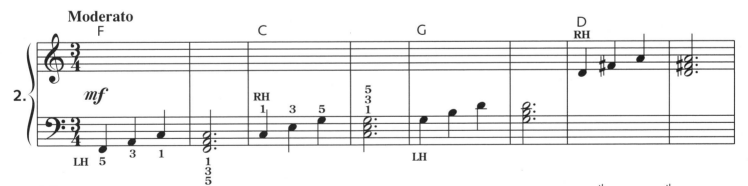

Moderato

2. *mf*

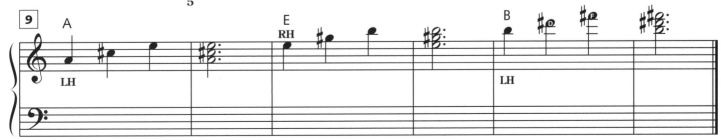

■ **Written Exercise:**
Write letter names on the correct keys to form each major five-finger pattern.

Notes that are spelled differently but are identical in sound are called **enharmonic.** F♯ and G♭ are enharmonic five-finger patterns.

D♭ Major

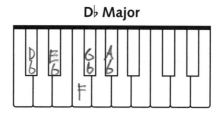

E♭ Major

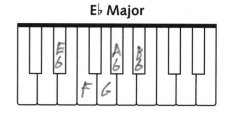

F♯ Major

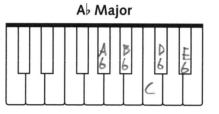

G♭ Major

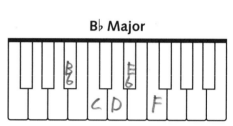

A♭ Major

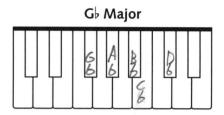

B♭ Major

Playing Major Five-Finger Patterns

Play the following exercise that uses major five-finger patterns beginning on black keys.

🔊 **2-4**

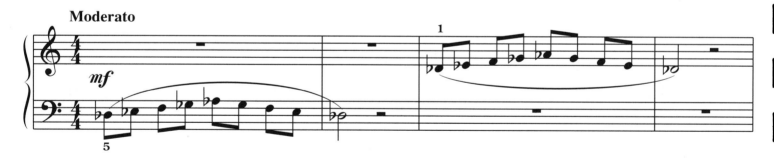

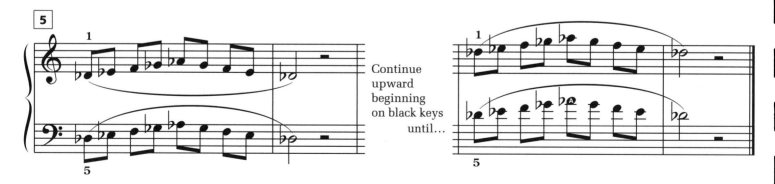

Continue upward beginning on black keys until…

Playing Major Five-Finger Patterns and Chords

Play the following exercises that use major five-finger patterns and chords beginning on black keys.

🔊 2-5

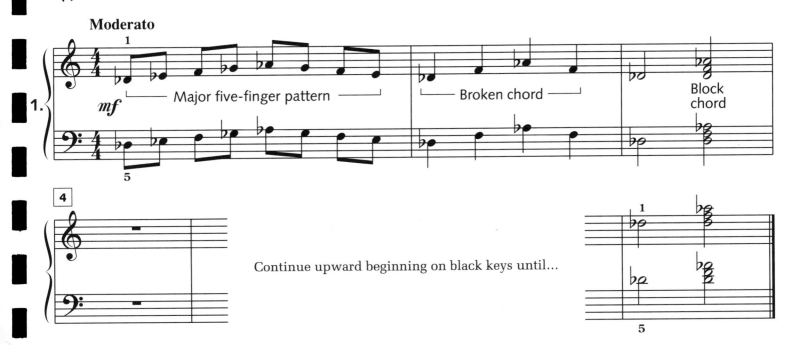

Moderato

1. Major five-finger pattern — Broken chord — Block chord

4 Continue upward beginning on black keys until...

🔊 2-6

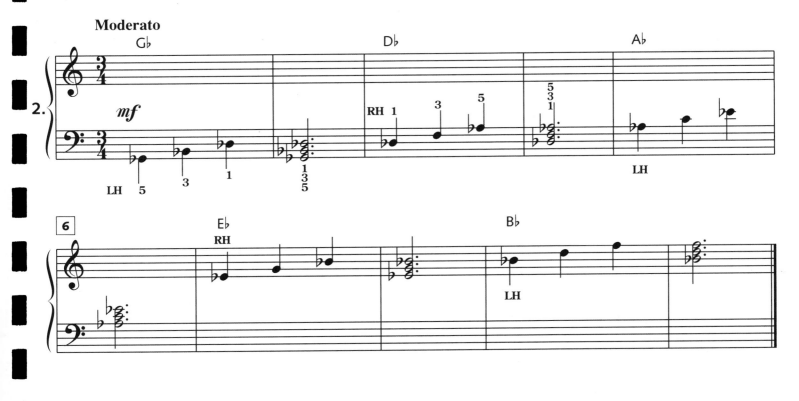

Moderato

2. G♭   D♭   A♭

6 E♭   B♭

♪olo Repertoire

Before playing:
- Tap the rhythm hands together.

While playing:
- Keep the LH softer than the RH.
- Observe the dynamics to create an echo effect.

DANCE

🔊 2-7

Moderato

Joachim van der Hofe
(c. 1612)

Before playing:

- Find one place where the LH crosses over the RH to play one note. Name and play this note.
- Find and practice the three measures where the hands play together.
- Map the piece using the first ending, repeat sign and second ending.

While playing:

- Think of the melody as being one long line divided between the hands.

BRIGHT LIGHTS BOOGIE

Gayle Kowalchyk
E. L. Lancaster

left hand plays note and comes back

TEACHER ACCOMPANIMENT: *(Student plays 1 octave higher)*

"Bright Lights Boogie" from BOOGIE 'N' BLUES, Book 1, by Gayle Kowalchyk and E. L. Lancaster
Copyright © MCMXCI by Alfred Publishing Co., Inc.

Major Five-Finger Patterns ■ Unit 3   **47**

New Time Signature

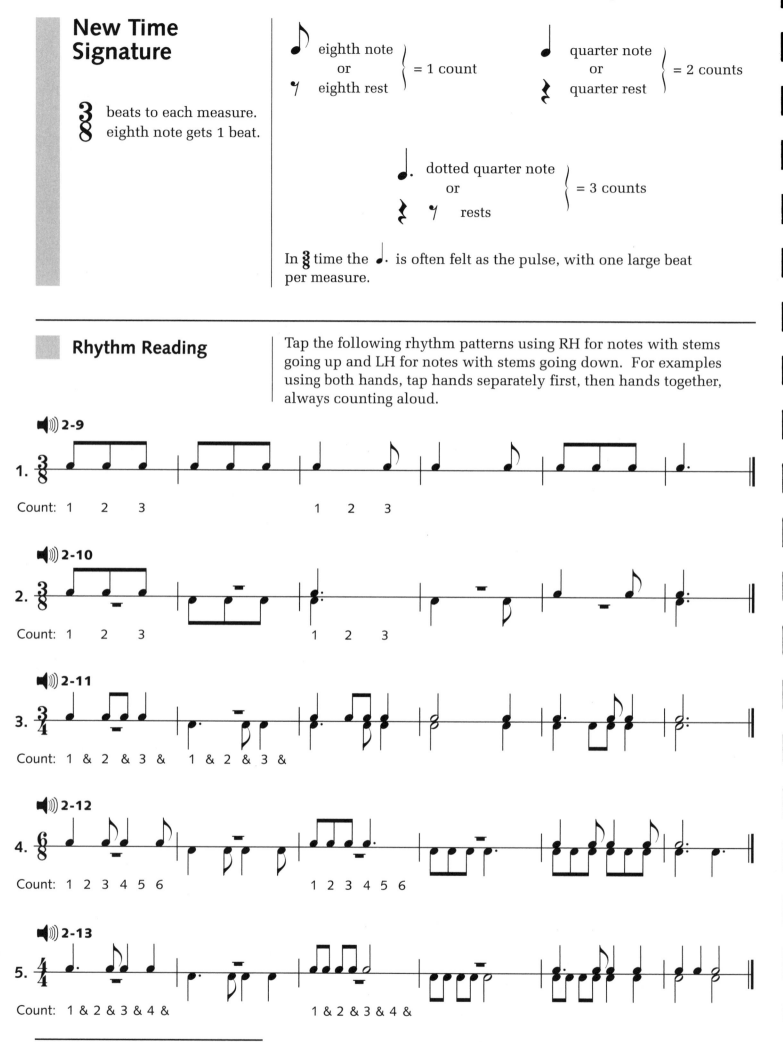

♪ eighth note
   or
𝄾 eighth rest
} = 1 count

♩ quarter note
   or
𝄽 quarter rest
} = 2 counts

$\frac{3}{8}$ beats to each measure.
eighth note gets 1 beat.

♩. dotted quarter note
    or
𝄽 𝄾 rests
} = 3 counts

In $\frac{3}{8}$ time the ♩. is often felt as the pulse, with one large beat per measure.

Rhythm Reading

Tap the following rhythm patterns using RH for notes with stems going up and LH for notes with stems going down. For examples using both hands, tap hands separately first, then hands together, always counting aloud.

🔊 2-9

1. $\frac{3}{8}$

Count: 1   2   3   1   2   3

🔊 2-10

2. $\frac{3}{8}$

Count: 1   2   3   1   2   3

🔊 2-11

3. $\frac{3}{4}$

Count: 1 & 2 & 3 &   1 & 2 & 3 &

🔊 2-12

4. $\frac{6}{8}$

Count: 1 2 3 4 5 6   1 2 3 4 5 6

🔊 2-13

5. $\frac{4}{4}$

Count: 1 & 2 & 3 & 4 &   1 & 2 & 3 & 4 &

Technique

Transpose means to perform at a pitch other than the original. Each pitch must be raised or lowered by precisely the same interval, resulting in a change of key.

🔊 **2-14**

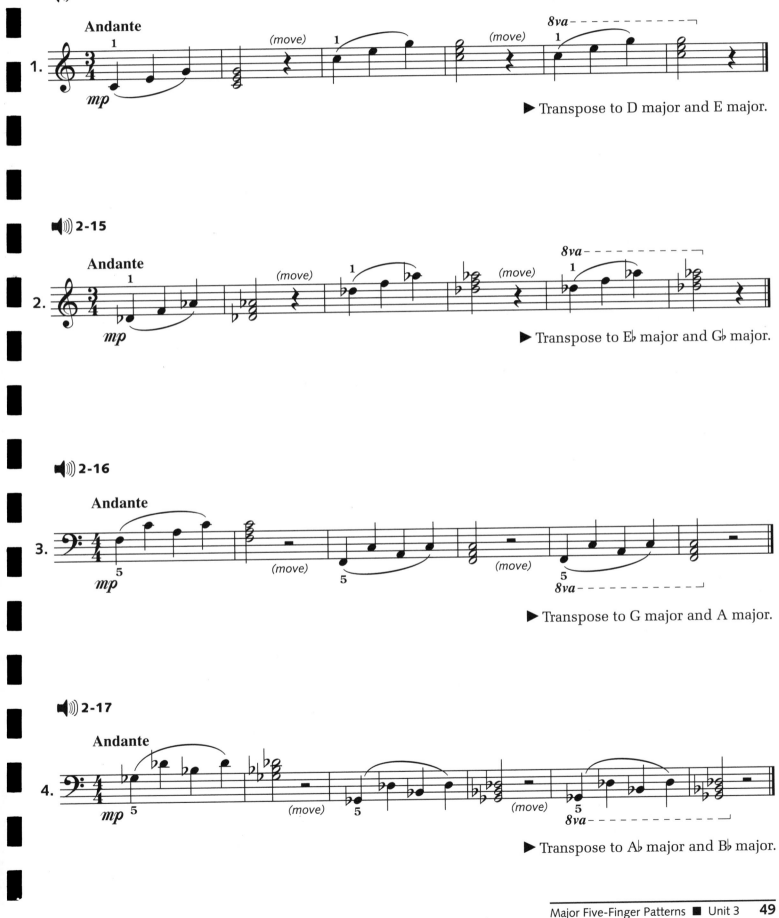

▶ Transpose to D major and E major.

🔊 **2-15**

▶ Transpose to E♭ major and G♭ major.

🔊 **2-16**

▶ Transpose to G major and A major.

🔊 **2-17**

▶ Transpose to A♭ major and B♭ major.

Identify the key of each example. Use the indicated tempo, dynamics and articulation as you play these exercises.

Use the following practice directions:

1. Tap and count aloud.
2. Play and count aloud.
3. Play and say note names.

An **accent sign** (>) over or under a note means play that note louder.

TURKISH MARCH

2-18

Ludwig van Beethoven
(1770–1827)

2-19

► Transpose to F major.

🔊 2-20

Allegro

3.

p *leggiero* (lightly)

5

▶ Transpose to D♭ major.

🔊 2-21

Andante

4.

mf

f

5

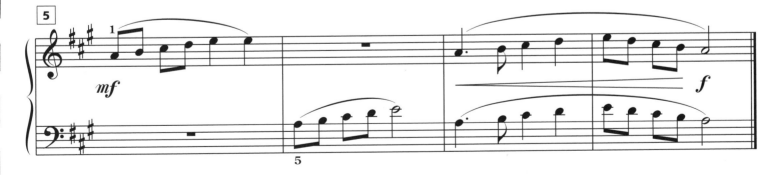

mf

f

▶ Transpose to C major.

Harmonization

Harmonize each of the melodies by playing tonic (**I**) or dominant (**V**) on the first beat of every measure.

- Use tonic when most of the melody notes are 1, 3 and 5.
- Use dominant when most of the melody notes are 2, 4 and 5.
- Begin and end each harmonization using tonic.

Dominant almost always precedes tonic at the end of the piece.

◀))) 2-22

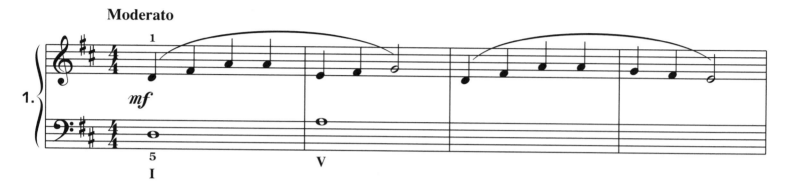

▶ Transpose to E major.

◀))) 2-23

▶ Transpose to C major.

2-24

3.

▶ Transpose to B♭ major.

2-25

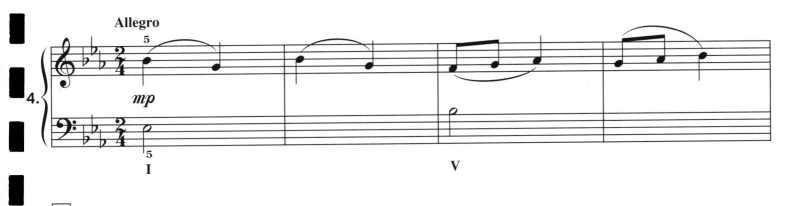

4.

▶ Transpose to D♭ major.

Duet Repertoire

WALTZ
(THE CHILDREN'S MUSICAL FRIEND)
Secondo—Teacher

🔊 2-26

Heinrich Wohlfahrt (1797–1883)
Op. 87, No. 39

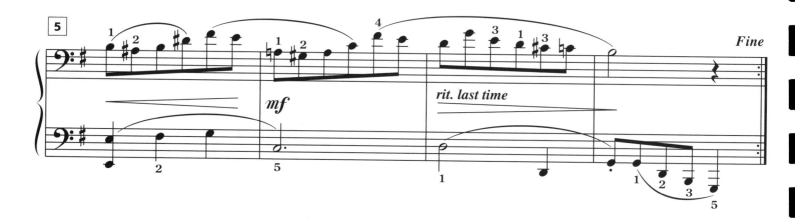

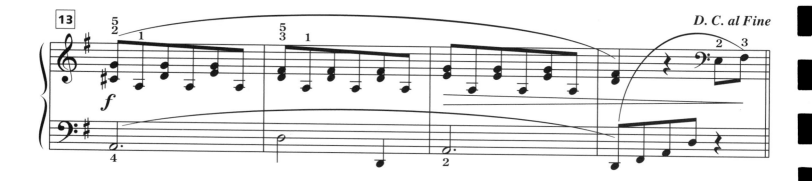

WALTZ
(THE CHILDREN'S MUSICAL FRIEND)
Primo—Student

D. C. (da capo) al Fine means repeat from the beginning and play to **Fine** (the end).

🔊 2-26

Heinrich Wohlfahrt (1797–1883)
Op. 87, No. 39

Tranquillo (tranquil)
♩=88
RH one octave higher than written throughout

LH two octaves higher than written throughout

*E*nsemble Repertoire

Play the four-part ensemble using the indicated chords to complete parts 3 and 4.

Part 1: Melody
Part 2: Countermelody (one octave higher than written throughout)
Part 3: Two-hand accompaniment
Part 4: Roots of chords (one octave lower than written throughout)

BARCAROLLE

2-27

E. L. Lancaster

Five-Finger Improvisation (Major)

Improvise an 8-measure melody using notes from the indicated five-finger pattern as the teacher plays each accompaniment. Listen to the 4-measure introduction to establish the tempo, mood and style before beginning the melody. You can use the suggested rhythm for your improvisation or create your own rhythm to complement the accompaniment.

1. Using a RH D major five-finger pattern, begin and end your melody on the D above middle C.

🔊 2-28

TEACHER ACCOMPANIMENT

2. Using a RH F major five-finger pattern, begin and end your melody on the F above middle C.

🔊 2-29

TEACHER ACCOMPANIMENT

Major Five-Finger Pattern Review

Objectives

Upon completion of this unit the student will be able to:

1. Play major five-finger patterns and major triads beginning on any key.
2. Perform solo repertoire that utilizes major five-finger patterns.
3. Sight-read and transpose melodies in major five-finger patterns.
4. Harmonize melodies with root position chords.
5. Create two-hand accompaniments from chord symbols.
6. Perform four-part ensembles with partners.

Assignments

Week of 9/14

Write your assignments for the week in the space below.

- Play triads moving up half steps

- be at piano Wednesday

- play triads crossing over (start with block chords then play broken)

9/21 2 octave scales:
C, G, D, A, E   (pg 347)

★↑ practice these
123 45   123   123 4   123

- thumbs play tonic, 3rd finger plays together

- pg 69 and 70

- Little Scherzo (rep piece)

★ - scale quiz Monday

- Harmonization 2-44

- play Happy Birthday by ear, start on Middle C

Major Five-Finger Pattern Groups

Major five-finger patterns can be divided into groups by the color of the keys in their **I** or tonic chords.

B = Black key   W = White key

Group 1 (C, G, F)

Tonic Chord: W W W

Five-Finger Patterns:
C, G — W W W W W
  F — W W W B W

Play the following:

▶ Transpose to G and F.

Group 2 (D, A, E)

Tonic Chord: W B W

Five-Finger Patterns:
D, A — W W B W W
   E — W B B W W

Play the following:

▶ Transpose to A and E.

Group 3 (D♭, A♭, E♭)

Tonic Chord: B W B

Five-Finger Patterns:
D♭, A♭ — B B W B B
   E♭ — B W W B B

Play the following:

▶ Transpose to A♭ and E♭.

Group 4 (B♭, B, G♭ or F♯)

Tonic Chord:
   B♭ — B W W
    B — W B B
G♭ or F♯ — B B B

Five-Finger Patterns:
   B♭ — B W W B W
    B — W B B W B
G♭ or F♯ — B B B W B

Play the following:

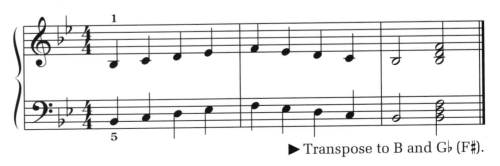

▶ Transpose to B and G♭ (F♯).

Playing Major Chords

Play the following exercises that use major chords with alternating hands:

🔊 2-30

🔊 2-31

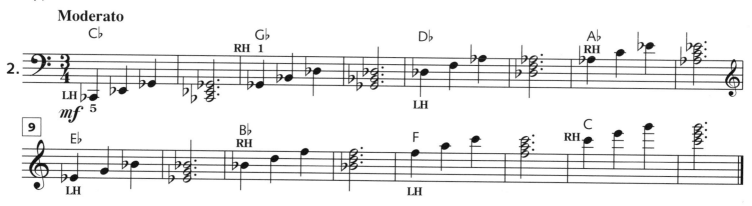

Playing Major Five-Finger Patterns and Broken Chords

Play the following exercise that uses major five-finger patterns and broken chords:

🔊 2-32

Continue upward by half steps until. . .

Sixteenth Notes

When a sixteenth note is written alone it has two flags. When written in pairs or groups of four, they are joined with two beams.

Four sixteenth notes are played in the time of one quarter note:

Count: 1 e & a = ♩
or Four six-teenth notes

Rhythm Reading

Tap the following rhythm patterns using RH for notes with stems going up and LH for notes with stems going down. For examples using both hands, tap hands separately first, and then hands together, always counting aloud.

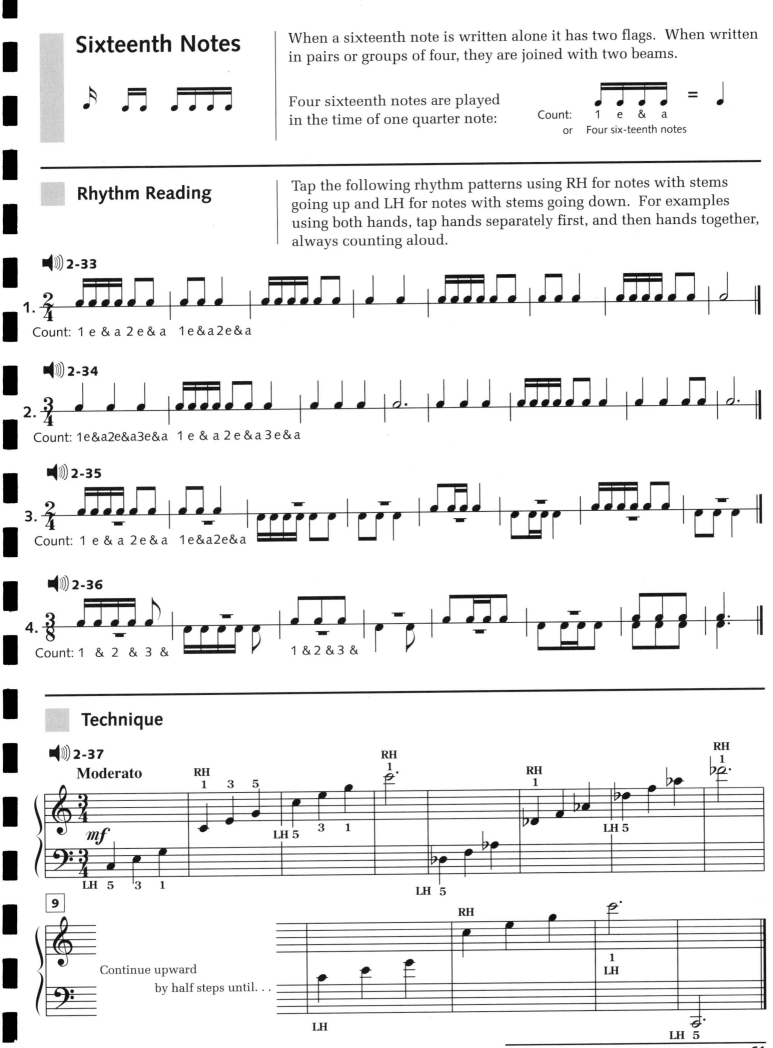

2-33

1. Count: 1 e & a 2 e & a   1 e & a 2 e & a

2-34

2. Count: 1 e & a 2 e & a 3 e & a   1 e & a 2 e & a 3 e & a

2-35

3. Count: 1 e & a 2 e & a   1 e & a 2 e & a

2-36

4. Count: 1 & 2 & 3 &   1 & 2 & 3 &

Technique

2-37

Moderato

mf

9

Continue upward by half steps until. . .

Reading

Identify the key of each example. Use the indicated tempo, dynamics and articulation as you play these exercises.

Use the following practice directions:
1. Tap RH and count aloud; then LH.
2. Play hands separately and count aloud.
3. Tap hands together and count aloud.
4. Play hands together and count aloud.

STUDY
(THE FIRST TERM AT THE PIANO)

2-38

Moderato

Béla Bartók
(1881–1945)

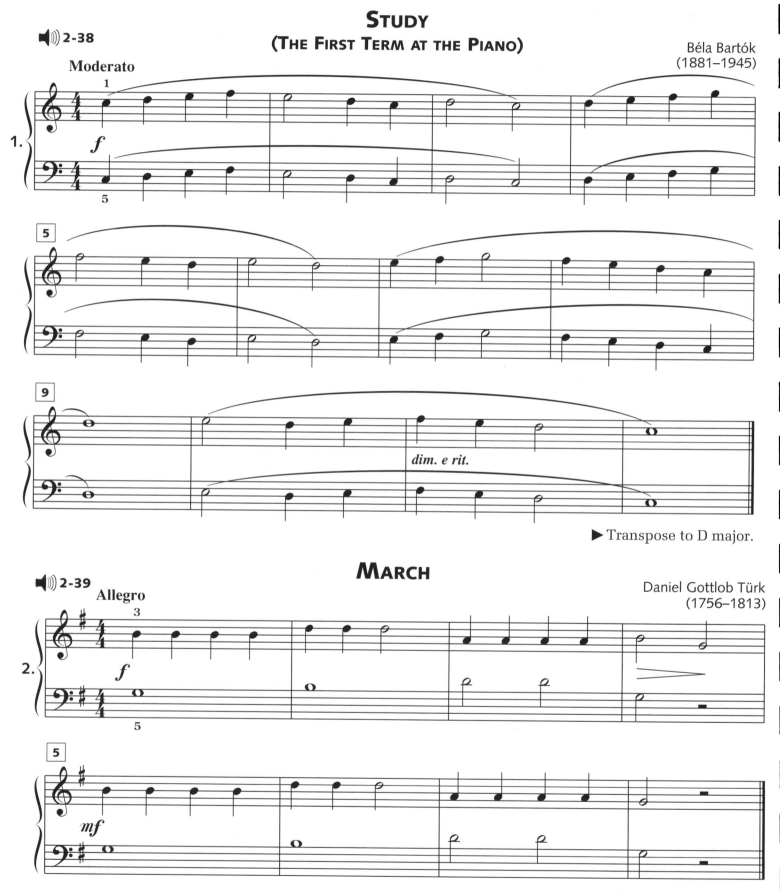

► Transpose to D major.

MARCH

2-39

Allegro

Daniel Gottlob Türk
(1756–1813)

► Transpose to F major.

2-40

Maestoso

3.

▶ Transpose to A major.

2-41

Moderato

4.

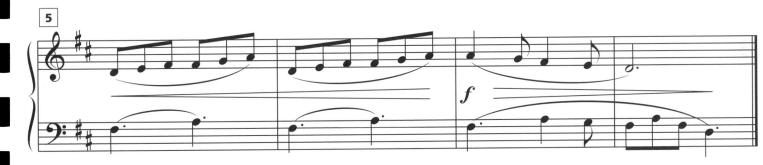

5.

▶ Transpose to C major.

ETUDE

Carl Czerny
(1791–1857)

2-42

Allegretto

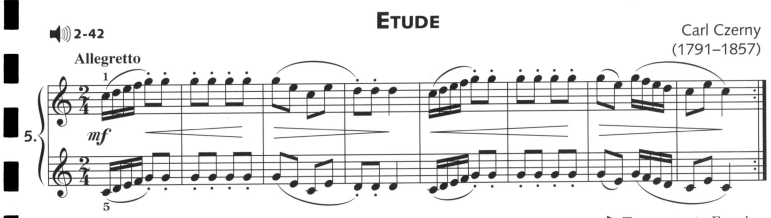

5.

▶ Transpose to F major.

Solo Repertoire

Before playing:

- Notice that the LH is written in treble clef.
- Tap the finger numbers in rhythm, first hands separately, and then together.
- Identify the measures with slurs.

A **tenuto** mark (–) means to hold the note for its full value.

While playing:

- Listen carefully for slurs and staccato notes.
- Stress the notes that have a tenuto marking and hold them for their full value.
- Slightly separate the notes that have both a staccato dot and a tenuto marking.

LITTLE SCHERZO

◀))) 2-43

E. L. Lancaster

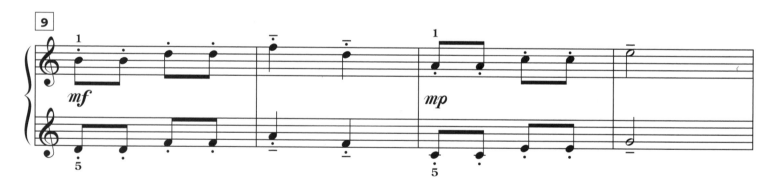

Harmonization

Harmonize each of the melodies by playing the indicated root-position chords. In measures where no chords are indicated, the last chord from the previous measure is repeated on beat one.

🔊 2-44

🔊 2-45

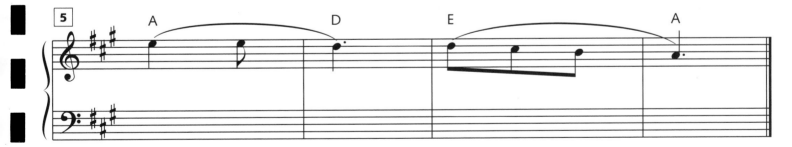

Playing by Ear

Using notes in the major five-finger pattern, play the following melodies. If you are unfamiliar with a melody, learn it by listening to the audio file or MIDI file.

🔊 2-46 When the Saints Go Marching In (Key of F, start on F)

🔊 2-47 Go Tell Aunt Rhody (Key of D, start on F♯)

Ensemble Repertoire

FORTY-FINGER ENSEMBLE

Part 1

2-48

Lively

E. L. Lancaster

Part 2

2-48

Lively

E. L. Lancaster

Part 3

 2-48

Lively
Both hands one octave higher than written throughout

E. L. Lancaster

Part 4

 2-48

Lively
Both hands two octaves lower than written throughout

E. L. Lancaster

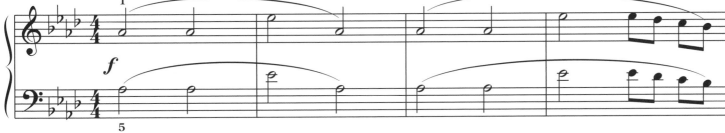

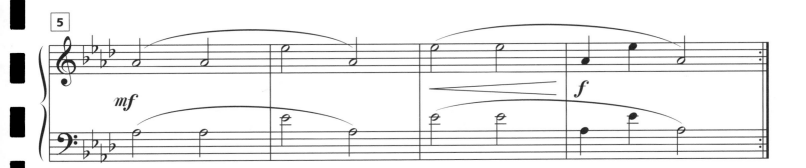

Harmonization with Two-Hand Accompaniment

Using the indicated chords, create a two-hand accompaniment for the following melody by continuing the pattern given in the first three measures.

🔊 2-49

Moderato

Germany

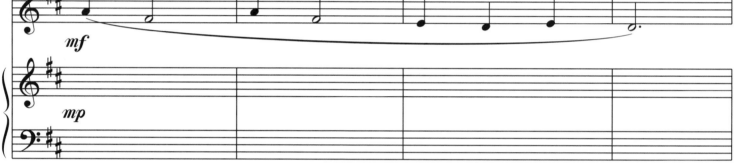

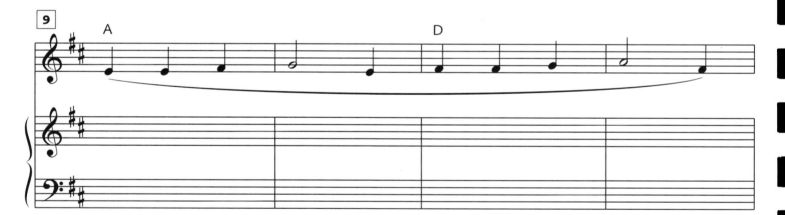

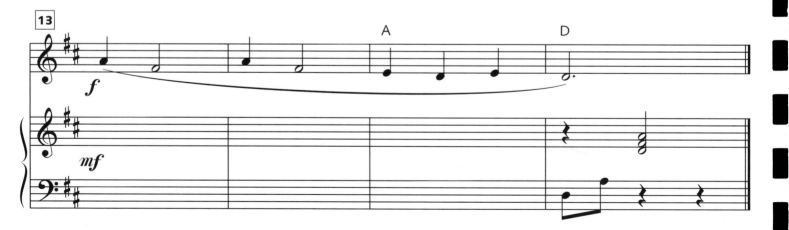

Review Worksheet

Name _Jacob Mick_   Date _9/23/20_

1. Begin on each given key and build an ascending major five-finger
   pattern. Write the names of the keys in the blanks.

   G _A_ _B_ _C_ _D_

   A _B_ _C#_ _D_ _E_

   D♭ _E♭_ _F_ _G♭_ _A♭_

   B♭ _C_ _D_ _E♭_ _F_

---

2. Identify each major five-finger pattern from its black-white key
   sequence. Write the name of the five-finger pattern in the blank.

W	W	W	B	W	_F_
W	B	B	W	W	_E_
B	W	W	B	B	_E♭_
B	B	B	W	B	_F#_

---

3. Identify each major triad by writing its name on the line.

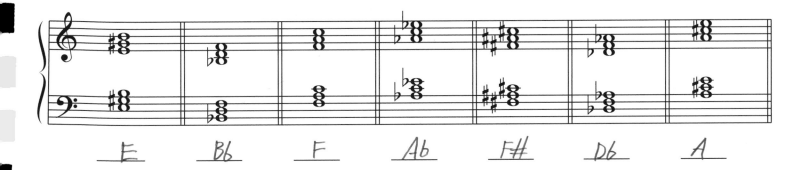

_E_   _B♭_   _F_   _A♭_   _F#_   _D♭_   _A_

4. Identify the major chords from their black-white key sequence.
    Write the names of the chords in the blanks.

B	W	B	E♭	A♭	D♭
W	B	W	D	A	E
W	W	W	C	F	G

5. Draw a line to connect the major key on the left with its
    corresponding key signature on the right.

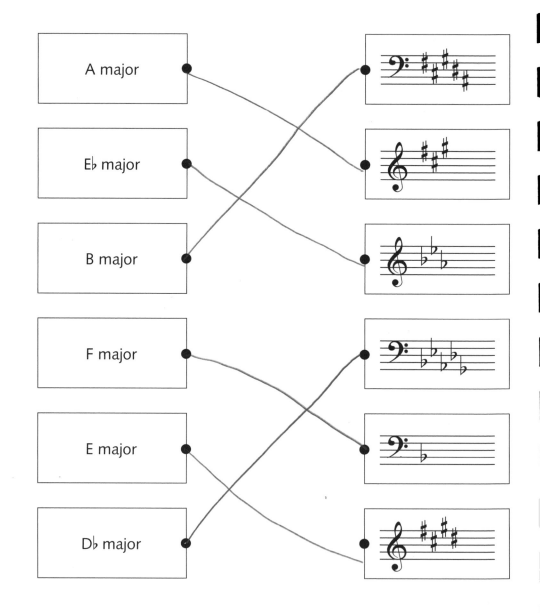

Minor Five-Finger Patterns

Objectives

Upon completion of this unit the student will be able to:

1. Play minor five-finger patterns and minor triads beginning on any key.
2. Perform solo repertoire that utilizes minor five-finger patterns.
3. Sight-read and transpose melodies in minor five-finger patterns.
4. Harmonize minor melodies with tonic and dominant tones as an accompaniment.
5. Create four-part ensembles from chord symbols.

Assignments

Week of 9/88

Write your assignments for the week in the space below.

- Erie Canal part 3 (pg 83)

- rep piece: Dream Echoes (pg 116)

•notes: dominant 7 chord - 2 notes   (V7)

    I chord - C E G

    dom 7 - F G

    I chord - D F# A

    dom 7 - G A

    I chord - E G# B

    dom 7 - A B

4 types of chords: major

    minor - lower 3rd

    augmented - raise 5th

    diminished - lower 3rd and 5th

Minor Five-Finger Patterns

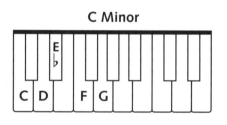

WHOLE STEP · HALF STEP · WHOLE STEP · WHOLE STEP

A minor five-finger pattern is a series of five notes having a pattern of *whole step, half step, whole step, whole step.*

The first note of the pattern is the tonic (**i**). The fifth note of the pattern is the dominant (**V**).

LH five-finger patterns are fingered 5 4 3 2 1.
RH five-finger patterns are fingered 1 2 3 4 5.

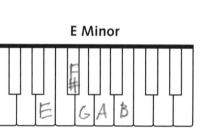

■ **Written Exercise:**
Write letter names on the correct keys to form each minor five-finger pattern.

Example:

C Minor

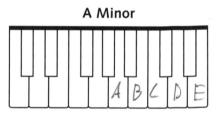

D Minor

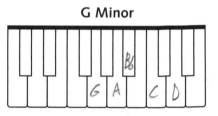

G Minor

E Minor

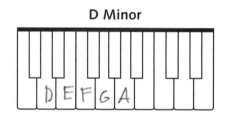

A Minor

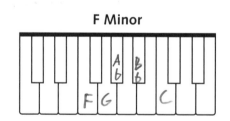

F Minor

B Minor

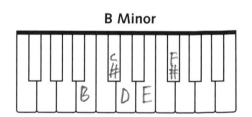

Major and Minor Five-Finger Patterns

Major five-finger patterns become minor five-finger patterns when the third (middle note) is lowered a half step.

Major Five-Finger Pattern:

Minor Five-Finger Pattern:

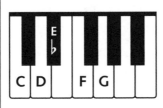

Playing Major and Minor Five-Finger Patterns

Play the following exercise that uses major and minor five-finger patterns.

◀))) **3-1**

Continue upward beginning on white keys until. . .

■ **Written Exercise:**

Write letter names on the correct keys to form each minor five-finger pattern.

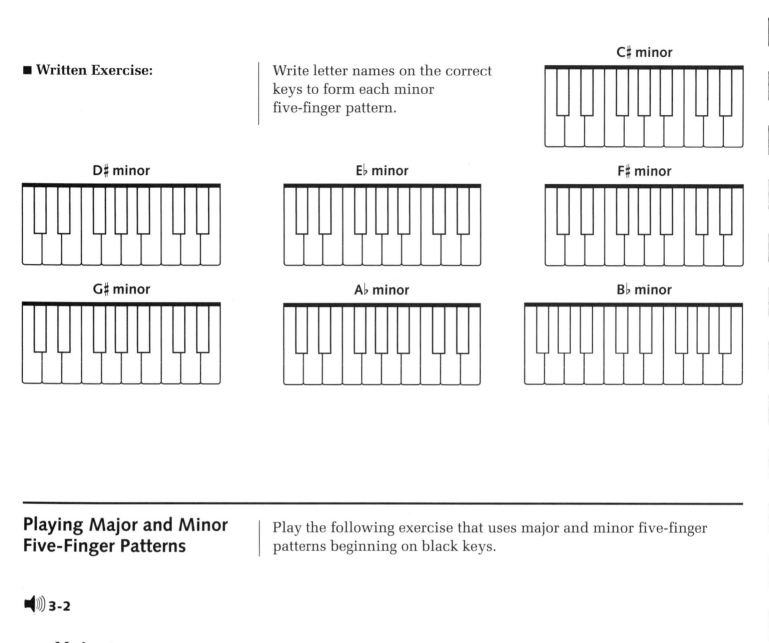

Playing Major and Minor Five-Finger Patterns

Play the following exercise that uses major and minor five-finger patterns beginning on black keys.

Minor Chords

Major chords become minor chords when the third (middle note) is lowered a half step.

Major Chord

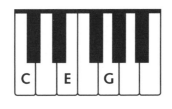

Minor Chord

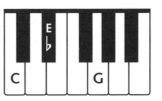

Playing Minor Five-Finger Patterns and Chords

Play the following exercises that use minor five-finger patterns and chords.

🔊 3-3

Moderato

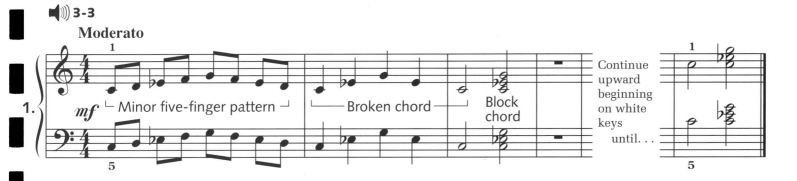

Minor five-finger pattern — Broken chord — Block chord

Continue upward beginning on white keys until...

🔊 3-4

Moderato

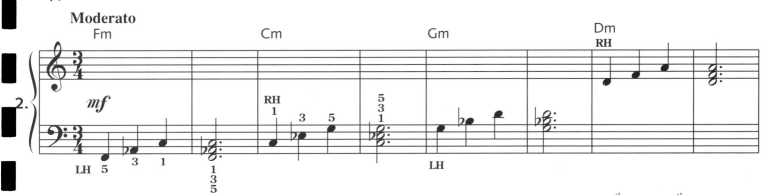

Playing Minor Five-Finger Patterns and Chords

Play the following exercises that use minor five-finger patterns and chords beginning on black keys.

🔊 **3-5**

🔊 **3-6**

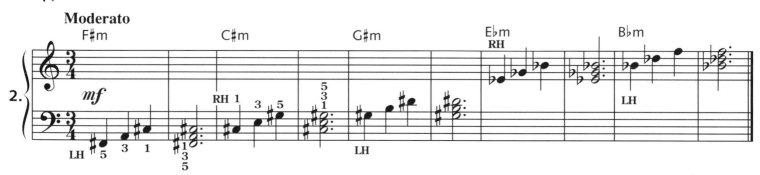

Reading

Identify the key of each example. Use the indicated tempo, dynamics and articulation as you play these exercises.

Use the following practice directions:

1. Tap RH and count aloud; then LH.
2. Play hands separately and count aloud.
3. Tap hands together and count aloud.
4. Play hands together and count aloud.

STUDY

🔊 **3-7**

Ferdinand Beyer (1803–1863)
Op. 101, No. 42

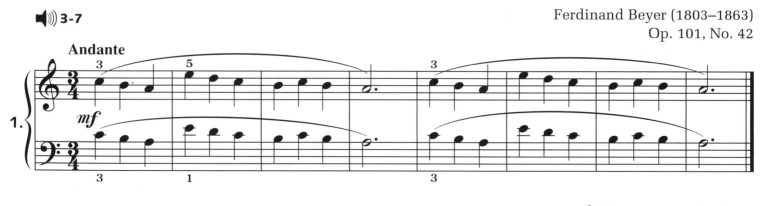

▶ Transpose to G minor.

LITTLE STUDY
(MUSICAL ABC)

Heinrich Wohlfahrt
(1797–1883)

3-8

Andante con moto *(with motion)*

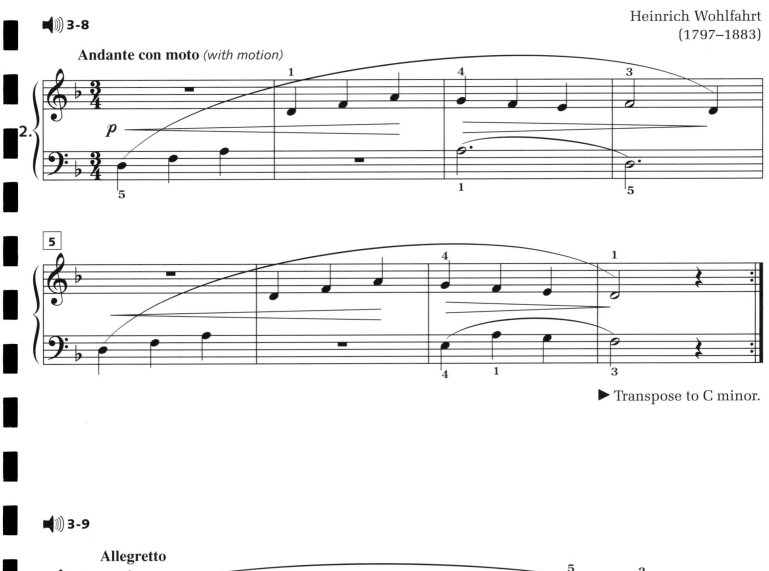

▶ Transpose to C minor.

3-9

Allegretto

▶ Transpose to G minor.

🔊 **3-10**

Flowing

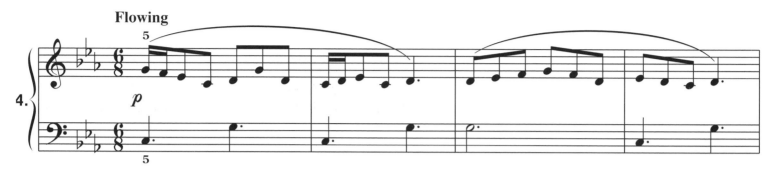

5.

 5

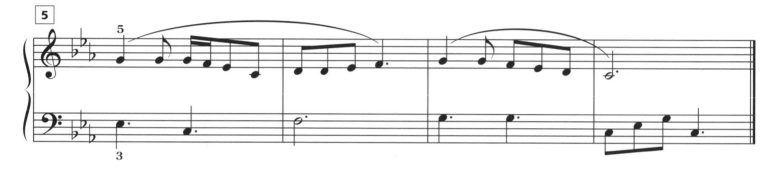

▶ Transpose to D minor.

Notes played between the main beats of a measure and held across the beat are called **syncopated notes.** In the second measure of this piece, the quarter note in the RH is syncopated.

When notes on the same line or space are joined by a curved line, they are called **tied notes** (♩ ♩). The key is held down for the *combined* values of both notes.

🔊 **3-11**

Animato (animated, lively)

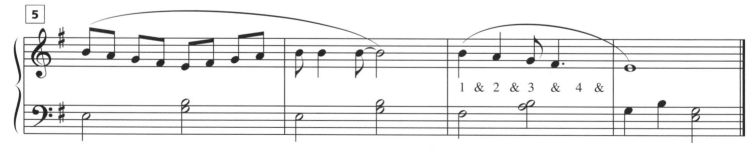

5.

1 & 2 & 3 & 4 &

5

1 & 2 & 3   & 4 &

▶ Transpose to D minor.

Relative Minor Keys

Every major key has a **relative minor key** that shares the *same key signature*. The name of the relative minor can be found by moving down (left) three half steps from the name of the major key. Always skip two keys and one alphabet letter.

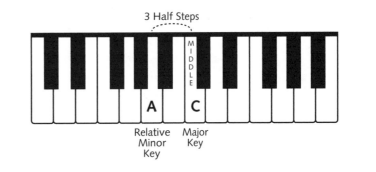

3 Half Steps

Relative Minor Key — A   Major Key — C

■ **Written Exercise:**
Write the name of each major key in the blank in the middle column. Write the name of its relative minor in the blank in the right column.

	Key Signature	Major Key	Minor Key
1.	𝄞	C	A
2.	𝄞 ♯♯	D	B
3.	𝄞 ♭♭♭	Ab	F
4.	𝄞 ♭	Bb	G
5.	𝄢 ♭	F	D
6.	𝄢 ♯	G	E
7.	𝄢 ♭♭♭	Eb	C

♪olo Repertoire

Before playing:
- Map the piece using *D.C. al Fine* and *Fine*.
- Notice the position change to the relative major in measures 9 and 10.
- Note that the LH is written in treble clef beginning in measure 10.
- Tap the finger numbers in rhythm, first hands separately, and then together.

While playing:
- Be aware of the two notes that are tied, with an accent on the first note.
- First practice hands separately. When playing hands together, notice how the LH imitates the RH.

ETUDE

Ferdinand Beyer (1803–1863)
Op. 101, No. 60

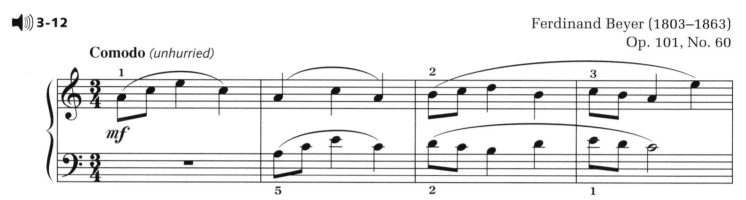

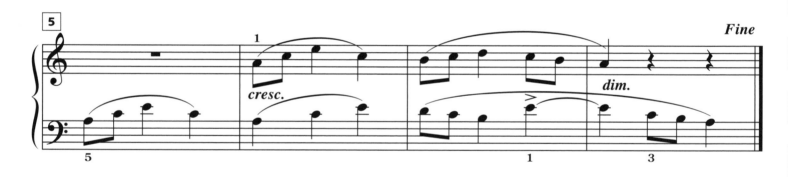

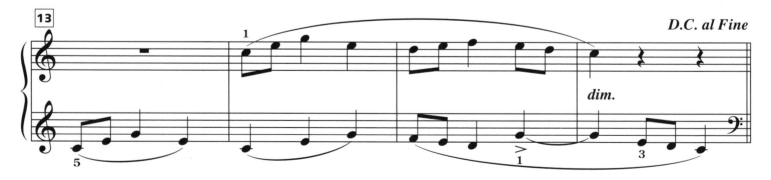

Technique

◀))) 3-13

Andante

▶ Transpose to D minor and E minor.

◀))) 3-14

Andante

▶ Transpose to G minor and A minor.

◀))) 3-15

Andante

▶ Transpose to D minor and F♯ minor.

◀))) 3-16

Andante

▶ Transpose to C♯ minor and G minor.

Harmonization

Harmonize each of the melodies by playing tonic (**i**) or dominant (**V**) on the first beat of every measure.

- Use tonic when most of the melody notes are 1, 3 and 5.
- Use dominant when most of the melody notes are 2, 4 and 5.
- Begin and end each harmonization using tonic.

Dominant almost always precedes tonic at the end of the piece.

▶ Transpose to A minor.

▶ Transpose to D minor.

▶ Transpose to C minor.

*E*nsemble Repertoire

Play the four-part ensemble using the indicated chords to complete parts 2, 3 and 4.

Part 1: Melody
Part 2: Broken chords (one octave higher than written throughout)
Part 3: Two-hand accompaniment
Part 4: Roots of chords

🔊 **3-20**

ERIE CANAL

keep doing same pattern

Minor Five-Finger Pattern Review

Objectives

Upon completion of this unit the student will be able to:

1. Play minor five-finger patterns and minor triads beginning on any key.

2. Perform solo repertoire that utilizes minor five-finger patterns.

3. Sight-read and transpose melodies in minor five-finger patterns.

4. Harmonize minor melodies with tonic and dominant tones as an accompaniment.

5. Perform duet repertoire with a partner.

6. Improvise melodies in minor five-finger patterns as the teacher plays an accompaniment.

Assignments

Week of 10/5

Write your assignments for the week in the space below.

notes:

I chord: C E G

5 7 chord: B F G   # practice these

I chord: D F# A

5 7 chord: C# G A

※ dominant 7th → left hand:
keep thumb on 5th, play 2nd
finger, slide pinky down half step

※ play I chord
2nd finger down
pinky down half step

- Cannon (pg 327)
- practice V VII chords
      - these are active

Playing Major and Relative Minor Five-Finger Patterns

Play the following exercise that uses major and relative minor five-finger patterns.

🔊 3-21

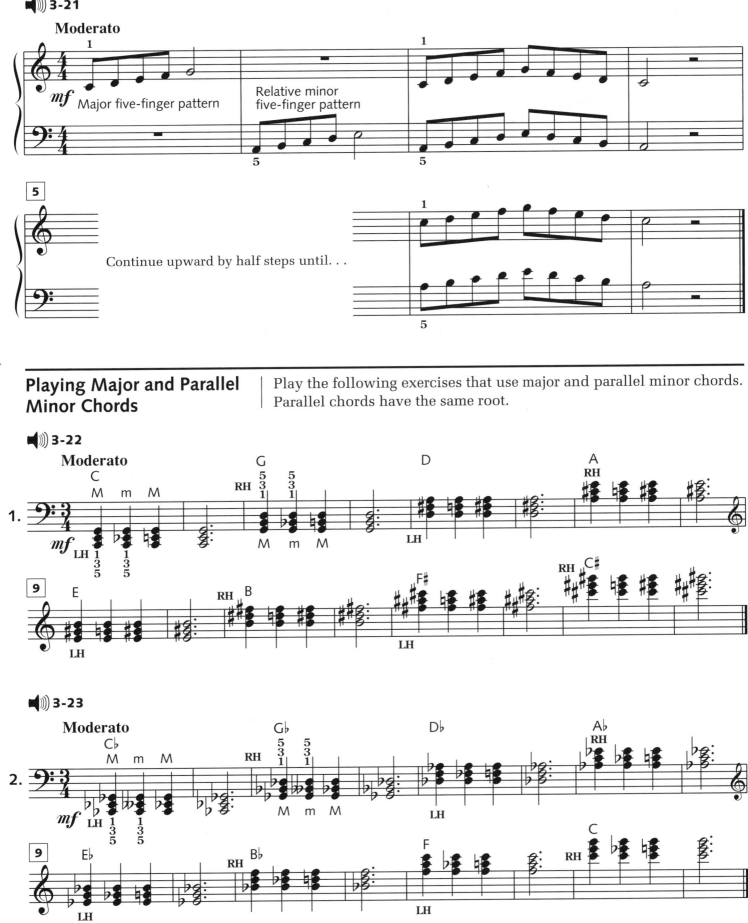

Continue upward by half steps until. . .

Playing Major and Parallel Minor Chords

Play the following exercises that use major and parallel minor chords. Parallel chords have the same root.

🔊 3-22

🔊 3-23

Eighth-Note Triplets

When three notes are grouped together with a figure "3" above or below the notes, the group is called a **triplet.** The three notes of an eighth-note triplet group equal one quarter note.

When a piece contains triplets, count "trip-a-let" or "1-and-a."

Rhythm Reading

Tap the following rhythm patterns using RH for notes with stems going up and LH for notes with stems going down. Tap hands separately first, and then hands together, always counting aloud.

◀))) 3-24

1.

Count: 1   2   3   Trip-a-let

◀))) 3-25

2.

Count: 1   2   3   4   1   2   3   Trip-a-let

◀))) 3-26

3.

◀))) 3-27

4.

◀))) 3-28

5.

Harmonization

Harmonize each of the melodies by playing tonic (**i**) or dominant (**V**) on the first beat of every measure.

- Use tonic when most of the melody notes are 1, 3 and 5.
- Use dominant when most of the melody notes are 2, 4 and 5.
- Begin and end each harmonization using tonic.

Dominant almost always precedes tonic at the end of the piece.

◀))) 3-29

Lively

1.

▸ Transpose to F minor.

◀))) 3-30

Allegro

2.

▸ Transpose to D minor.

◀))) 3-31

Moderato

3.

▸ Transpose to F♯ minor.

Solo Repertoire

¢ This time signature is **alla breve,** sometimes called "cut time." This indicates $\frac{2}{2}$ time. Count *one* for each half note, etc.

Before playing:
- Map the piece using *D.C. al Fine* and *Fine.*
- Locate and mark the measures where both hands change to a different position.
- Tap the rhythm with both hands.

While playing:
- Maintain a staccato touch throughout the piece.
- Observe the dynamics for an exciting performance!

TOCCATINA

3-32

E. L. Lancaster

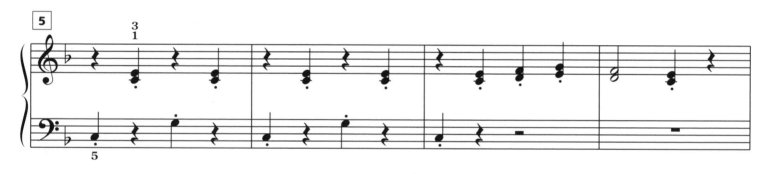

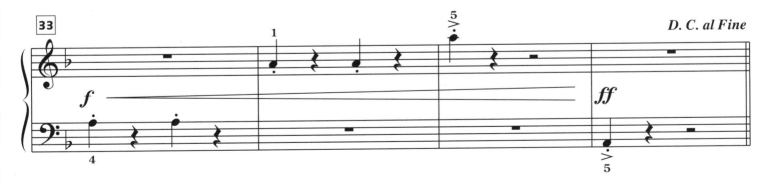

Reading

Identify the key of each example. Use the indicated tempo, dynamics and articulation as you play these exercises.

Use the following practice directions:

1. Tap RH and count aloud; then LH.
2. Play hands separately and count aloud.
3. Tap hands together and count aloud.
4. Play hands together and count aloud.

STUDY

3-33

Ferdinand Beyer (1803–1863)
Op. 101, No. 43

Moderato

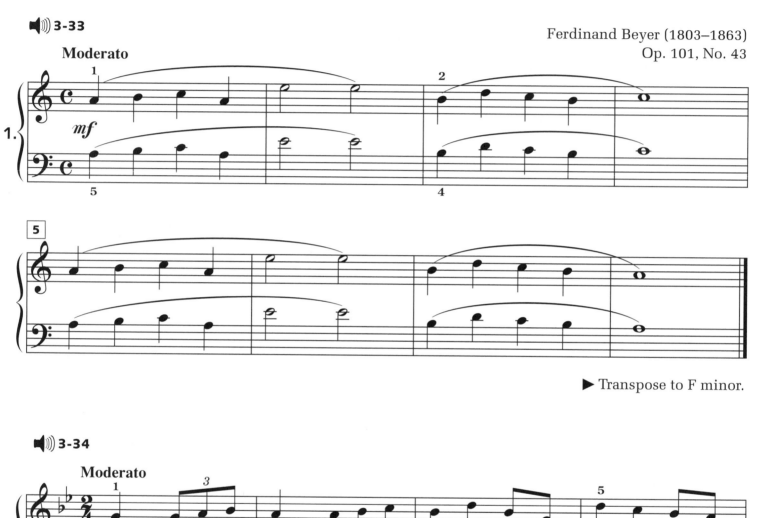

► Transpose to F minor.

3-34

Moderato

► Transpose to A minor.

🔊 **3-35**

Relaxed

▶ Transpose to C minor.

🔊 **3-36**

Moderato

▶ Transpose to C minor.

🔊 **3-37**

Allegretto

▶ Transpose to B minor.

Duet Repertoire

PRELUDE
(THE CHILDREN'S MUSICAL FRIEND)

Secondo—Teacher

🔊 3-38

Heinrich Wohlfahrt (1797–1883)
Op. 87, No. 2

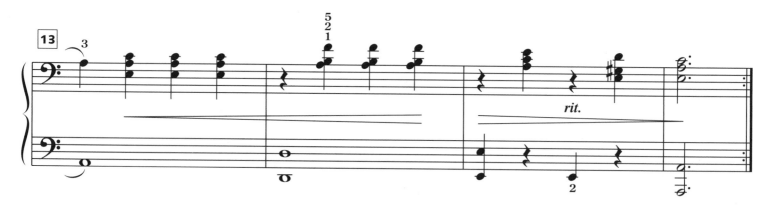

Some pieces begin with an **incomplete measure.** The first measure below has only one count. The three missing counts are found in the last measure.

PRELUDE
(THE CHILDREN'S MUSICAL FRIEND)
Primo—Student

3-38

Heinrich Wohlfahrt (1797–1883)
Op. 87, No. 2

Lento (slow)

RH one octave higher than written throughout

LH two octaves higher than written throughout

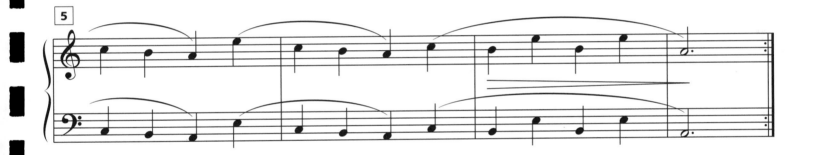

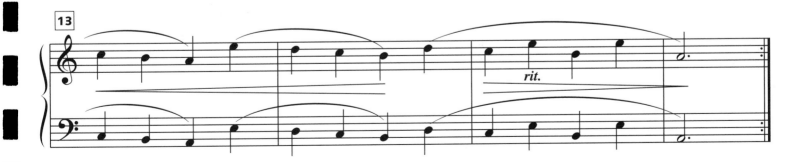

Five-Finger Improvisation (Minor)

Improvise an 8-measure melody using notes from the indicated five-finger pattern as the teacher plays each accompaniment. Listen to the 4-measure introduction to establish the tempo, mood and style before beginning the melody. You can use the suggested rhythm for your improvisation or create your own rhythm to complement the accompaniment.

1. Using a RH D minor five-finger pattern, begin and end your melody on the D above middle C.

◀))) 3-39

TEACHER ACCOMPANIMENT

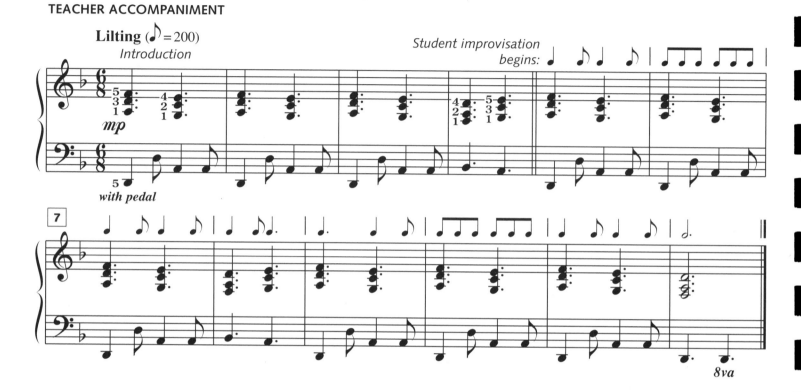

2. Using a RH G minor five-finger pattern, begin and end your melody on the G above middle C.

◀))) 3-40

TEACHER ACCOMPANIMENT

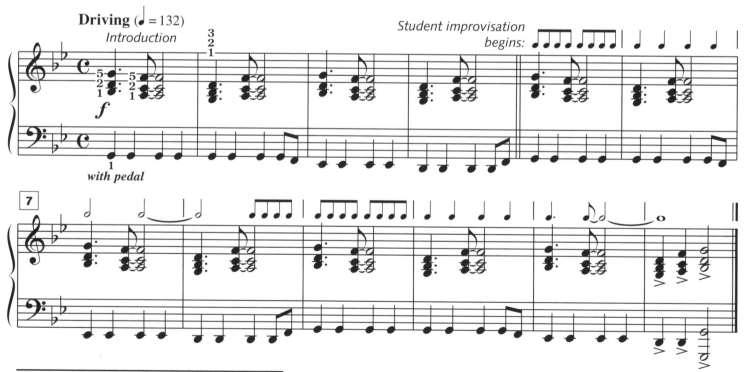

Review Worksheet

Name _____   Date _____

1. Begin on each given key and build an ascending minor five-finger
   pattern. Write the names of the keys in the blanks.

   B _____ _____ _____ _____ _____

   F _____ _____ _____ _____ _____

   E♭ _____ _____ _____ _____ _____

   C♯ _____ _____ _____ _____ _____

2. Identify each minor five-finger pattern from its black-white key
   sequence. Write the name of the five-finger pattern in the blank.

W	B	W	W	W	_____
B	B	W	W	B	_____
B	W	B	B	B	_____
W	W	B	B	W	_____

3. Identify each minor triad by writing its name on the line.

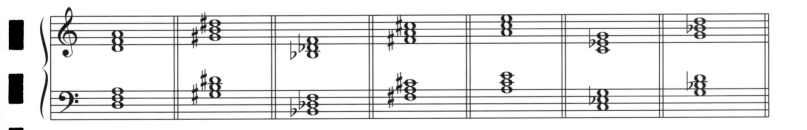

   _____   _____   _____   _____   _____   _____   _____

4. Identify the minor chords from their black-white key sequence.
   Write the names of the chords in the blanks.

B	**W**	**B**	____	____	____
W	**B**	**W**	____	____	____
W	**W**	**W**	____	____	____

5. Draw a line to connect the minor key on the left with its
   corresponding key signature on the right.

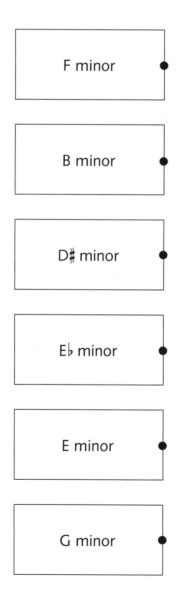

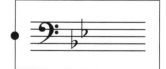

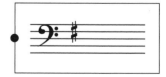

Chord Qualities

Objectives

Upon completion of this unit the student will be able to:

1. Play major, minor, augmented and diminished chords beginning on any key.
2. Perform solo and ensemble repertoire that uses various chord qualities.
3. Sight-read and transpose melodies with various chord qualities as an accompaniment.
4. Create two-hand accompaniments from chord symbols.

Assignments

Week of _____

Write your assignments for the week in the space below.

_____

_____

_____

_____

_____

_____

_____

_____

_____

_____

_____

_____

Augmented Chords

A major chord becomes **augmented** when the fifth is raised a half step. A plus sign (+) indicates an augmented chord.

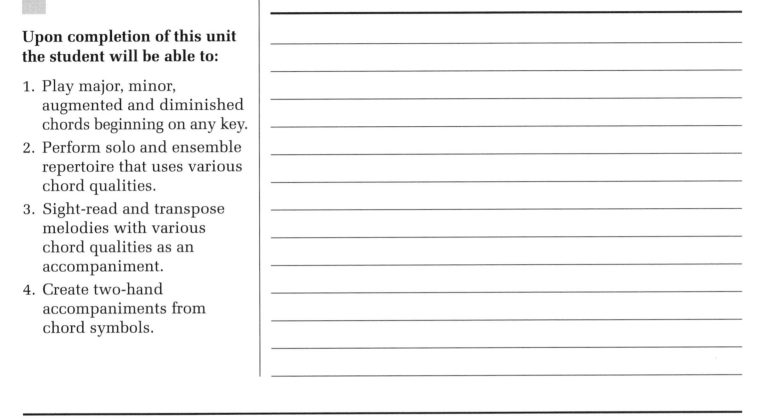

Playing Major and Augmented Chords

Play the following exercise that uses major (M) and augmented (A) chords.

🔊 4-1

Continue upward by half steps until. . .

Diminished Chords

A minor chord becomes **diminished** when the fifth is lowered a half step. A small circle (°) indicates a diminished chord.

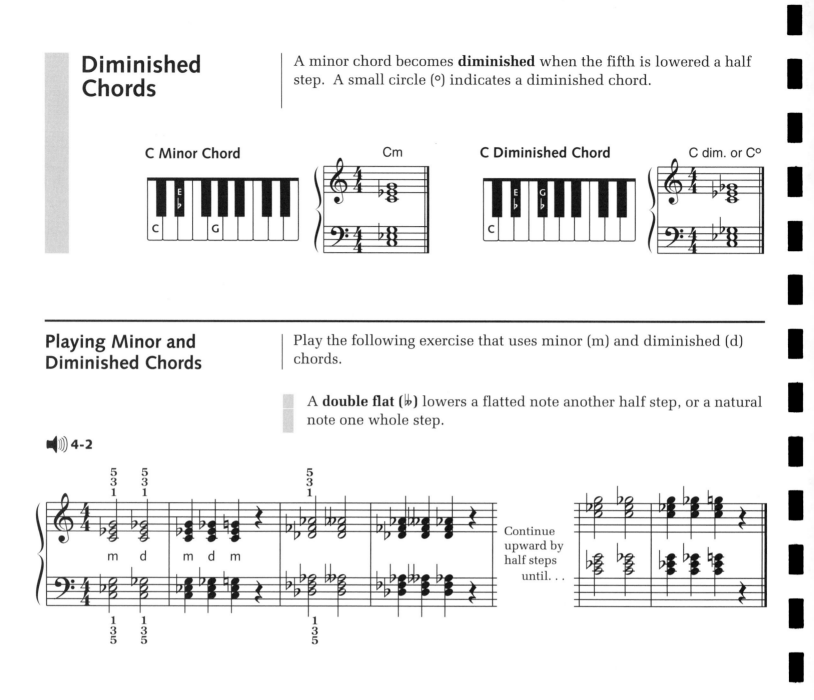

Playing Minor and Diminished Chords

Play the following exercise that uses minor (m) and diminished (d) chords.

A **double flat** (♭♭) lowers a flatted note another half step, or a natural note one whole step.

🔊 4-2

Playing Major, Augmented, Minor and Diminished Chords

Play the following exercise that uses major (M), augmented (A), minor (m) and diminished (d) chords.

A **double sharp** (𝄪) raises a sharped note another half step, or a natural note one whole step.

🔊 4-3

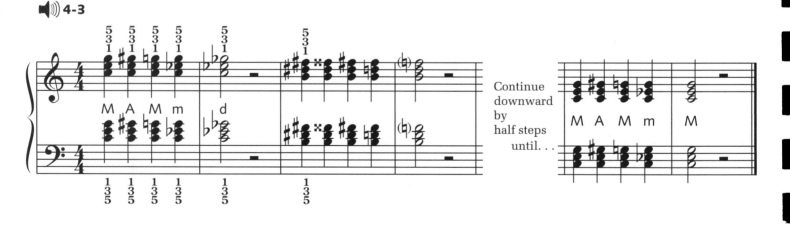

The Dotted Eighth Note

A dotted eighth note has the same value as an eighth note tied to a sixteenth note.

Rhythm Reading

Tap the following rhythm patterns using RH for notes with stems going up and LH for notes with stems going down. For exercises that use both hands, tap hands separately first, and then hands together, always counting aloud.

Solo Repertoire

Before playing:
- Block and name all the chords in the RH.
- Tap the finger numbers in rhythm with both hands.
- Circle each note that the LH plays by crossing over the RH.

While playing:
- Listen for accents as you play measures 15–16 and 30–31.
- Maintain the RH staccato throughout the piece.
- Observe the *crescendos* and *dimenuendos*.

🔊 4-10

TOPSY-TURVY

E. L. Lancaster

Vivo, giocoso *(lively, humorous)*

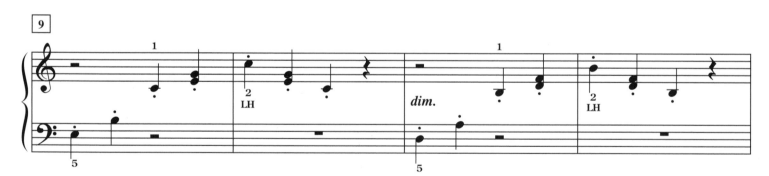

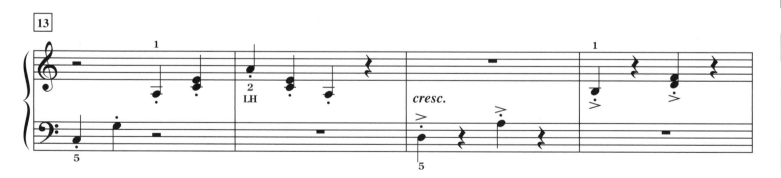

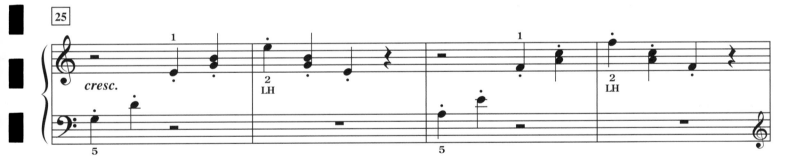

Reading

Identify the key of each example. Use the indicated tempo, dynamics and articulation as you play these exercises.

Use the following practice directions:

1. Tap RH and count aloud; then LH.
2. Play hands separately and count aloud.
3. Tap hands together and count aloud.
4. Play hands together and count aloud.

◀))) 4-11

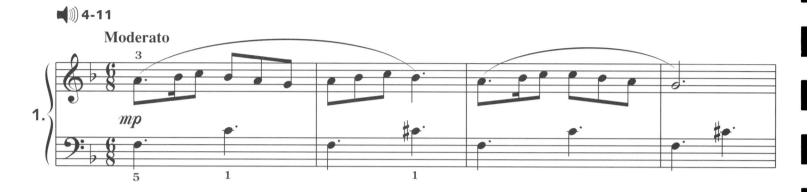

1.

5

▶ Transpose to G major.

◀))) 4-12

2.

4-13

Allegretto

3.

9

► Transpose to D major.

ALLEGRO

4-14

Alexander Reinagle
(1756–1809)

Allegro

4.

5

Technique

🔊 4-15

Moderato

1.

mf

5

Continue upward on white keys until. . .

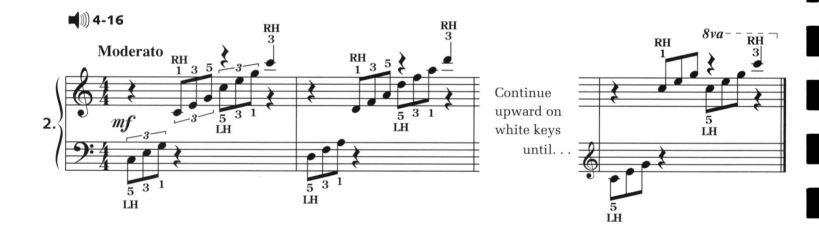

🔊 4-16

Moderato

2.

mf

Continue upward on white keys until. . .

🔊 4-17

Andante

3.

mp

▶ Transpose to E♭ and F.

🔊 4-18

Andante

4.

mp

▶ Transpose to F♯ and D.

Harmonization with Two-Hand Accompaniment

Using the indicated chords, create a two-hand accompaniment for the melodies by continuing the pattern given in the first two meas-

🔊 4-19

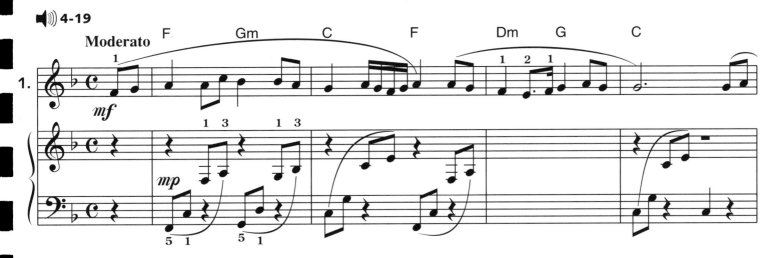

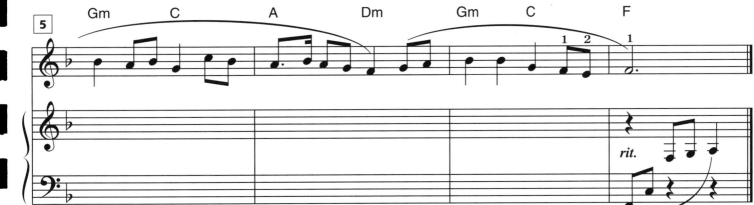

COUNTRY GARDENS

🔊 4-20

Percy Grainger
(1882–1961)

Major Scales in Tetrachord Position

Objectives

Upon completion of this unit the student will be able to:

1. Play major scales in tetrachord position.
2. Play exercises that utilize intervals up to an octave.
3. Use the damper pedal in performance.
4. Perform solo repertoire that uses intervals up to an octave.
5. Create two-hand accompaniments from chord symbols.
6. Sight-read melodies with intervals of 5ths, 6ths, 7ths and 8ths (octaves) as accompaniment.

Assignments

Week of _____

Write your assignments for the week in the space below.

_____

_____

_____

_____

_____

_____

_____

_____

_____

_____

_____

_____

_____

_____

Tetrachords and the Major Scale

A **tetrachord** is a series of four notes having a pattern of *whole step, whole step, half step.*

LH tetrachords are fingered 5 4 3 2.
RH tetrachords are fingered 2 3 4 5.

The **major scale** is made of two tetrachords joined by a whole step. Each scale begins and ends on a note of the same name as the scale, called the **keynote.** Any major scale can be formed by following this sequence of whole and half steps: W W H W W W H.

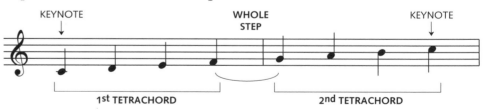

■ **Written Exercise:**   Write letter names on the correct keys to form each major scale. Then play using tetrachord position.

Example:

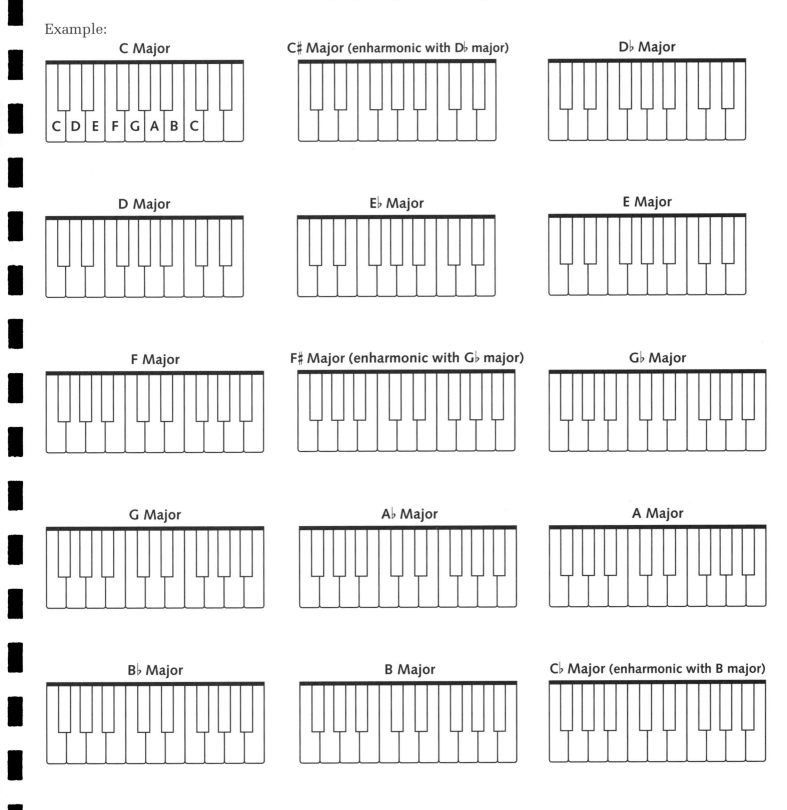

C Major

C# Major (enharmonic with D♭ major)

D♭ Major

D Major

E♭ Major

E Major

F Major

F# Major (enharmonic with G♭ major)

G♭ Major

G Major

A♭ Major

A Major

B♭ Major

B Major

C♭ Major (enharmonic with B major)

Playing Tetrachord Scales in Sharp Keys

Play the following major scales in tetrachord position while the teacher plays an accompaniment.

🔊 4-21

Moderate waltz tempo

41 **E Major**

51 **B Major**

61 **F♯ Major**

71 **C♯ Major**

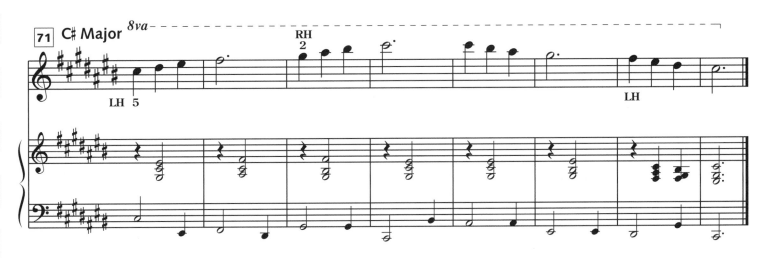

Playing Tetrachord Scales in Flat Keys

Play the following major scales in tetrachord position while the teacher plays an accompaniment.

🔊 4-22   **Moderate waltz tempo**

C♭ Major

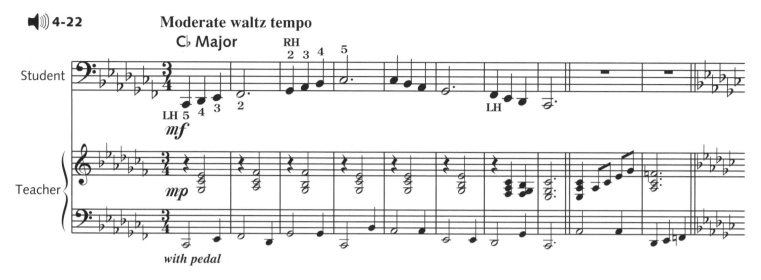

11 G♭ Major

21 D♭ Major

31 A♭ Major

41 **E♭ Major**

51 **B♭ Major**

F Major

61

71 **C Major**

Intervals of 6ths, 7ths and 8ths (octaves)

When you skip four white keys, the interval is a 6th.
6ths are written line-space or space-line.

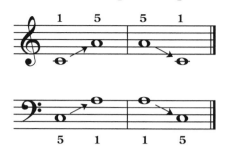
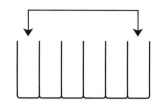

When you skip five white keys, the interval is a 7th.
7ths are written line-line or space-space.

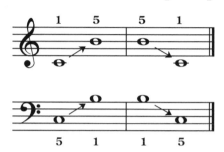
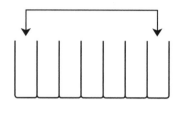

When you skip six white keys, the interval is an 8th (octave).
Octaves are written line-space or space-line.

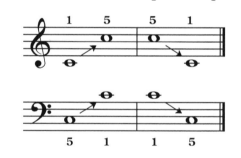
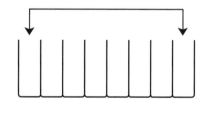

Play the following exercises that use intervals.

🔊 4-23

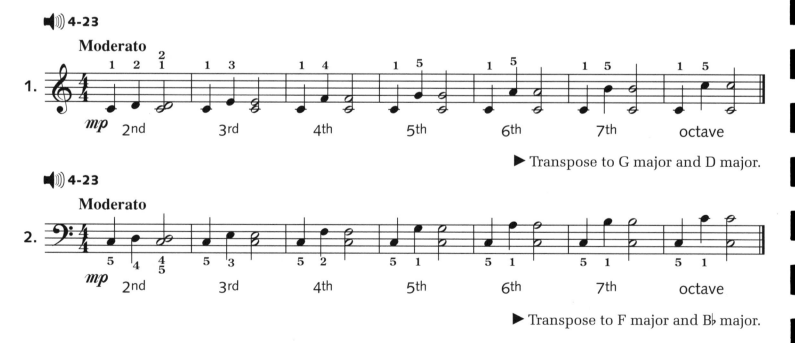

Moderato

1.

▶ Transpose to G major and D major.

🔊 4-23

Moderato

2.

▶ Transpose to F major and B♭ major.

The Damper Pedal

The right pedal is called the **damper pedal.** When you hold the damper pedal down, any tone you play continues after you release the key. The right foot is used on the damper pedal. Always keep your heel on the floor; use your ankle like a hinge.

This sign shows when the damper pedal is to be used:

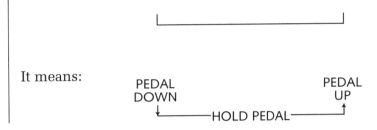

It means:

PEDAL DOWN   PEDAL UP

└───────HOLD PEDAL───────┘

Practice the following pedal exercise using intervals of 5ths, 6ths and 7ths. Notice how the damper pedal causes the tones to continue to sound, even after your hands have released the keys.

Press the pedal down as you play each group of notes. Hold it down through the rests.

Overlapping Pedal

The following sign is used to indicate **overlapping pedal.**

PLAY

PEDAL DOWN ∧ PEDAL DOWN

↑

At this point, the pedal comes up,
and it goes down again immediately!

Practice the following exercise. As you play each interval, let the pedal up and press it down again immediately. The pedal must come up exactly at the instant the notes come down, as if the pedal "comes up to meet the hand!" Careful listening is the key to successful pedaling.

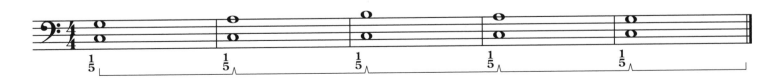

Technique

Harmonization with Two-Hand Accompaniment

Using the indicated chords, create a two-hand accompaniment for the melody by continuing the pattern given in the first two measures.

🔊 4-28

♩olo Repertoire

Before playing:
- Block the melodic fifths.
- Silently find each position change.
- Practice the cross overs in measures 13–14 and 29–30.

While playing:
- Observe the dynamics to create the echoes.
- Listen for clear pedal changes.

DREAM ECHOES

🔊 4-29

E. L. Lancaster

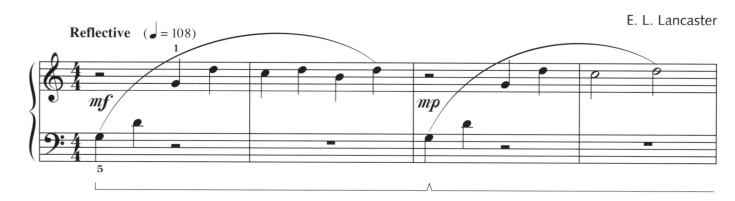

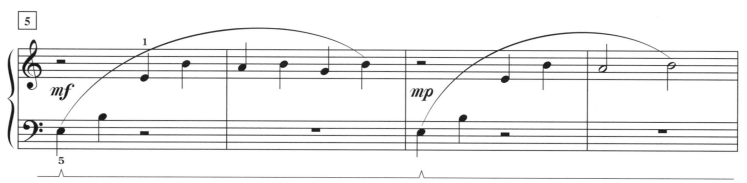

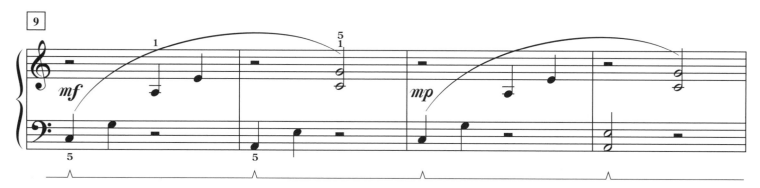

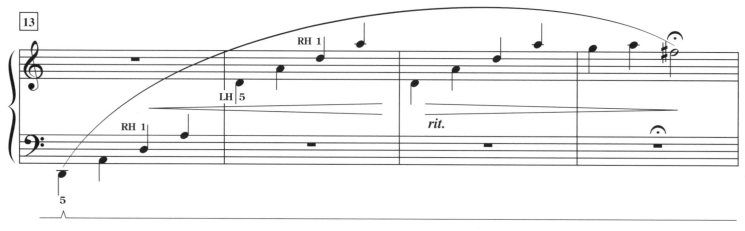

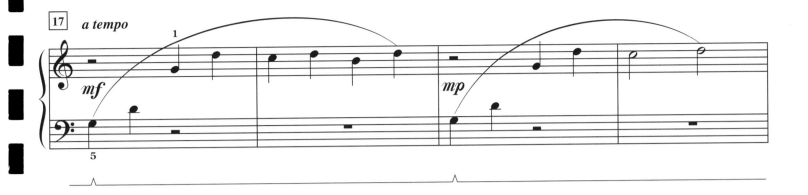

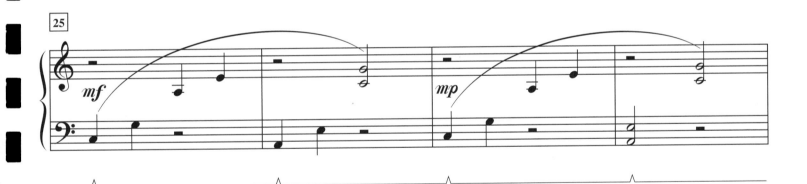

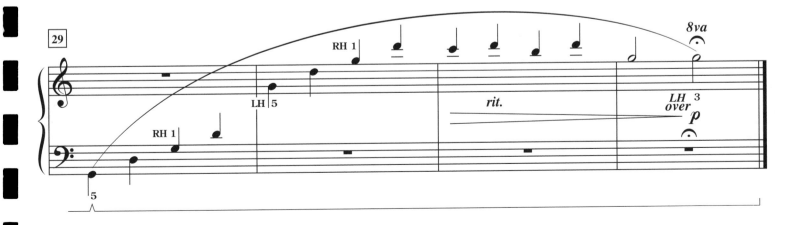

Identify the key of each example. Use the indicated tempo, dynamics and articulation as you play these exercises.

Use the following practice directions:

1. Tap RH and count aloud; then LH.
2. Play hands separately and count aloud.
3. Tap hands together and count aloud.
4. Play hands together and count aloud.

ON TOP OF OLD SMOKY

United States

🔊 4-32

5

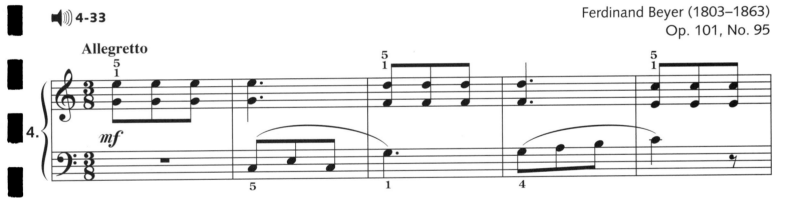

STUDY IN SIXTHS

Ferdinand Beyer (1803–1863)
Op. 101, No. 95

🔊 4-33

6

11

Major Scales (Group 1) and Triads of the Key

Objectives

Upon completion of this unit the student will be able to:

1. Build a triad on any note of the scale.

2. Play Group 1 major scales and arpeggios using traditional fingerings.

3. Perform solo repertoire that uses scale and arpeggio patterns.

4. Sight-read and transpose music that uses scale patterns.

5. Harmonize melodies with roots of chords.

6. Improvise scale melodies over roots of chords and root-position triads of the key.

Assignments

Week of 10/14

Write your assignments for the week in the space below.

- practice C and G arpeggios

Playing Triads of the Key

Triads may be built on any note of any scale. The sharps or flats in the key signature must be used when playing these triads. Triads of the key are identified by Roman numerals. These triads built on each scale degree are called **diatonic.**

Play triads of the key in C major.

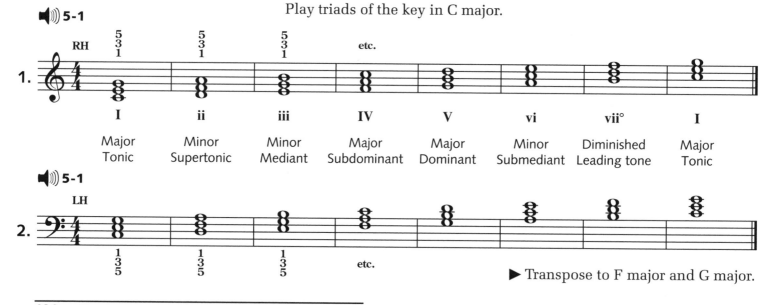

▶ Transpose to F major and G major.

Technique

Transpose to D, E, G, A and B major.

Transpose to D, E, F, G, and A major.

Practicing Major Scales (Group 1 Keys): C, G, D, A and E

The following principles will help you remember the fingering for the Group 1 major scales:

1. All five scales use the same fingering.
   RH: 1 2 3 1 2 3 4   1 2 3   1 2 3 4 5
   LH: 5 4 3 2 1   3 2 1   4 3 2 1   3 2 1
2. The fourth finger plays only once per octave in each scale.
3. Thumbs play on the tonic of each scale.
   (Note: Thumb must be substituted for finger 5 at the beginning and end of the scale.)
4. When playing hands together, finger 3 in each hand plays at the same time.

Practice Suggestions (Note: If you are just beginning major scales, you and your teacher may choose to practice the scale first for one octave rather than two.)

1. Build each scale in tetrachord position.
2. Block the scale as written below.
3. Play the scale hands separately using the correct fingering. (See pages 124–126.)

C Major

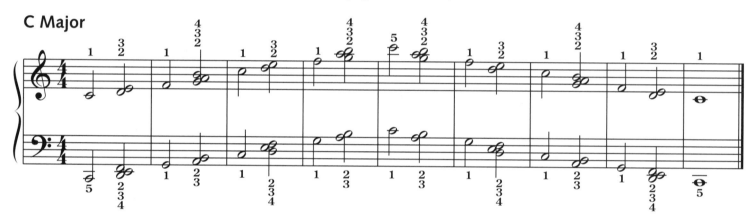

Scale Challenges

1. Play the scale in contrary motion as written below. (Notice that the same fingers in each hand play together.)
2. Play the scale hands together in parallel motion.
3. Play the scale (hands separately or together) *forte*, then *piano*.
4. Play the scale (hands separately or together) *staccato*, then *legato*.
5. Play the scale (hands separately or together) and *crescendo* when ascending, *diminuendo* when descending.

C Major

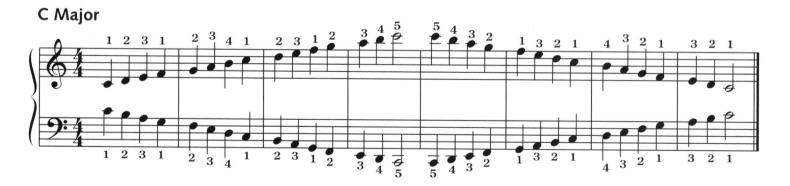

Practicing Major Arpeggios (Group 1 Keys): C, G, D, A and E

An **arpeggio** is a broken chord; pitches are sounded successively rather than simultaneously.

The following principles will help you remember the fingering for the Group 1 major arpeggios:

1. All five arpeggios use the same fingering in the RH.
   RH: 1 2 3   1 2 3 5
2. When playing the LH arpeggio, use finger 4 when there is one white key between the root and third of the broken chord. Use finger 3 when there are two white keys between the root and third of the broken chord.
   LH (C, G): 5 4 2 1   4 2 1
   LH (D, A, E): 5 3 2 1   3 2 1

Practice Suggestions (Note: If you are just beginning major arpeggios, you and your teacher may choose to practice the arpeggio for one octave rather than two.)

1. Play the blocked chords as written below.
2. Play the broken chords hand-over-hand as written below.
3. Play the arpeggio hands separately using the correct fingering. (See pages 124–126.)

C Major (blocked)

C Major (hand-over-hand)

Arpeggio Challenges

1. Play the arpeggio hands together in parallel motion.
2. Play the arpeggio (hands separately or together) *forte*, then *piano*.
3. Play the arpeggio (hands separately or together) *staccato*, then *legato*.
4. Play the arpeggio (hands separately or together) and *crescendo* when ascending, *diminuendo* when descending.

Playing Major Scales and Arpeggios

C Major

RH: 1 2 3 1 2 3 4   1 2 3 1 2 3 4 5
LH: 5 4 3 2 1 3 2   1 4 3 2 1 3 2 1

🔊 5-7

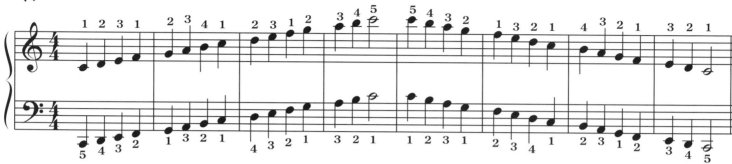

RH: 1 2 3   1 2 3 5
LH: 5 4 2   1 4 2 1

🔊 5-8

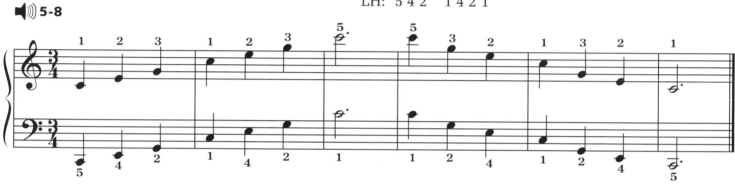

G Major   **Note:** A dot (•) above a fingering indicates a black key.

RH: 1 2 3 1 2 3 4̇   1 2 3 1 2 3 4 5̇
LH: 5 4 3 2 1 3 2̇   1 4 3 2 1 3 2̇ 1

🔊 5-9

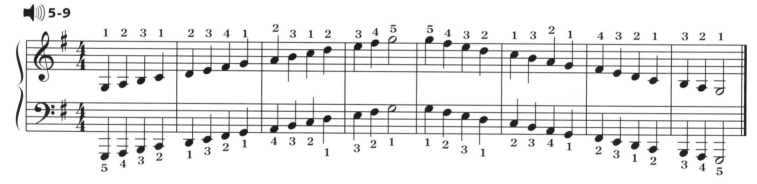

RH: 1 2 3   1 2 3 5
LH: 5 4 2   1 4 2 1

🔊 5-10

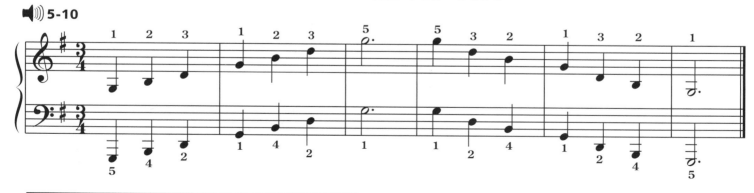

D Major

RH: 1 2 3̇ 1 2 3 4   1 2 3̇ 1 2 3 4 5
LH: 5 4 3̇ 2 1 3̇ 2   1 4 3̇ 2 1 3̇ 2 1

🔊 5-11

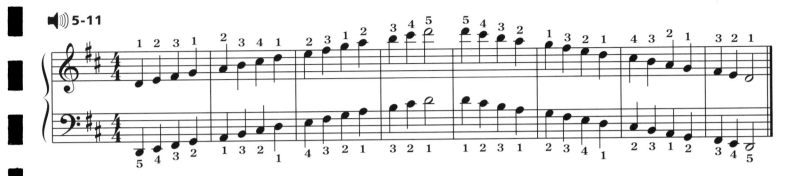

RH: 1 2̇ 3   1 2̇ 3 5
LH: 5 3̇ 2   1 3̇ 2 1

🔊 5-12

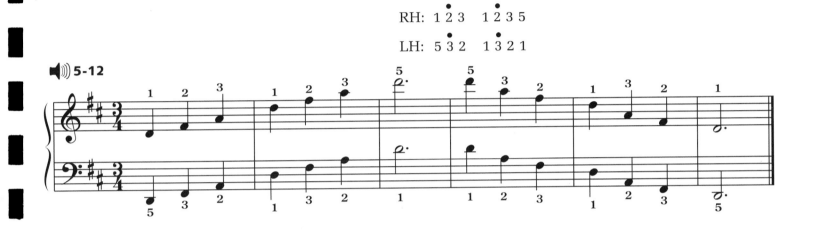

A Major

RH: 1 2 3̇ 1 2 3̈ 4   1 2 3̇ 1 2 3̈ 4 5
LH: 5 4 3̇ 2 1 3̈ 2   1 4 3̇ 2 1 3̈ 2 1

🔊 5-13

RH: 1 2̇ 3   1 2̇ 3 5
LH: 5 3̇ 2   1 3̇ 2 1

🔊 5-14

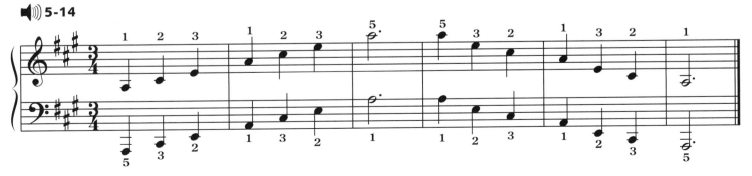

Playing Major Scales and Arpeggios (continued)

E Major

RH: 1 2 3 1 2 3 4   1 2 3 1 2 3 4 5

LH: 5 4 3 2 1 3 2   1 4 3 2 1 3 2 1

🔊 5-15

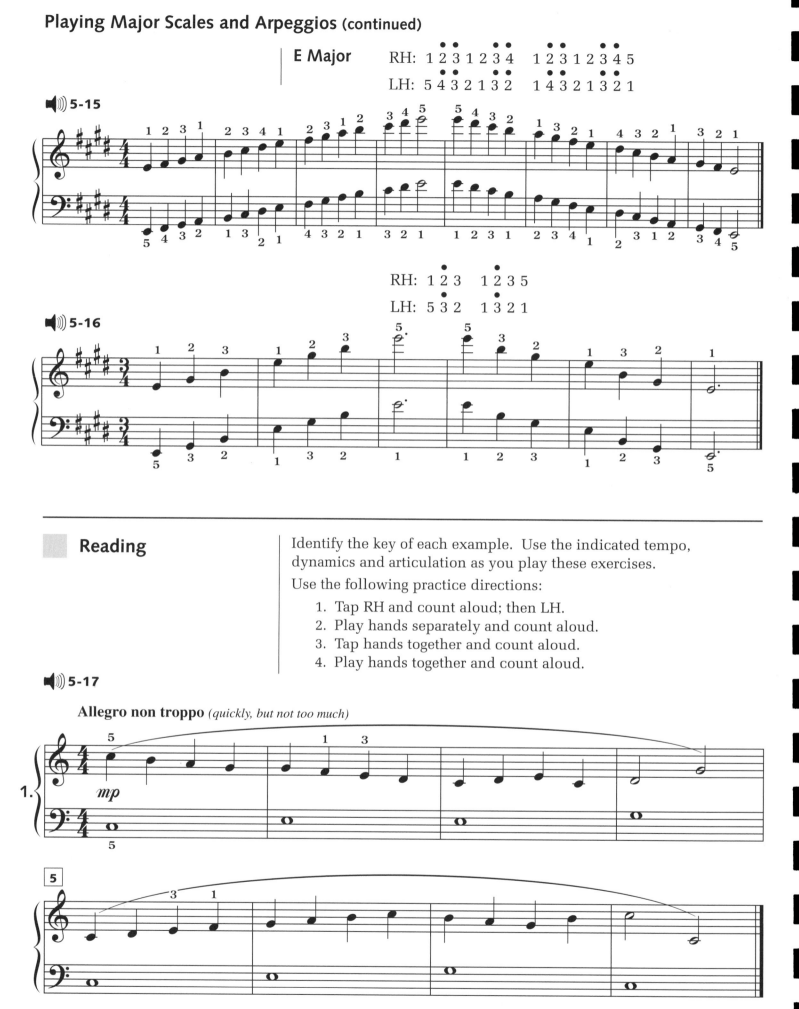

RH: 1 2 3   1 2 3 5

LH: 5 3 2   1 3 2 1

🔊 5-16

Reading

Identify the key of each example. Use the indicated tempo, dynamics and articulation as you play these exercises.

Use the following practice directions:

1. Tap RH and count aloud; then LH.
2. Play hands separately and count aloud.
3. Tap hands together and count aloud.
4. Play hands together and count aloud.

🔊 5-17

Allegro non troppo *(quickly, but not too much)*

1.

▶ Transpose to D major.

---

126   Unit 9 ■ Major Scales (Group 1) and Triads of the Key

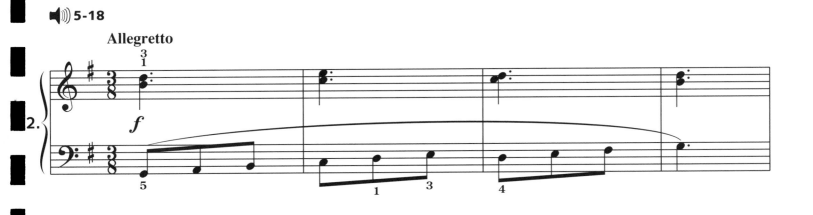

🔊 5-18

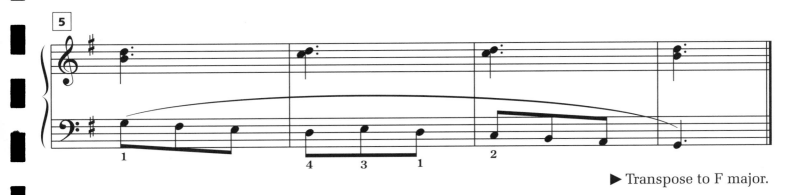

▶ Transpose to F major.

🔊 5-19

▶ Transpose to C major.

♪olo Repertoire

Before playing:
- Find two places where the RH plays a G major scale.
- Tap the rhythm hands together.
- Find the place where the LH changes octaves. Practice the move.

While playing:
- Play the LH a little louder than the RH in measures 9–12.

MORNING SALUTE

🔊 5-20

Cornelius Gurlitt (1820–1901)
Op. 117, No. 13

Before playing:
- Practice the RH scale passages using the indicated fingering.
- Practice the LH chord changes.

While playing:
- Play the RH a little louder than the LH.
- Add small *crescendos* and *diminuendos* to follow the rise and fall of the RH scale passages.

GERMAN DANCE

Ludwig van Beethoven
(1770–1827)

🔊 5-21

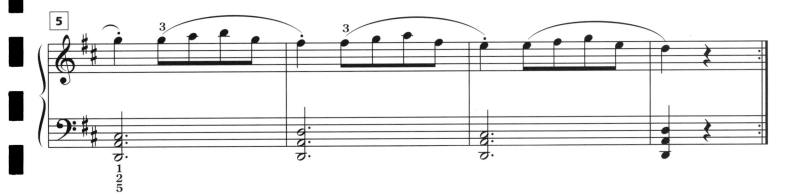

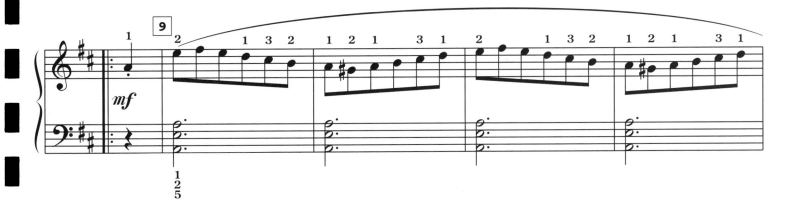

Harmonization

Harmonize each melody below, using the root of the indicated triads.

🔊 5-22

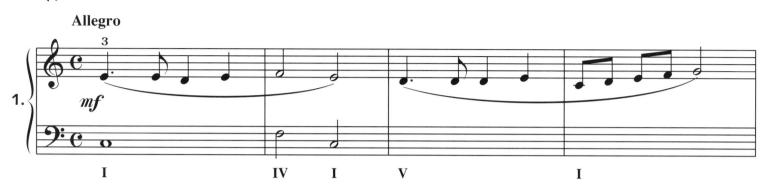

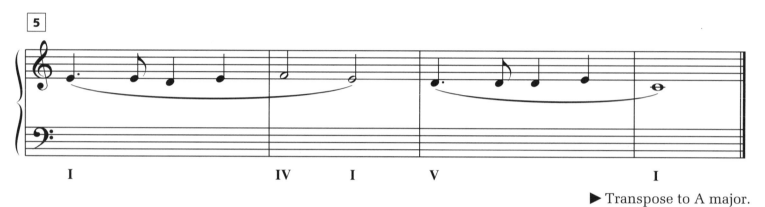

▶ Transpose to A major.

NOW THE DAY IS OVER

🔊 5-23

Joseph Barnby
(1838–1896)

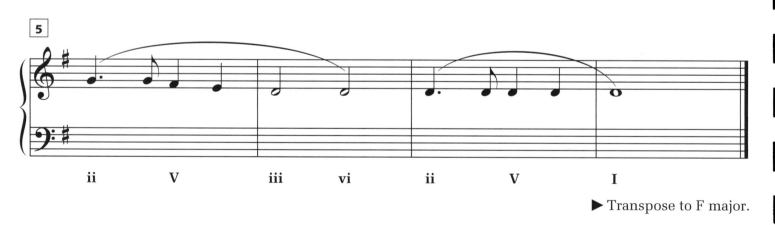

▶ Transpose to F major.

5-24

▶ Transpose to E major.

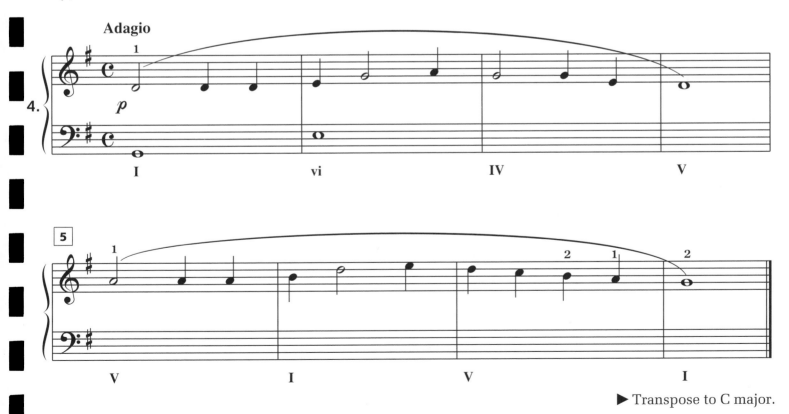5-25

▶ Transpose to C major.

Improvisation from Chord Symbols

Continue the RH melodic **sequence** (a short musical motive stated successively, beginning on different pitches) for the chord progression below while the LH plays the root-position chords.

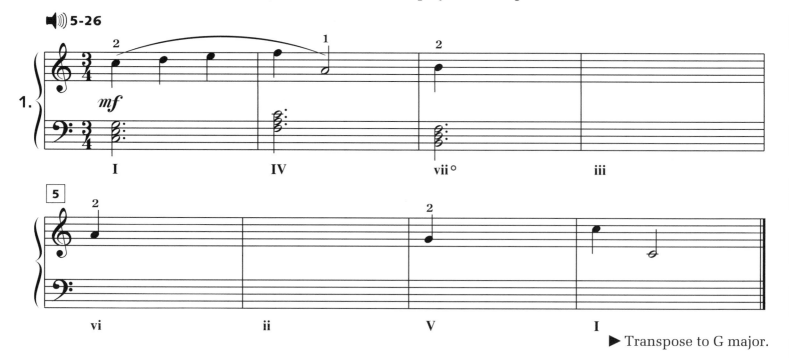

1.

I IV vii° iii

vi ii V I

▶ Transpose to G major.

Improvise a RH melody for the chord progression below while the LH plays the root of the indicated chords. Begin and end each phrase with the given notes. You can use the suggested rhythm for your improvisation or create your own rhythm to complement the accompaniment. Notate your favorite improvisation.

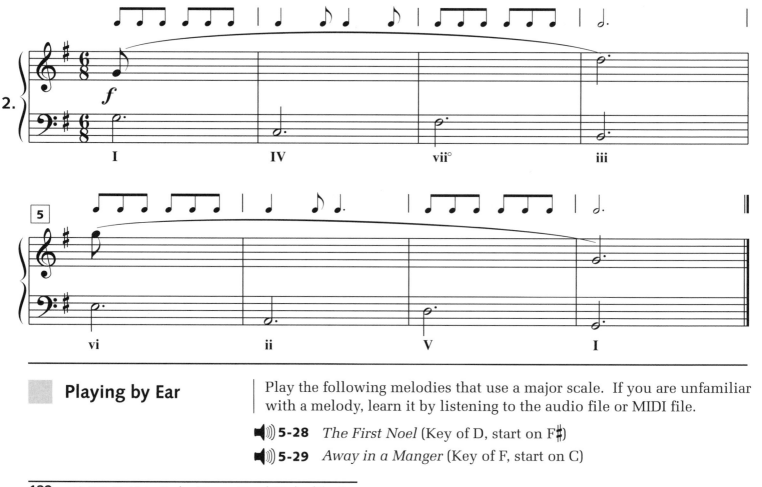

2.

I IV vii° iii

vi ii V I

Playing by Ear

Play the following melodies that use a major scale. If you are unfamiliar with a melody, learn it by listening to the audio file or MIDI file.

◀)) **5-28** *The First Noel* (Key of D, start on F♯)

◀)) **5-29** *Away in a Manger* (Key of F, start on C)

Review Worksheet

Name _____   *Date* _____

1. Identify each major scale below by writing its name on the indicated
   line. Write the correct RH fingering on the line above the staff and
   the correct LH fingering on the line below the staff.

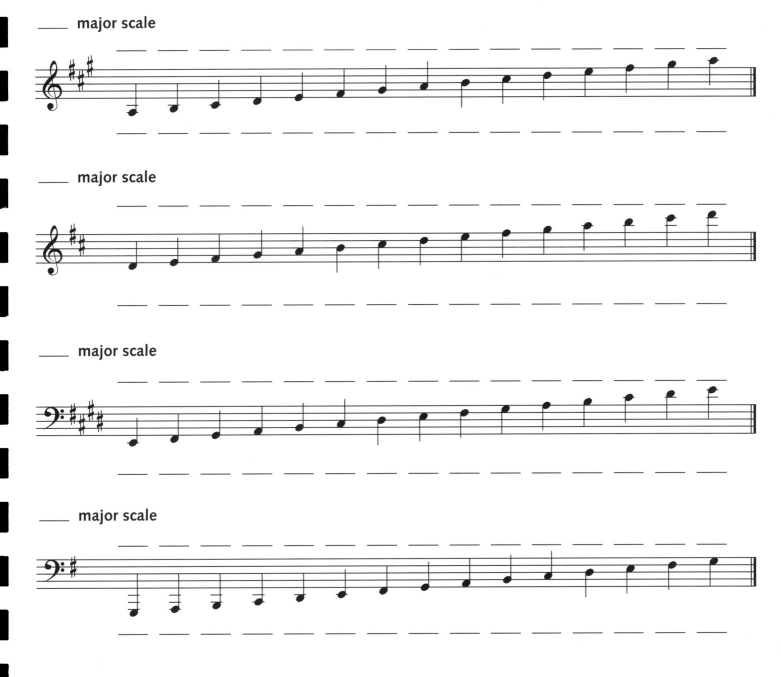

____ **major scale**

____ **major scale**

____ **major scale**

____ **major scale**

2. Identify each major key by writing its name on the line above the
   staff. Write the Roman numeral name for the given triad in that
   key on the line below the staff.

3. Identify each major key signature below by writing its name on the indicated line. Following the key signature, write the notes for that major scale on the staff, using whole notes. Write the sharps or flats from the key signature in front of the appropriate notes.

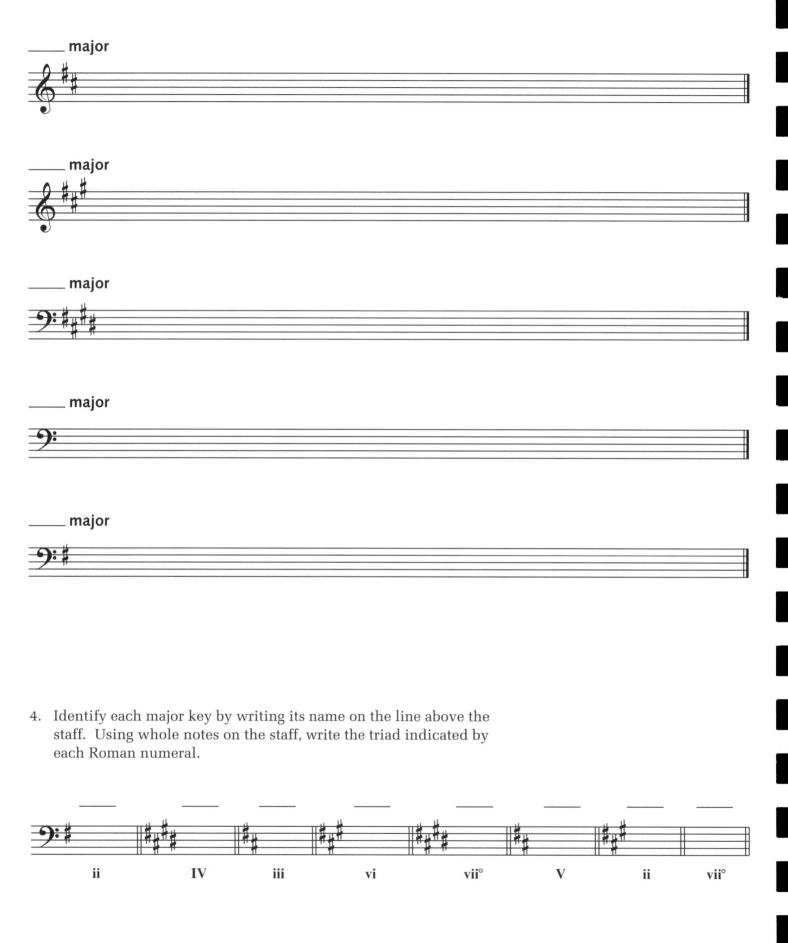

4. Identify each major key by writing its name on the line above the staff. Using whole notes on the staff, write the triad indicated by each Roman numeral.

Major Scales (Group 2) & Triads and Inversions

Objectives

Upon completion of this unit the student will be able to:

1. Play triads in root position, first inversion and second inversion.
2. Play Group 2 major scales and arpeggios using traditional fingerings.
3. Perform solo repertoire that uses triads and inversions.
4. Sight-read music that uses triads and inversions.
5. Harmonize melodies with the bottom notes of triads and inversions.
6. Create two-hand accompaniments from chord symbols.

Assignments

Week of 10/19

Write your assignments for the week in the space below.   11/12

- D♭ major hands together

- practice   I   IV   I   V⁷   I
- rep piece (p. 144) due Saturday

Playing Triads of the Key

Triads may be built on any note of any scale. The sharps or flats in the key signature must be used when playing these triads. Triads of the key are identified by Roman numerals.

Play triads of the key in F major. Note the quality of each chord.

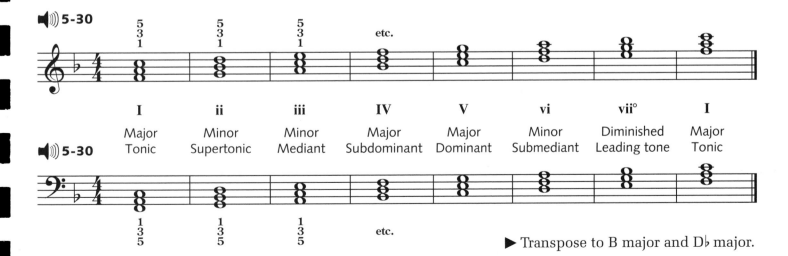

I	ii	iii	IV	V	vi	vii°	I
Major Tonic	Minor Supertonic	Minor Mediant	Major Subdominant	Major Dominant	Minor Submediant	Diminished Leading tone	Major Tonic

▶ Transpose to B major and D♭ major.

Triads: First Inversion

When the root of the chord is moved to the top and the third becomes the lowest note of the triad, it is said to be in the **first inversion.**

C E G becomes E G C

The root is always the top note of the interval of a 4th.

🔊 **5-31**

Play the following first-inversion triads in the key of C with RH, using 1 2 5 on each triad. Repeat with LH one octave lower, using 5 3 1 on each triad.

▶ Transpose to G and F.

🔊 **5-32**

Play with RH, using the indicated fingering. Repeat with LH one octave lower, using 5 3 1 on each triad.

Triads: Second Inversion

Any first-inversion triad may be inverted again by moving the lowest note to the top. All letter names are the same, but the root is in the middle and the fifth is the lowest note of the triad. This is called the **second inversion.**

E G C becomes G C E

From root position, you can find second inversion by moving the top note down one octave.

The root is always the top note of the interval of a 4th.

Play the following second-inversion triads in the key of C with RH, using 1 3 5 on each triad. Repeat with LH one octave lower, using 5 2 1 on each triad.

🔊 **5-33**

▶ Transpose to G and F.

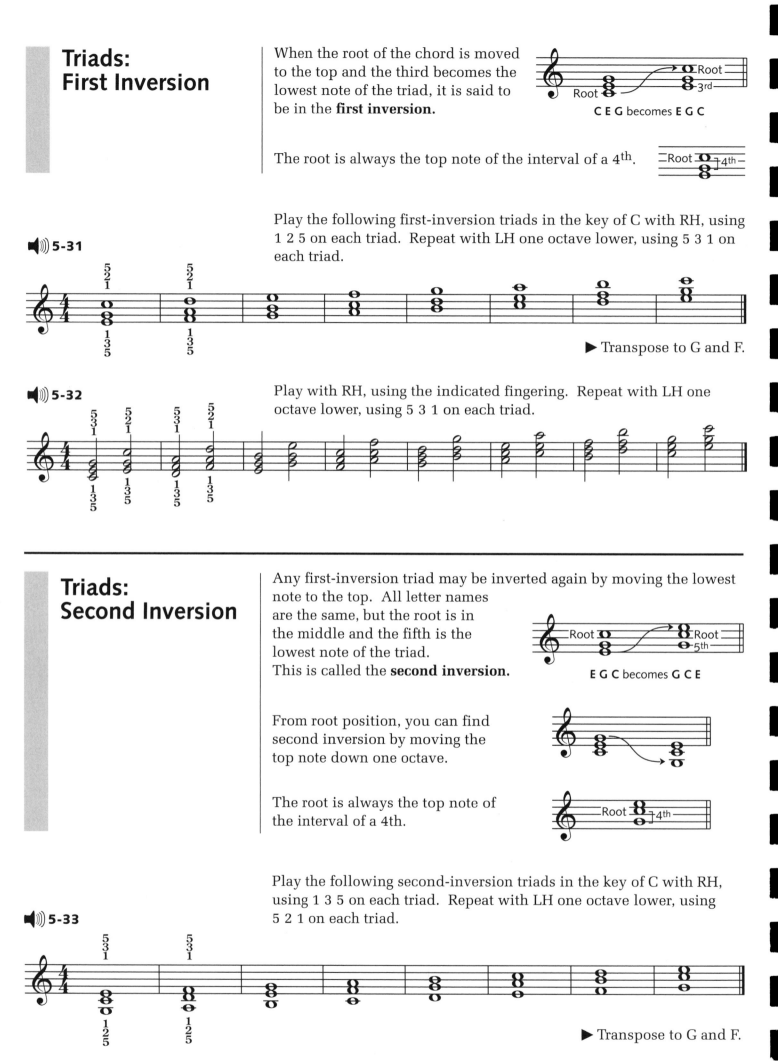

Triads: in All Positions

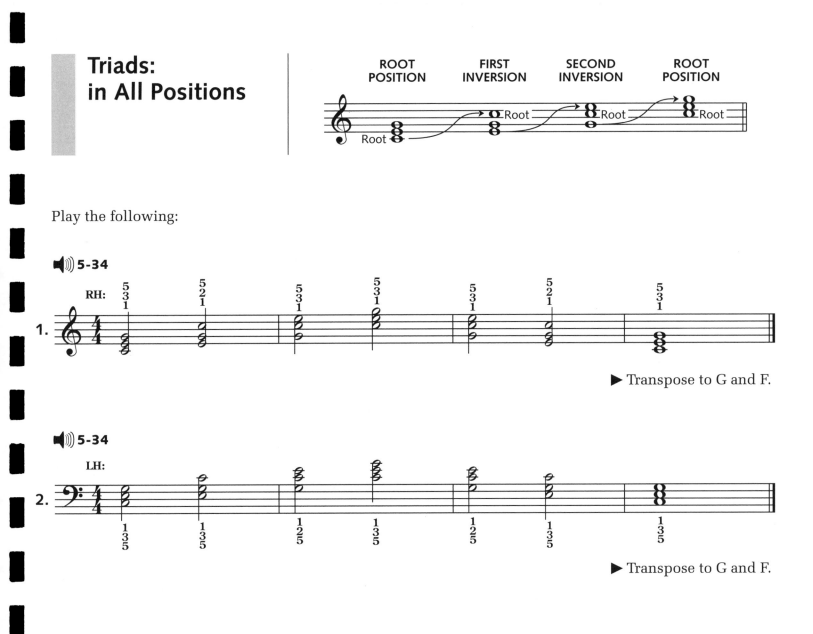

Play the following:

🔊 5-34

RH:

1.

▶ Transpose to G and F.

🔊 5-34

LH:

2.

▶ Transpose to G and F.

Naming Triads and Inversions

Roman numerals identify the scale degrees on which triads are built within a key.

Numbers to the right of the Roman numerals indicate the intervals between the lowest note and each of the other notes of the chord.

In the first inversion, the number 3 is usually omitted.

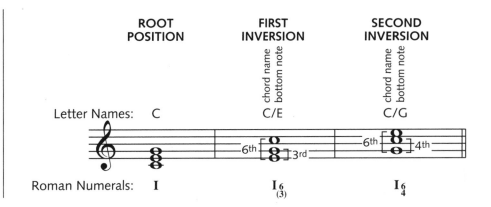

Playing Triads and Inversions with the Left Hand

Play these diatonic triads and inversions in the key of C major.

🔊 5-35

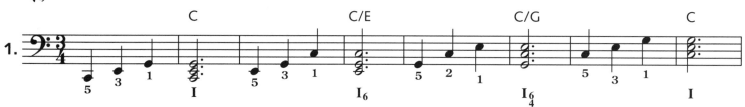

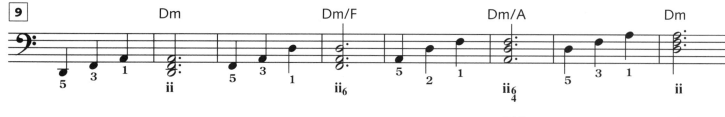

Continue upward on white keys until . . .

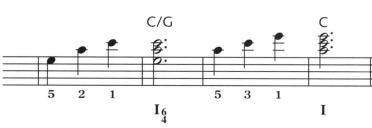

🔊 5-36

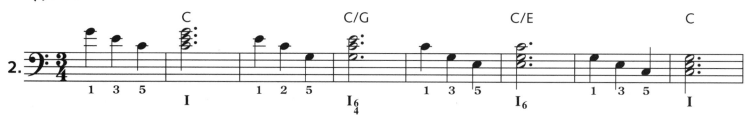

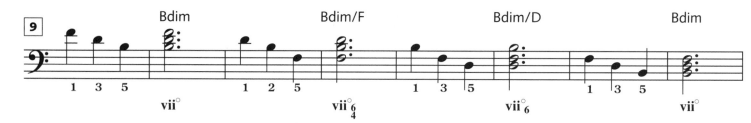

Continue downward on white keys until . . .

Playing Triads and Inversions with the Right Hand

Play these diatonic triads and inversions in the key of C major.

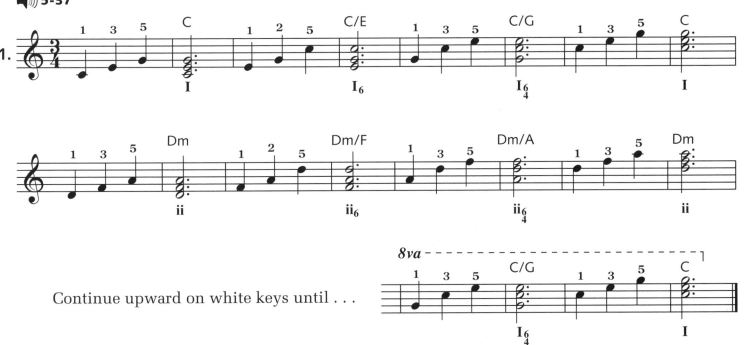

Continue upward on white keys until . . .

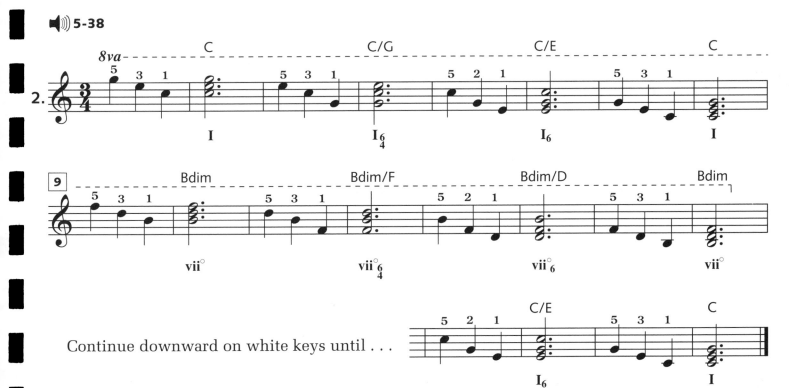

Continue downward on white keys until . . .

Technique

Practicing Major Scales
(Group 2 Keys):
F, B, G♭ (F♯) and D♭

The following principles will help you remember the fingering for the Group 2 major scales:

1. Fingers 2 and 3 play the two-black-key groups (or white-key equivalents).
   - In the key of F major, fingers 2 and 3 play D and E.
   - In the keys of G-flat and D-flat major, fingers 2 and 3 play D♭ and E♭.
   - In the keys of B and F-sharp major, fingers 2 and 3 play C♯ and D♯.
2. Fingers 2, 3 and 4 play the three-black-key groups (or white-key equivalents).
   - In the key of F major, fingers 2, 3 and 4 play G, A and B♭.
   - In the keys of G-flat and D-flat major, fingers 2, 3 and 4 play Gb, Ab and Bb.
   - In the keys of B and F-sharp major, fingers 2, 3 and 4 play F♯, G♯ and A♯.
3. When playing scales hands together, thumbs play at the same time on white keys (except on the first and last notes of F and B).

See page 122 for scale practice suggestions and challenges.

Practicing Major Arpeggios
(Group 2 Keys):
F, B, G♭ (F♯) and D♭

The following principles will help you remember the fingering for the Group 2 major arpeggios:

1. Arpeggios in the keys of F, B and G-flat major use the same fingering in the right hand.
   RH: 1 2 3   1 2 3 5

   When playing the LH arpeggios, use finger 4 when there is one white key between the root and third of the broken chord. Use finger 3 when there are two white keys between the root and third of the broken chord.
   LH: (F) 5 4 2 1   4 2 1
   LH: (B, G♭) 5 3 2 1   3 2 1

2. For the D♭ major arpeggio:
   - Thumbs play the white keys. In addition to the thumbs, only fingers 2 and 4 are used.
   - In the right hand, the fourth finger plays the root.
     RH: 4 1 2   4 1 2 4
   - In the left hand, the second finger plays the root.
     LH: 2 1 4   2 1 4 2

See page 123 for arpeggio practice suggestions and challenges.

Playing Major Scales and Arpeggios

F Major **Note:** A dot (•) above a fingering indicates a black key.

RH: 1 2 3 4̇ 1 2 3 1 2 3 4̇ 1 2 3 4

LH: 5 4 3 2 1 3 2 1 4̇ 3 2 1 3 2 1

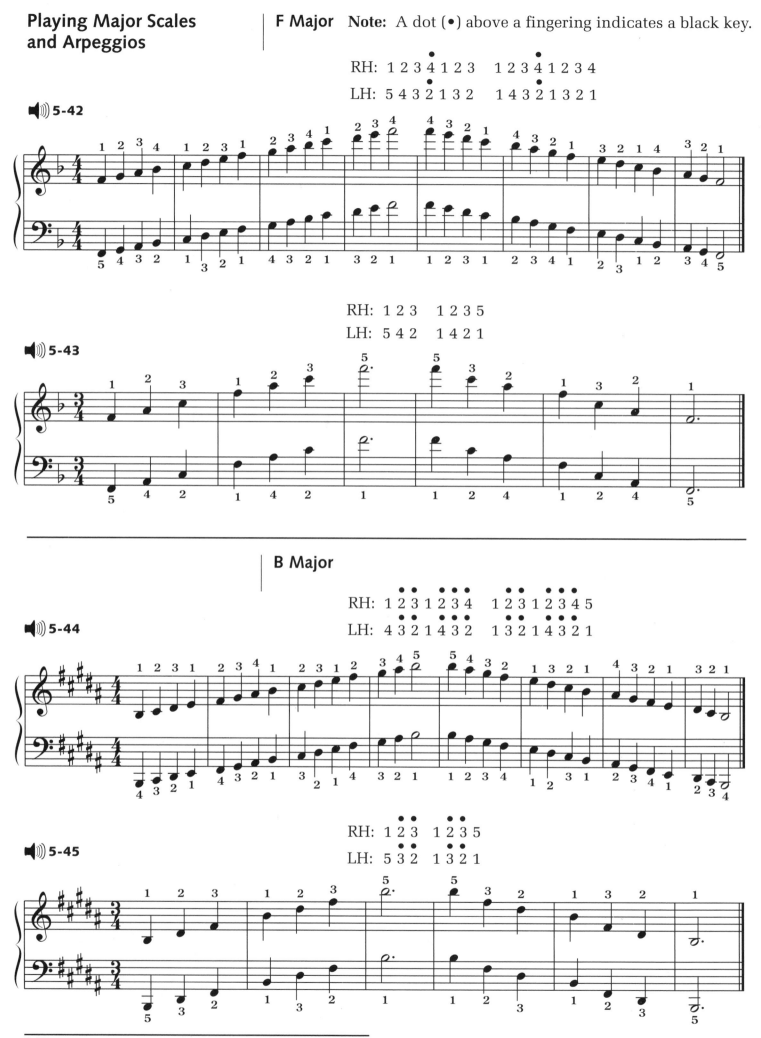

RH: 1 2 3 1 2 3 5

LH: 5 4 2 1 4 2 1

B Major

RH: 1̇ 2̇ 3 1 2̇ 3̇ 4 1̇ 2̇ 3 1 2̇ 3̇ 4 5

LH: 4̇ 3̇ 2 1 4̇ 3̇ 2 1 3̇ 2 1 4̇ 3̇ 2 1

RH: 1̇ 2̇ 3 1̇ 2̇ 3 5

LH: 5 3̇ 2 1 3̇ 2 1

142   Unit 10 ■ Major Scales (Group 2) & Triads and Inversions

G♭ Major (enharmonic to F♯ major)

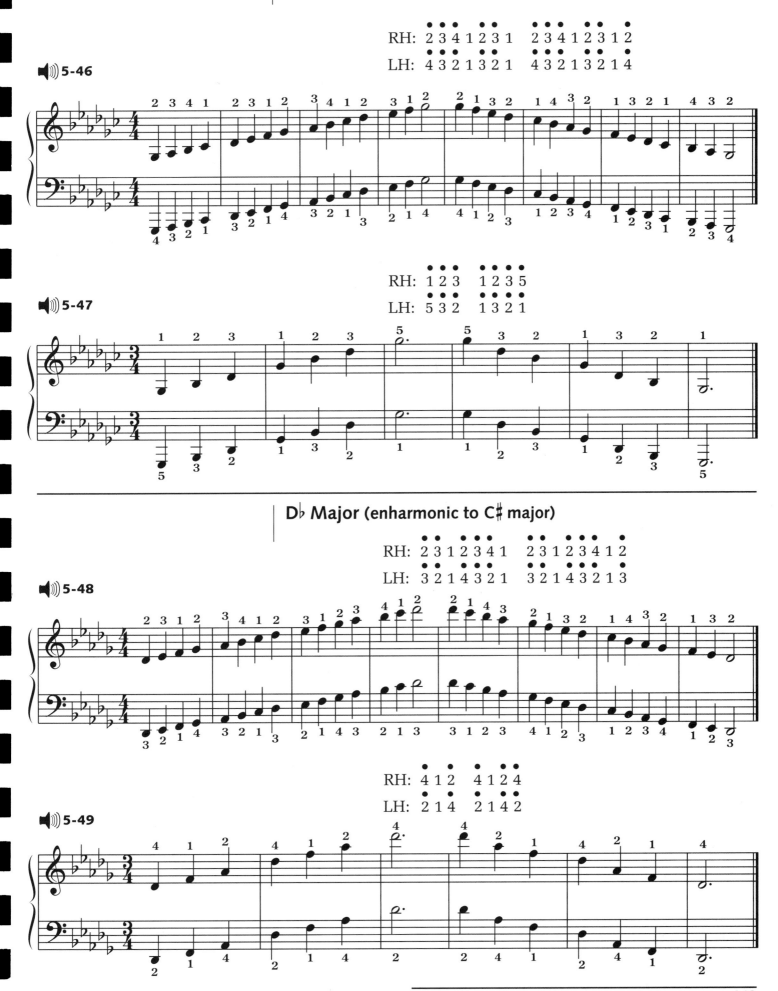

RH: 2 3 4 1 2 3 1   2 3 4 1 2 3 1 2
LH: 4 3 2 1 3 2 1   4 3 2 1 3 2 1 4

5-46

RH: 1 2 3   1 2 3 5
LH: 5 3 2   1 3 2 1

5-47

D♭ Major (enharmonic to C♯ major)

RH: 2 3 1 2 3 4 1   2 3 1 2 3 4 1 2
LH: 3 2 1 4 3 2 1   3 2 1 4 3 2 1 3

5-48

RH: 4 1 2   4 1 2 4
LH: 2 1 4   2 1 4 2

5-49

Solo Repertoire

Simile as used in this piece means to continue using the pedal in the same way.

Before playing:
- Find one measure where the LH and RH chord inversions are different.
- Block the LH and RH chords.
- Tap the rhythm with the correct hands and fingers.

While playing:
- Play legato so that the triplet figure divided between the hands sounds like one line.

ETUDE

🔊 5-50

Cornelius Gurlitt
(1820–1901)

Allegretto

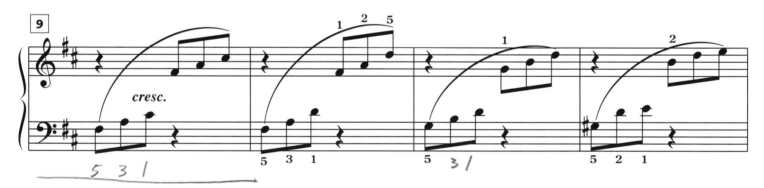

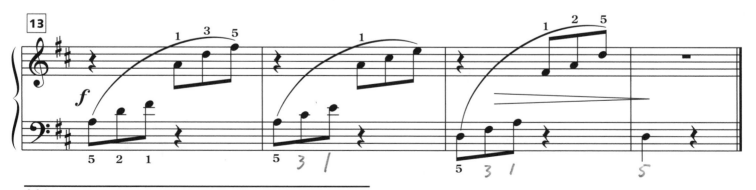

Harmonization

Harmonize the following melody using the bottom note of each triad and inversion.

🔊 5-51

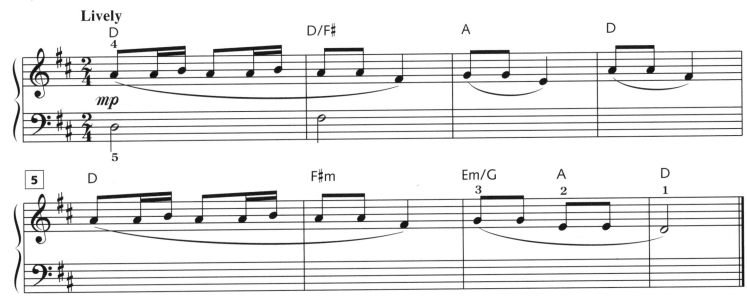

Harmonization with Two-Hand Accompaniment

Using the indicated chords, create a two-hand accompaniment for the melody by continuing the pattern given in the first three measures.

TEMPO DI MENUETTO
(SONATA IN G)

Ludwig van Beethoven (1770–1827)
Op. 49, No. 2

🔊 5-52

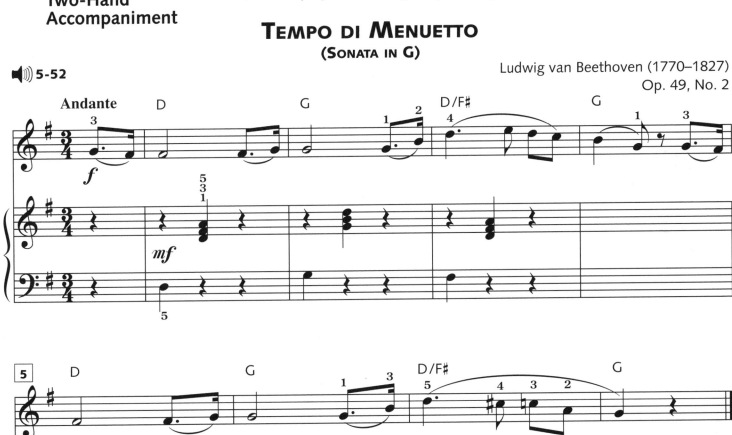

Reading

Identify the key of each example. Use the indicated tempo, dynamics and articulation as you play these exercises.

Use the following practice directions:

1. Tap RH and count aloud; then LH.
2. Play hands separately and count aloud.
3. Tap hands together and count aloud.
4. Play hands together and count aloud.

5-53

Alla marcia *(in march style)*

1.

5-54

Slow march tempo

2.

🔊 **5-55**

5

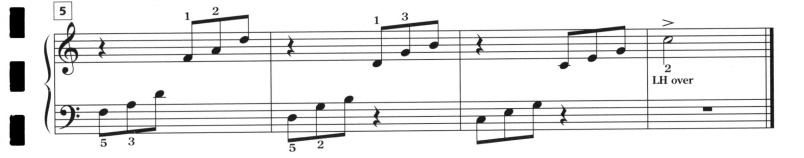

🔊 **5-56**

5

The Dominant and Dominant Seventh Chords

Objectives

Upon completion of this unit the student will be able to:

1. Play I–V$^6_3$–I and I–V$^6_5$–I chord progressions in all major keys.

2. Perform solo repertoire that uses tonic and dominant harmonies.

3. Sight-read and transpose music that uses tonic and dominant chords.

4. Harmonize and transpose melodies with tonic and dominant chords.

5. Create two-hand accompaniments from Roman numerals.

6. Improvise melodies over tonic and dominant chords.

Assignments

Week of 10/12

Write your assignments for the week in the space below.

pg 154 and 155

G and C arpeggios

Tonic and Dominant

In the key of C, the **I** chord (tonic) is the C triad. The **V** chord (dominant) is the G triad.

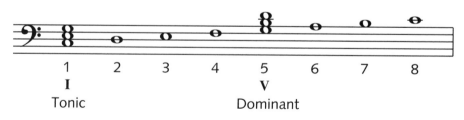

1 2 3 4 5 6 7 8
I V
Tonic Dominant

To make chord progressions easier to play and sound better, the **V** chord may be played in first inversion by moving the two top notes down an octave.

V V$^6_{(3)}$

Playing the I–V$_6^{(3)}$–I Progression

Play the following chord progression:

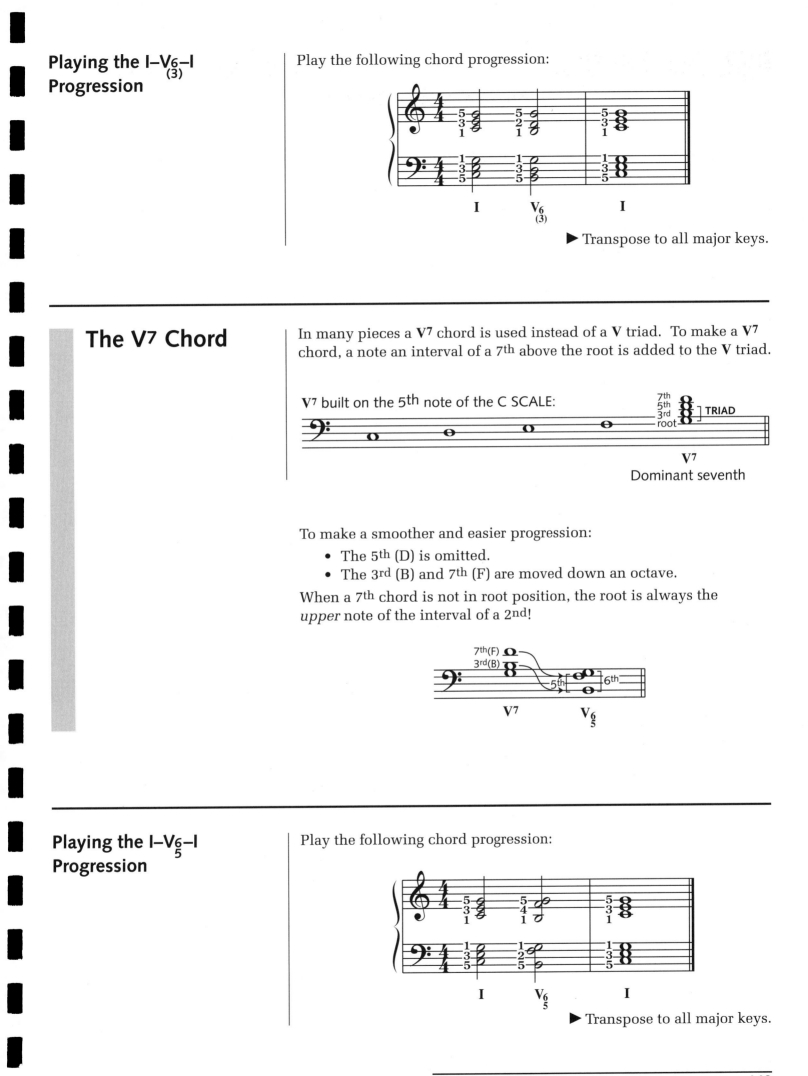

I V$_6$ (3) I

▶ Transpose to all major keys.

The V^7 Chord

In many pieces a **V^7** chord is used instead of a **V** triad. To make a **V^7** chord, a note an interval of a 7th above the root is added to the **V** triad.

V^7 built on the 5th note of the C SCALE:

7th
5th
3rd
root] TRIAD

V^7
Dominant seventh

To make a smoother and easier progression:
- The 5th (D) is omitted.
- The 3rd (B) and 7th (F) are moved down an octave.

When a 7th chord is not in root position, the root is always the *upper* note of the interval of a 2nd!

7th(F)
3rd(B)
5th
6th

V^7 V$_5^6$

Playing the I–V$_5^6$–I Progression

Play the following chord progression:

I V$_5^6$ I

▶ Transpose to all major keys.

Playing the I–V⁶₅–I Chord Progression
(continued)

Use the following steps to play the **I–V⁶₅–I** chord progression exercise:

1. Top note remains the same
2. Middle note moves *up* a half step
3. Bottom note moves *down* a half step.
4. Play hands separately first, then hands together.

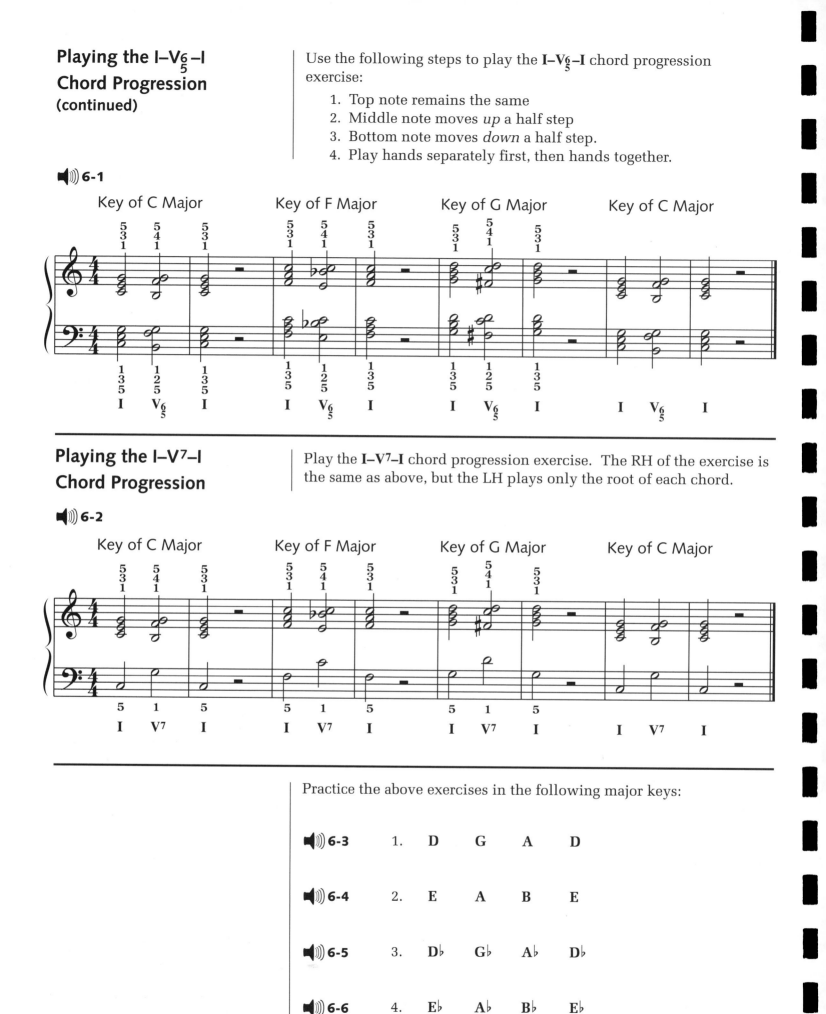

6-1

Playing the I–V⁷–I Chord Progression

Play the **I–V⁷–I** chord progression exercise. The RH of the exercise is the same as above, but the LH plays only the root of each chord.

6-2

Practice the above exercises in the following major keys:

6-3   1.   D   G   A   D

6-4   2.   E   A   B   E

6-5   3.   D♭   G♭   A♭   D♭

6-6   4.   E♭   A♭   B♭   E♭

Solo Repertoire

Before playing:
- Find the I and V$^6_5$ chords in the LH.
- Practice the RH jump between measures 8 and 9.
- Practice the LH in measures 3 and 11, noticing the different positions of the V7 chord.

While playing:
- Keep the tempo steady.
- Listen for clear, crisp staccato.
- Play the RH a little louder than the LH.

MARCH

Louis Köhler
(1820–1886)

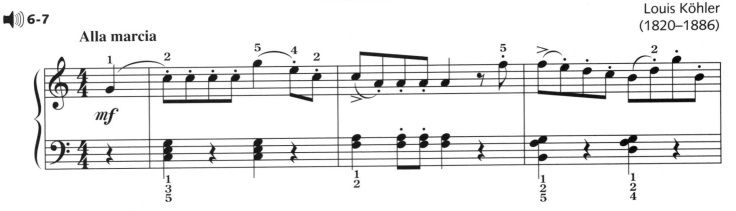

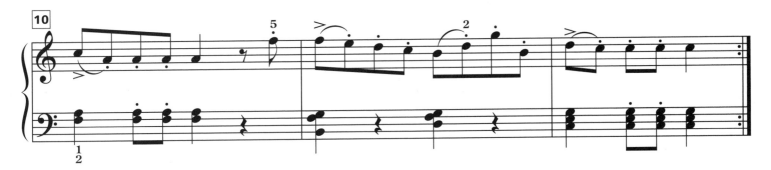

Reading

Identify the key of each example. Use the indicated tempo, dynamics and articulation as you play these exercises.

Use the following practice directions:
1. Tap RH and count aloud; then LH.
2. Play hands separately and count aloud.
3. Tap hands together and count aloud.
4. Play hands together and count aloud.

ALLEGRETTO

🔊 6-8

Cornelius Gurlitt (1820–1901)
Op. 117, No. 5

▶ Transpose to G major.

DANCE

🔊 6-9

Carl Czerny (1791–1857)
Op. 823, No. 11

▶ Transpose to D major.

Block Chords and Broken Chords

Chords are often used as follows:

- **Block chords** (all notes together)

- **Broken chords** (one note at a time)

🔊 6-10

3.

🔊 (continues)

▶ Transpose to A major.

🔊 6-11

4.

▶ Transpose to F major.

Harmonization Using Tonic and Dominant Chords

Rules for Harmonization:

Harmonize each of the melodies with tonic (**I**) or dominant (**V** or **V7**).
- Use tonic when most of the melody notes are scale tones 1, 3 and 5.
- Use dominant when most of the melody notes are scale tones 2, 4, 5 and 7.
- Begin and end each harmonization on tonic.
- Dominant almost always precedes tonic at the end of a piece.

Using tonic (**I**) and dominant (**V7** or **V$^6_5$**) chords, harmonize the following melodies with block or broken chords as indicated. Write the letter name of each chord on the line above the staff and the Roman numeral name of each chord on the line below the staff.

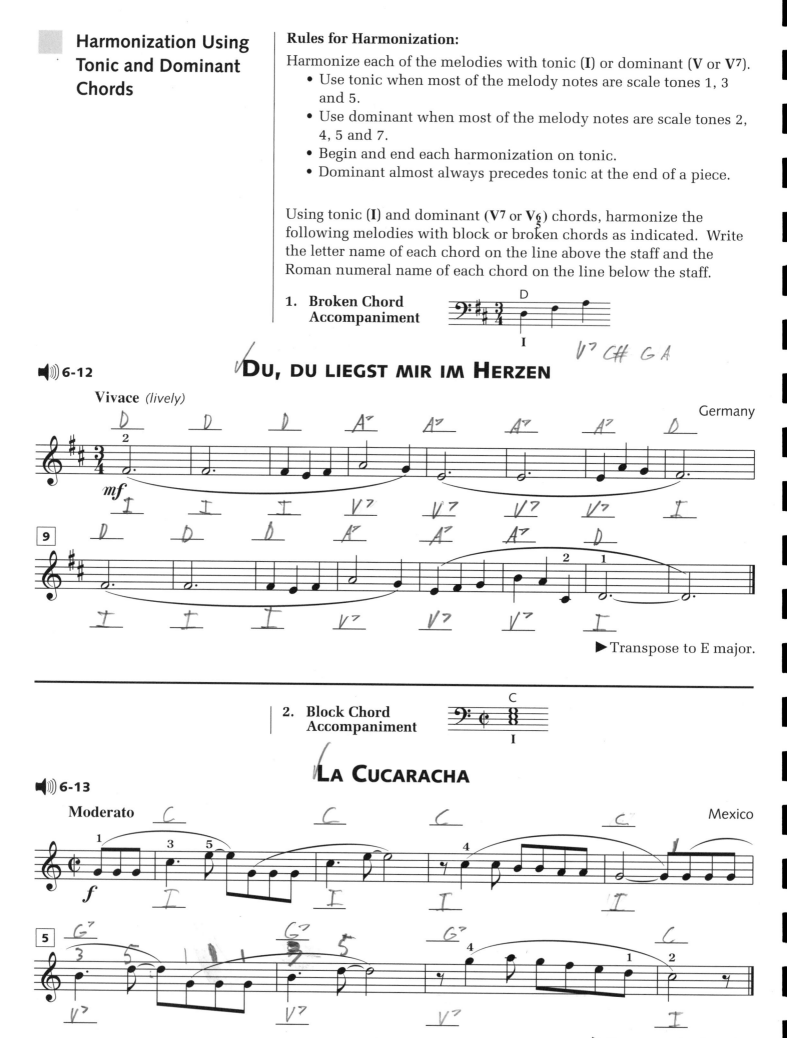

1. **Broken Chord Accompaniment**

🔊 6-12

DU, DU LIEGST MIR IM HERZEN

Vivace *(lively)*

Germany

▶ Transpose to E major.

2. **Block Chord Accompaniment**

🔊 6-13

LA CUCARACHA

Moderato

Mexico

▶ Transpose to A major.

3. Block Chord Accompaniment

BOOLA BOOLA

🔊 6-14

Allan M. Hirsch

Alla marcia

► Transpose to C major.

4. Block Chord Accompaniment

SLEEP, BABY, SLEEP

🔊 6-15

Moderately slow

United States

► Transpose to G major.

Harmonization with Two-Hand Accompaniment

Using the indicated chords, create a two-hand accompaniment for the melody by continuing the pattern given in the first two measures.

HUSH LITTLE BABY

🔊 6-16

Moderato

United States

Improvisation from Chord Symbols

Using the chord progressions below, improvise RH melodies while the LH plays the suggested accompaniment style. (First play the LH chord progression using the suggested accompaniment style and observing the indicated meter.) You can use the suggested rhythm for your improvisation or create your own rhythm to complement the accompaniment. Notate your favorite improvisation.

Rules for Improvisation:

1. When the tonic chord is used, play mostly scale tones 1, 3 and 5 in the melody.

2. When the dominant chord is used, play mostly scale tones 2, 4, 5 and 7 in the melody.

3. Most improvisations begin and end on tonic.

4. The ear should always be the final guide in determining which melody notes to play.

◀))) 6-17

Key of D major

1. **Block Chord Accompaniment**

◀))) 6-18

Key of E♭ major

2. **Broken Chord Accompaniment**

The Subdominant Chord

Objectives

Upon completion of this unit the student will be able to:

1. Play I–IV$\frac{6}{4}$–I chord progressions in all major keys.

2. Perform solo repertoire that uses tonic, dominant and subdominant harmonies.

3. Sight-read and transpose music that uses tonic, dominant and subdominant chords.

4. Create two-hand accompaniments from chord symbols.

5. Harmonize and transpose melodies with tonic, dominant and subdominant chords.

6. Improvise melodies with the five-finger blues pattern over a 12-bar blues accompaniment.

7. Perform four-part ensembles with partners.

Assignments

Week of 11/2

Write your assignments for the week in the space below.

- practice I IV I V⁷ I chord progression
- rep piece (pg 144) due Saturday
- 12 bar blues (pg 167)

- Kum-ba-yah (pg 175)
- Ode to Joy (168)

pg 218 or 268 (2 hand accompaniment)

Tonic and Subdominant

In the key of C, the **I** chord (tonic) is the C triad. The **IV** chord (subdominant) is the F triad.

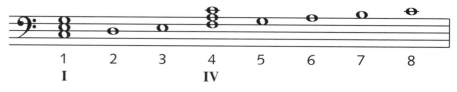

To make chord progressions easier to play and sound better, the **IV** chord may be played in the second inversion by moving the top note of the **IV** chord down an octave.

Playing the I–IV⁶₄–I Chord Progression

Play the following chord progression:

▶ Transpose to all major keys.

Use the following steps to play the **I–IV⁶₄–I** chord-progression exercise:

1. Top note moves up a whole step.
2. Middle note moves up a half step.
3. Bottom note remains the same.
4. Play hands separately first, then hands together.

🔊 **6-19**

Playing the I–IV–I Chord Progression

Play the **I–IV–I** chord progression exercise. The RH of the exercise is the same as above, but the LH plays only the root of each chord.

🔊 **6-20**

Practice the above exercises in the following major keys:

🔊 **6-21**	1.	D	G	A	D
🔊 **6-22**	2.	E	A	B	E
🔊 **6-23**	3.	D♭	G♭	A♭	D♭
🔊 **6-24**	4.	E♭	A♭	B♭	E♭

♪olo Repertoire

Before playing:
- Find the I, IV and V chords.
- Find all repeat signs.
- Locate places where the hands change positions.
- Tap the rhythm, first hands separately, then hands together.

While playing:
- Listen carefully for slurs and staccato notes.
- Play the RH a little louder than the LH.

MINUET IN F MAJOR

6-25

Leopold Mozart
(1719–1787)

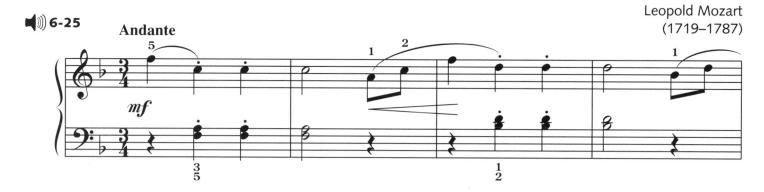

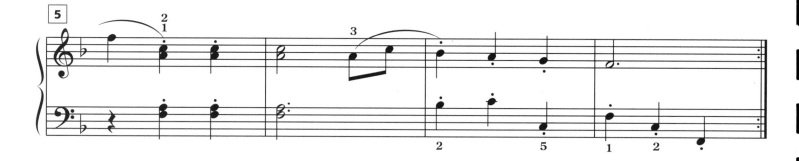

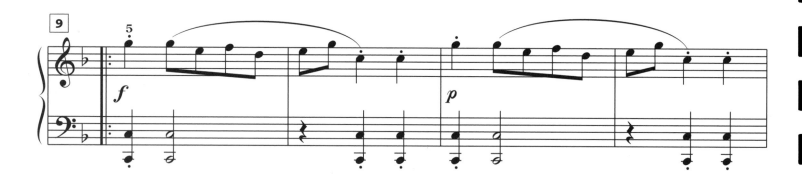

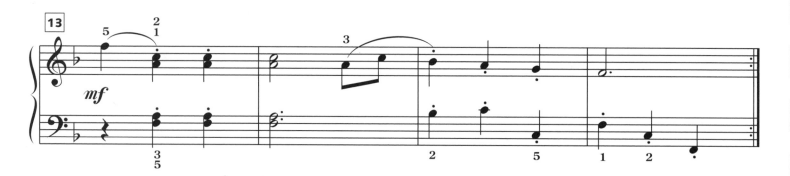

Harmonization with Two-Hand Accompaniment

Using the indicated chords, create a two-hand accompaniment for the following melody by continuing the pattern given in the first two measures.

THE STREETS OF LAREDO

🔊 6-26

United States

▶ Transpose to G major.

Alberti Bass and Waltz Bass Accompaniment

Chords are often used as follows:

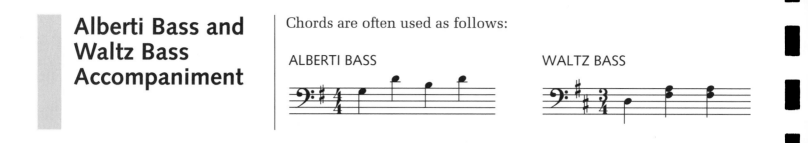

ALBERTI BASS

WALTZ BASS

Reading

Practice Suggestions: See page 152.

🔊 **6-27**

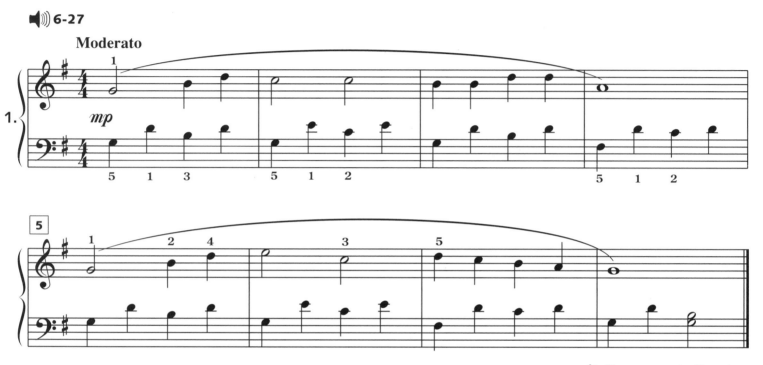

1.

Moderato

mp

► Transpose to F major.

🔊 **6-28**

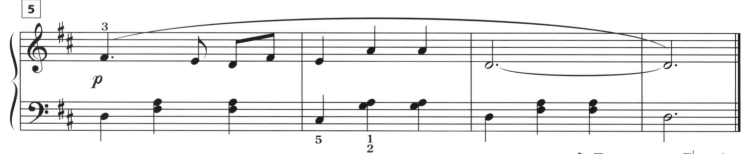

2.

Moderato

mf

p

► Transpose to E♭ major.

🔊 **6-29**

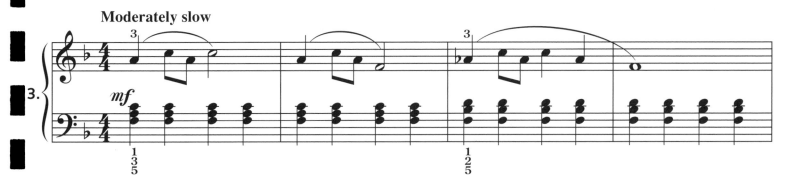

3.

5

▶ Transpose to G major.

STUDY

🔊 **6-30**

Ferdinand Beyer (1803–1863)
Op. 101, No. 66

Allegretto

4.

mf *dolce* (sweetly)

5

▶ Transpose to B♭ major.

Harmonization

Rules for Harmonization:

Harmonize each of the melodies with tonic (**I**), dominant (**V** or **V7**) or subdominant (**IV**).

- Use tonic when most of the melody notes are scale tones 1, 3 and 5.
- Use dominant when most of the melody notes are scale tones 2, 4, 5 and 7.
- Use subdominant when most of the melody notes are scale tones 1, 4 and 6.
- Dominant almost always precedes tonic at the end of a piece.

Using tonic (I), dominant (V7 or V$\frac{6}{5}$) and subdominant (IV or IV$\frac{6}{4}$) chords, harmonize the following melodies with the indicated accompaniment style. Write the letter name of each chord on the line above the staff and the Roman numeral name of each chord on the line below the staff.

1. Broken Chord Accompaniment

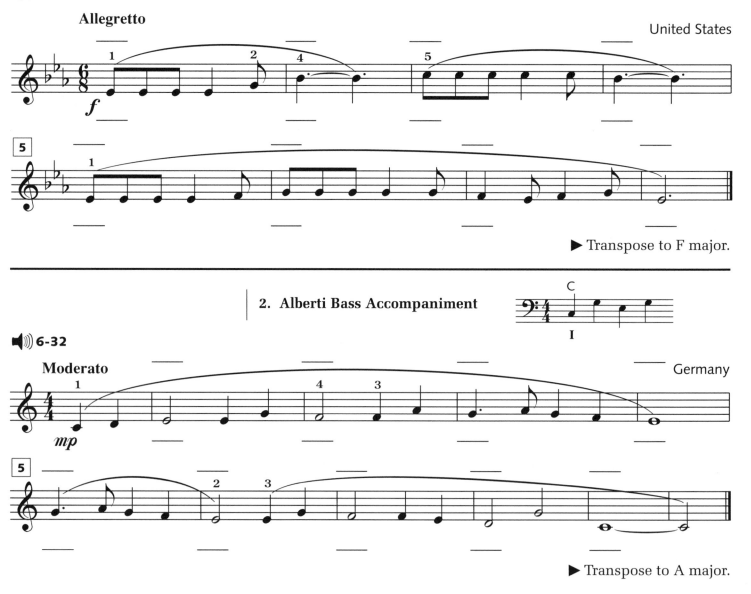

◀))) 6-31

SALLY GO ROUND

Allegretto

United States

f

▶ Transpose to F major.

---

2. Alberti Bass Accompaniment

◀))) 6-32

Moderato

Germany

mp

▶ Transpose to A major.

3. Block Chord Accompaniment

MICHAEL, ROW THE BOAT ASHORE

🔊 6-33

Andante moderato

United States

► Transpose to E major.

4. Block Chord Accompaniment

RUSSIAN DANCE
(THE NUTCRACKER SUITE)

🔊 6-34

Molto vivace

Peter Ilyich Tchaikovsky
(1840–1893)

Harmonization
(continued)

Write the Roman numeral name of each chord on the line below the staff.

5. Block Chord Accompaniment

🔊 6-35
NEW RIVER TRAIN

United States

Lively

mf

▶ Transpose to D major.

6. Broken Chord Accompaniment

🔊 6-36
SILENT NIGHT

Franz Grüber
(1787–1863)

Gently, moderately slow

p

▶ Transpose to C major.

Playing by Ear

Play the following melodies. If you are unfamiliar with a melody, learn it by listening to the audio file or MIDI file. Then harmonize the melodies using I, IV and V⁷ chords in block style.

🔊 **6-37** *If You're Happy and You Know It* (Key of F, start on C)

🔊 **6-38** *Alouette* (Key of G, start on G)

🔊 **6-39** *For He's a Jolly Good Fellow* (Key of D, start on D)

🔊 **6-40** *Up on the Housetop* (Key of C, start on G)

12-Bar Blues Improvisation

The blues accompaniment follows a strict 12-bar pattern.
Using block chords, play the 12-bar blues pattern with the left hand.

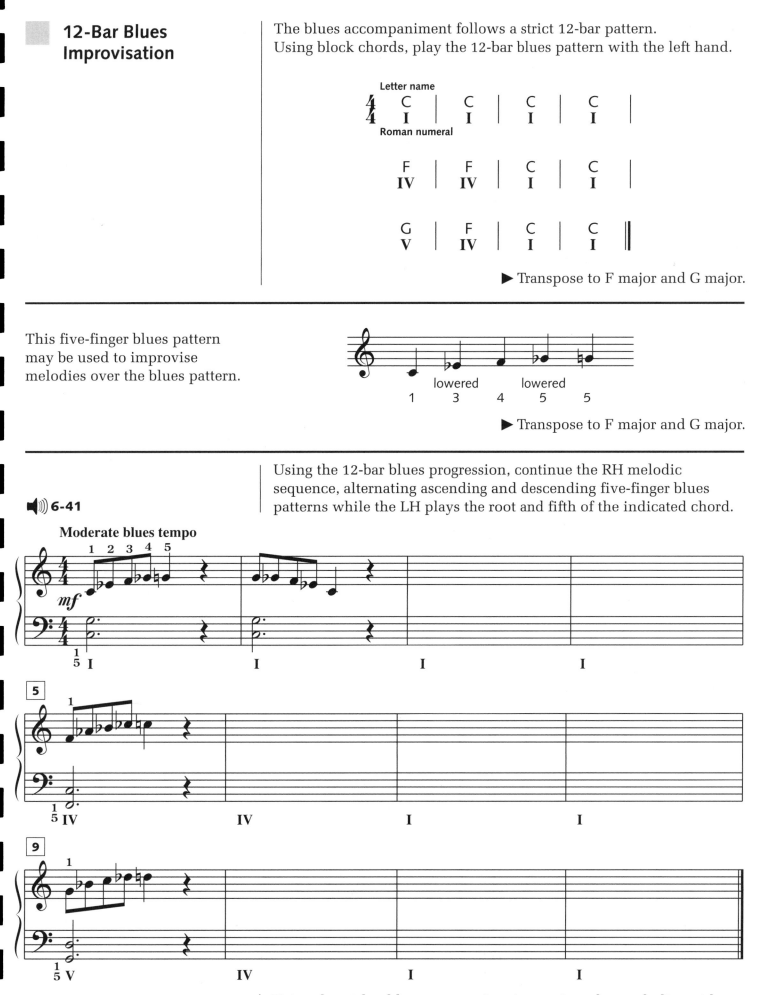

Letter name
$\frac{4}{4}$ C | C | C | C |
I | I | I | I |
Roman numeral

F | F | C | C |
IV | IV | I | I |

G | F | C | C ‖
V | IV | I | I

▶ Transpose to F major and G major.

This five-finger blues pattern may be used to improvise melodies over the blues pattern.

lowered   lowered
1   3   4   5   5

▶ Transpose to F major and G major.

Using the 12-bar blues progression, continue the RH melodic sequence, alternating ascending and descending five-finger blues patterns while the LH plays the root and fifth of the indicated chord.

🔊 6-41

Moderate blues tempo

Using the 12-bar blues progression, improvise other melodies with the five-finger blues pattern.

ℰnsemble Repertoire

1. Play the four-part single-line ensemble.
2. Harmonize measures 1–8 of Part 1 with I, IV and V chords using a block-chord accompaniment.

ODE TO JOY
(SYMPHONY NO. 9)

Ludwig van Beethoven (1770–1827)
Arranged from Op. 125

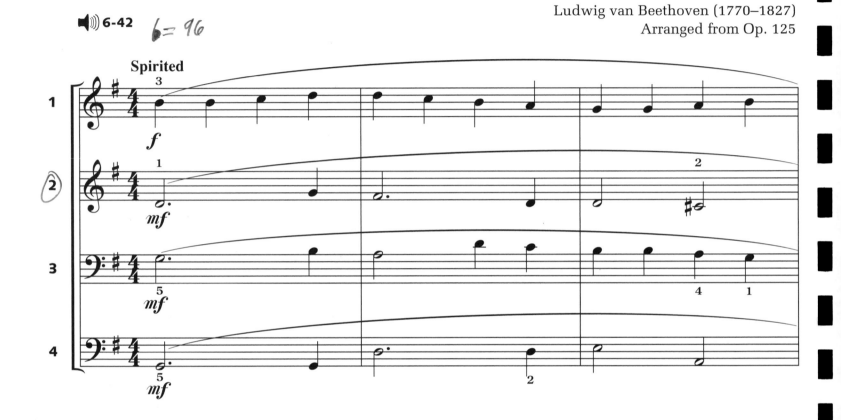

Primary Chords in Major Keys

Objectives

Upon completion of this unit the student will be able to:

1. Play I–IV$_4^6$–I–V$_5^6$–I chord progressions in all major keys.

2. Perform solo repertoire that uses scale patterns and chords.

3. Sight read and transpose music that uses tonic, dominant, and subdominant chords.

4. Create two-hand accompaniments from chord symbols.

5. Harmonize and transpose melodies with tonic, dominant, and subdominant chords.

6. Improvise melodies over tonic, dominant, and subdominant chords.

Assignments

Week of _____

Write your assignments for the week in the space below.

_____

_____

_____

_____

_____

_____

_____

_____

_____

_____

_____

_____

_____

_____

_____

_____

Playing the I–IV$_4^6$–I–V$_5^6$–I Chord Progression

Play hands separately first, then together.

🔊 7-1

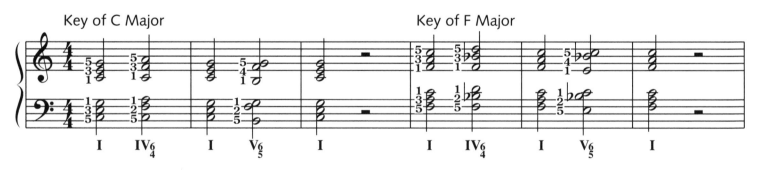

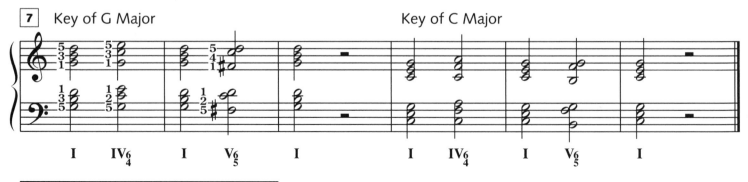

Playing the I–IV–I–V⁷–I Chord Progression

Play the **I–IV–I–V⁷–I** chord progression exercise. The RH of the exercise is the same as the previous example, but the LH plays only the root of each chord.

🔊 **7-2**

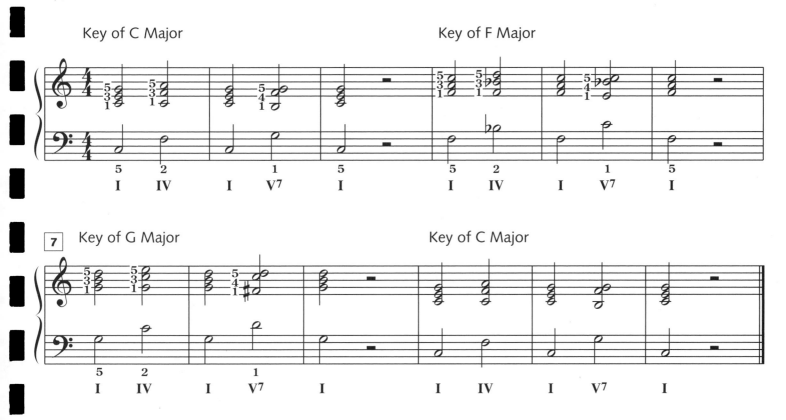

Key of C Major

Key of F Major

Key of G Major

Key of C Major

Practice the exercise on page 170 and the above exercise in the following major keys:

🔊 **7-3**

1.   **D**   **G**   **A**   **D**

🔊 **7-4**

2.   **E**   **A**   **B**   **E**

🔊 **7-5**

3.   **D♭**   **G♭**   **A♭**   **D♭**

🔊 **7-6**

4.   **E♭**   **A♭**   **B♭**   **E♭**

due 11/2

♪olo Repertoire

Before playing:
- Block the LH intervals in each measure, carefully noting all accidentals.
- Notice that both hands are written in the bass clef in measures 25 and 26.
- Find and play the first RH note of each measure with the correct fingering.

While playing:
- Observe the crescendo and diminuendo signs to shape the musical line.
- Listen for clear pedal changes.

🔊))) 7-7

MOONLIT SHORES

Randall Hartsell

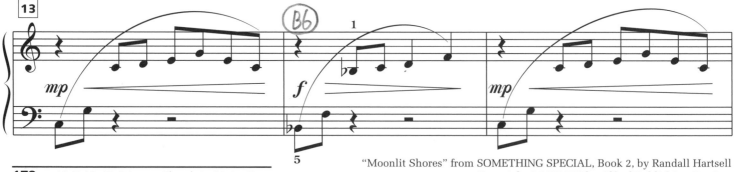

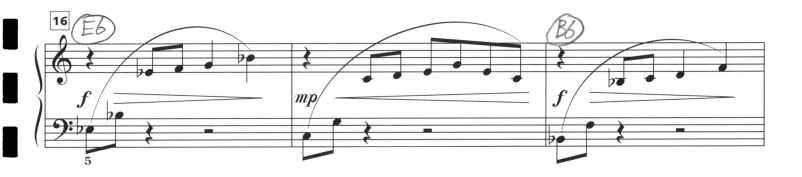

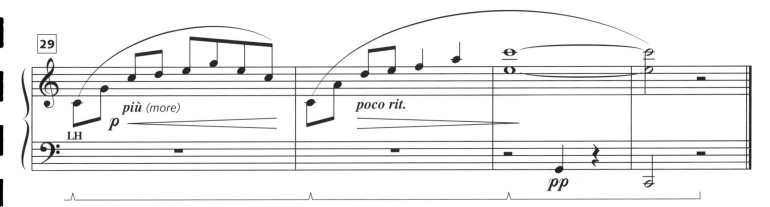

Reading

Identify the key of each example. Use the indicated tempo, dynamics and articulation as you play these exercises.

Use the following practice directions:

1. Tap RH and count aloud; then LH.
2. Play hands separately and count aloud.
3. Tap hands together and count aloud.
4. Play hands together and count aloud.

MARCH

🔊 7-8

Daniel Gottlob Türk
(1756–1813)

Allegro moderato

MELODY

🔊 7-9

Louis Köhler (1820–1886)
Op. 218, No. 8

Moderato

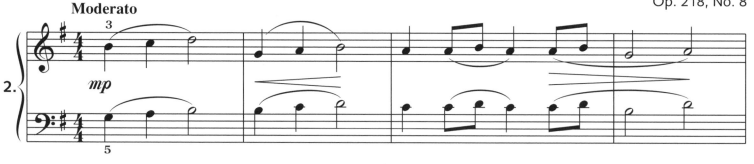

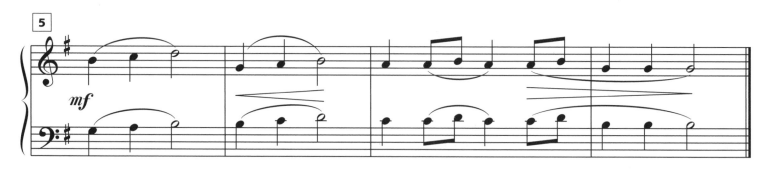

▶ Transpose to A major.

KUM-BA-YAH!

Traditional

*Finger substitution: while holding the key down with finger 4, shift to finger 5.

▶ Transpose to E♭ major.

7-11

▶ Transpose to B♭ major.

Playing Intervals

Play the following exercises that use intervals:

7-12

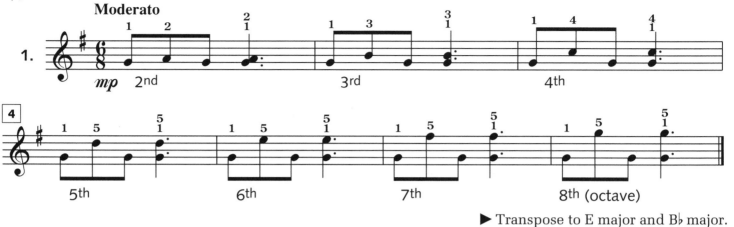

1. Moderato

2nd   3rd   4th

5th   6th   7th   8th (octave)

▶ Transpose to E major and B♭ major.

7-13

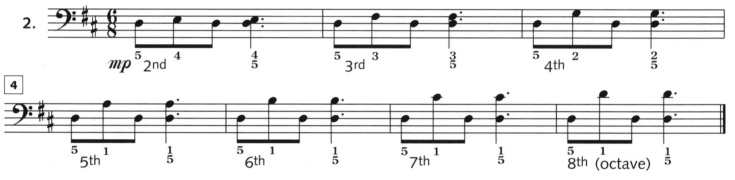

2. Moderato

2nd   3rd   4th

5th   6th   7th   8th (octave)

▶ Transpose to A major and F major.

7-14

3. Moderato

7-15

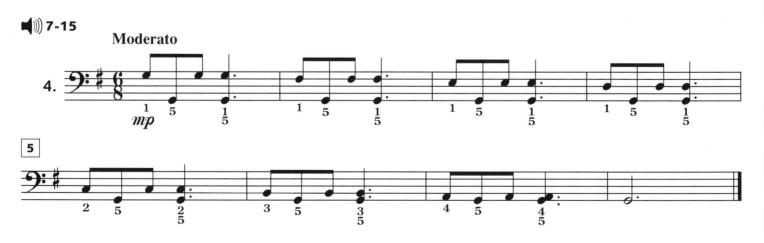

4. Moderato

Harmonization with Two-Hand Accompaniment

Using the indicated chords, create a two-hand accompaniment for the following melody by continuing the pattern given in the first two measures.

DONA NOBIS PACEM

7-16

Anonymous

Harmonization

1. Use the bottom note of each indicated chord to harmonize the following melody.

MINUET IN G MAJOR
(NOTEBOOK FOR ANNA MAGDALENA)

🔊 7-17

Johann Sebastian Bach
(1685–1750)

Using tonic (I), dominant (V⁷ or V⁶₅) and subdominant (IV or IV⁶₄) chords, harmonize the following melodies with the indicated accompaniment style. In the first example, write the Roman numeral name of each chord on the line below the staff.

2. **Block Chord Accompaniment**

WHEN THE SAINTS GO MARCHING IN

🔊 7-18

Traditional

▶ Transpose to E major.

3. **Waltz Style Accompaniment**

LULLABY

🔊 7-19

Johannes Brahms (1833–1897)
Op. 49, No. 4

▶ Transpose to F major.

4. **Block Chord Accompaniment**

NOBODY KNOWS THE TROUBLE I'VE SEEN

🔊 7-20

United States

▶ Transpose to G major.

Improvisation from Chord Symbols

Using the chord progressions below, improvise RH melodies while the LH plays appropriate accompaniment styles. (First play the LH chord progression using the suggested accompaniment style and observing the indicated meter.) You can use the suggested rhythm for your improvisation or create your own rhythm to complement the accompaniment. Notate your favorite improvisation.

Rules for Improvisation:

1. When the tonic chord is used, play mostly scale tones 1, 3 and 5 in the melody.

2. When the dominant chord is used, play mostly scale tones 2, 4, 5 and 7 in the melody.

3. When the subdominant chord is used, play mostly scale tones 1, 4 and 6 in the melody.

4. Most improvisations begin and end on tonic.

5. The ear should always be the final guide in determining which melody notes to play.

1. **Broken Chord Accompaniment**

🔊 7-21

Key of C major

🔊 7-22

Key of A major

2. **Broken Chord Accompaniment**

Review Worksheet

Name _____   *Date* _____

1. In each measure below, draw a whole note above the given note
    to make the indicated harmonic interval.

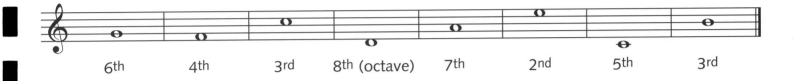

      6th   4th   3rd   8th (octave)   7th   2nd   5th   3rd

2. Identify the major and minor keys represented by each of the
    following key signatures by writing the major key and the
    minor key on the blanks between the staffs.

3. Identify the quality of each chord by writing M for major,
    A for augmented, m for minor or d for diminished on the
    lines below the staff.

4. Identify each major scale below by writing its name on the indicated line.
   Write the correct RH fingering on the lines above the staff and the correct
   LH fingering on the lines below the staff.

_____ major

_____ major

_____ major

_____ major

5. Identify each major key by writing its name on the line above the staff.
   Using whole notes on the staff, write the triad indicated by each Roman numeral.

ii   IV   iii   I   vi   vii°   iii   vi

6. Using whole notes, write the indicated chord in root position,
   first inversion and second inversion.

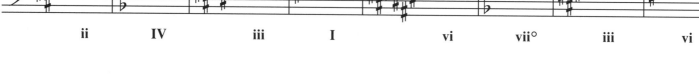

G major   F minor   A♭ minor   E major   C♯ minor

Root 1st 2nd   Root 1st 2nd   Root 1st 2nd   Root 1st 2nd   Root 1st 2nd

Minor Scales in Tetrachord Position

Objectives

Upon completion of this unit the student will be able to:

1. Play natural, harmonic and melodic minor scales in tetrachord position.
2. Play exercises that utilize intervals up to an octave.
3. Perform solo repertoire that uses minor scale patterns.
4. Sight-read and transpose music in minor keys.
5. Create a four-part ensemble from chord symbols.

Assignments

Week of _____

Write your assignments for the week in the space below.

_____

_____

_____

_____

_____

_____

_____

_____

_____

_____

_____

_____

_____

_____

_____

_____

_____

_____

_____

_____

Minor Scales

Every major key has a **relative minor key** that has the same key signature. The relative minor begins on the 6th tone of the major scale.

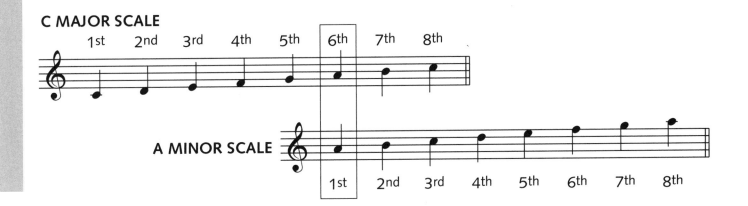

The Key of A Minor
(Relative to C Major)

There are three kinds of minor scales: the **natural**, the **harmonic** and the **melodic.** The harmonic minor is the most frequently used of the three.

Practice each of the following scales using tetrachord position. Transpose to E, D, B and G minor.

1. The Natural Minor Scale

This scale uses *only* the tones of the relative major scale.

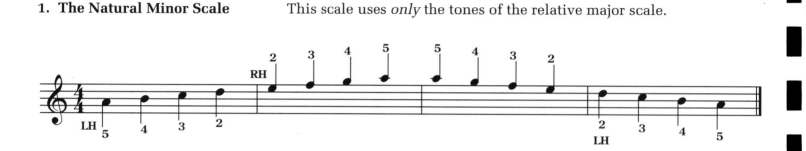

2. The Harmonic Minor Scale

The 7th tone (G) is raised one half step, ascending *and* descending.

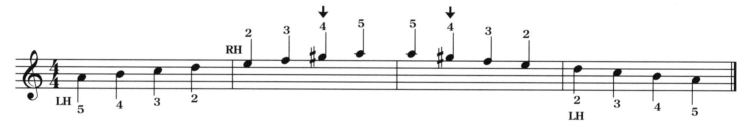

3. The Melodic Minor Scale

In the ascending scale, the 6th (F) and 7th (G) tones are raised one half step. The descending scale is the same as the natural minor.

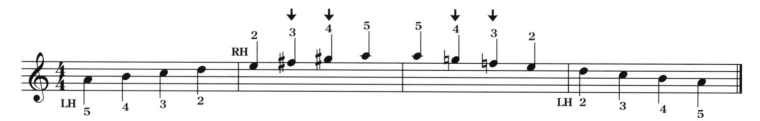

■ **Written Exercise:**
Write letter names on the correct keys to form
each harmonic minor scale.

Then play using tetrachord position.

Example:

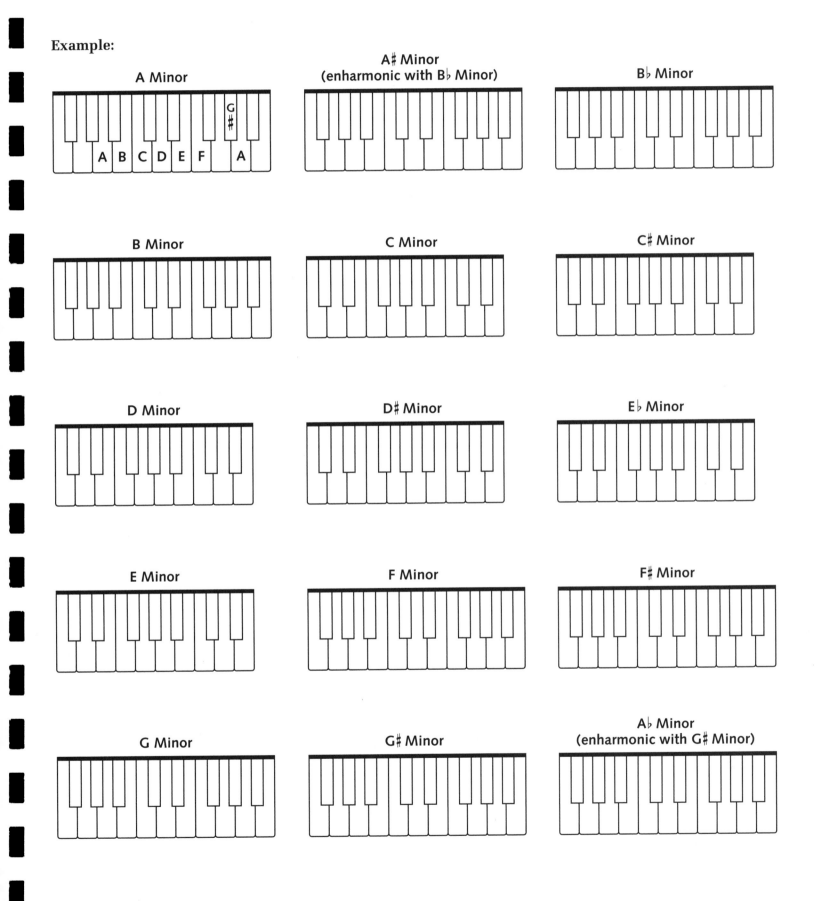

Playing Harmonic Minor Tetrachord Scales in Sharp Keys

Play the following harmonic minor scales in tetrachord position while the teacher plays an accompaniment.

🔊 7-23

C# Minor

G# Minor

D# Minor

A# Minor

Playing Harmonic Minor Tetrachord Scales in Flat Keys

Play the following harmonic minor scales in tetrachord position while the teacher plays an accompaniment.

🔊)) 7-24

C Minor

G Minor

D Minor

A Minor

Technique

♪olo Repertoire

Before playing:
- Tap the rhythm hands together, making sure to give quarter notes and rests their full value.
- Find the places where the hands move to different positions.

While playing:
- Listen for even sixteenth notes.

LITTLE FANTASY STUDY

🔊 **7-29**

Alec Rowley (1892–1958)
Op. 13, No. 2

Vivace

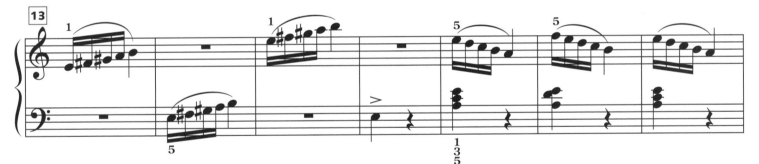

Reading

Identify the key of each example. Use the indicated tempo, dynamics and articulation as you play these exercises.

Use the following practice directions:

1. Tap RH and count aloud; then LH.
2. Play hands separately and count aloud.
3. Tap hands together and count aloud.
4. Play hands together and count aloud.

🔊 7-30

Andante moderato

1.

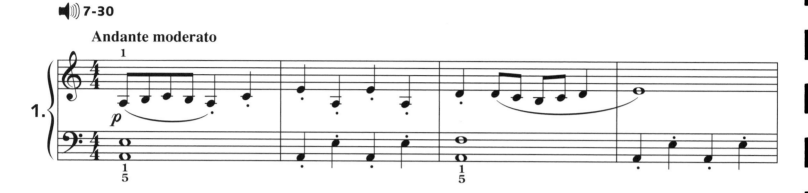

5

▶ Transpose to G minor.

🔊 7-31

Moderately fast

2.

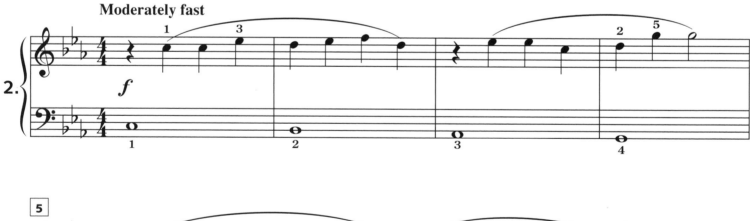

5

7-32

Mysteriously

3.

7

► Transpose to A minor.

7-33

Andante moderato

4.

5

*E*nsemble Repertoire

Play the four-part ensemble using the indicated chords to complete parts 2, 3 and 4.

Part 1: Melody
Part 2: Descending broken chords (one octave higher than written throughout)
Part 3: Two-Hand Accompaniment
Part 4: Roots of chords (one octave lower than written throughout)

WAYFARING STRANGER

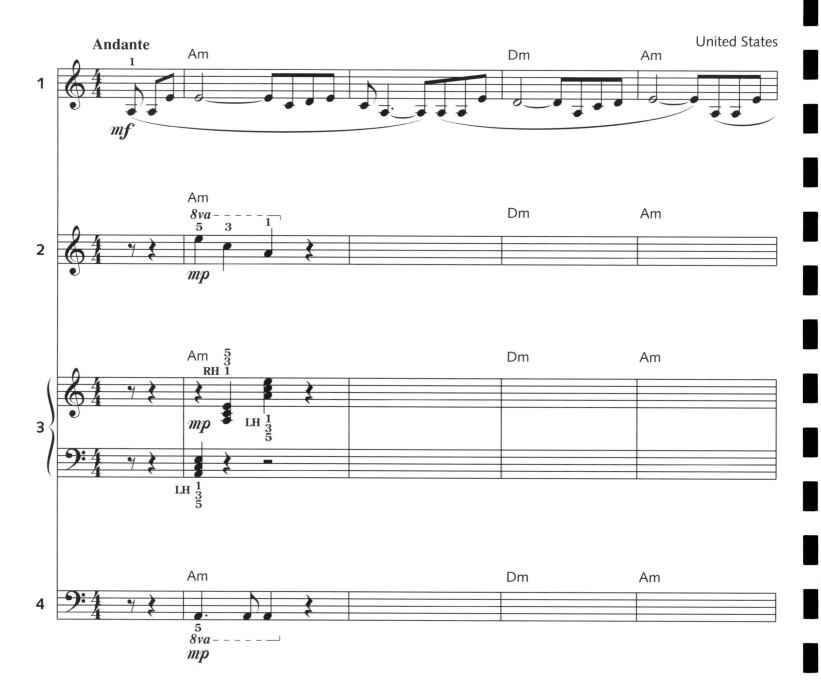

Minor Scales (Group I) and Triads of the Key

Objectives

Upon completion of this unit the student will be able to:

1. Build a triad of the key on any note of the harmonic minor scale.
2. Play Group 1 harmonic minor scales and minor arpeggios using traditional fingering.
3. Perform solo repertoire that uses minor scale patterns.
4. Harmonize melodies with roots of chords.
5. Sight-read music that uses minor scale patterns.
6. Improvise minor scale melodies over roots of chords and root-position triads of the key.

Assignments

Week of _____

Write your assignments for the week in the space below.

_____

_____

_____

_____

_____

_____

_____

_____

_____

_____

_____

_____

Playing Triads of the Key in Harmonic Minor

Triads may be built on any note of any scale. The sharps or flats in the key signature, as well as the raised seventh in harmonic minor, must be used when playing these triads. Triads of the key are identified by Roman numerals.

Play triads of the key in A harmonic minor. Note the quality of each chord.

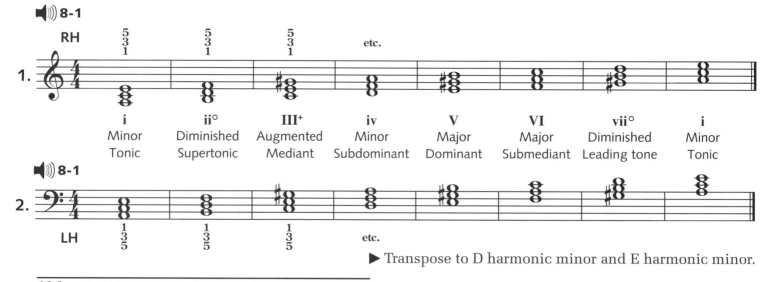

▶ Transpose to D harmonic minor and E harmonic minor.

Technique

Practicing Minor Scales (Group 1 Keys): A, E, D, G and C

The following principles will help you remember the fingering for the Group 1 minor scales:

1. All five scales use the same fingering.
   RH: 1 2 3   1 2 3 4   1 2 3   1 2 3 4 5
   LH: 5 4 3 2 1   3 2 1   4 3 2 1   3 2 1
2. The fourth finger plays only once per octave in each scale.
3. Thumbs play on the tonic of each scale.
   (Note: Thumb must be substituted for finger 5 at the beginning and end of the scale.)
4. When playing hands together, finger 3 in each hand plays at the same time.

Practice Suggestions (Note: If you are just beginning minor scales, you and your teacher may choose to practice the scale first for one octave rather than two.)

1. Build each scale in tetrachord position.
2. Play the scale hands separately using the correct fingering. (See pages 199–201.)

See page 122 for additional scale practice suggestions and challenges.

Practicing Minor Arpeggios (Group 1 Keys): A, E, D, G and C

The following principle will help you remember the fingering for the Group 1 minor arpeggios:

All five arpeggios use the same fingering in the RH.
RH: 1 2 3   1 2 3 5
LH: 5 4 2   1 4 2 1

Practice Suggestions (Note: If you are just beginning minor arpeggios, you and your teacher may choose to practice the arpeggio for one octave rather than two.)

See page 123 for additional arpeggio practice suggestions and challenges.

Playing Harmonic Minor
Scales and Arpeggios

A Minor

RH: 1 2 3 1 2 3 4 1 2 3 1 2 3 4 5
LH: 5 4 3 2 1 3 2 1 4 3 2 1 3 2 1

🔊 8-7

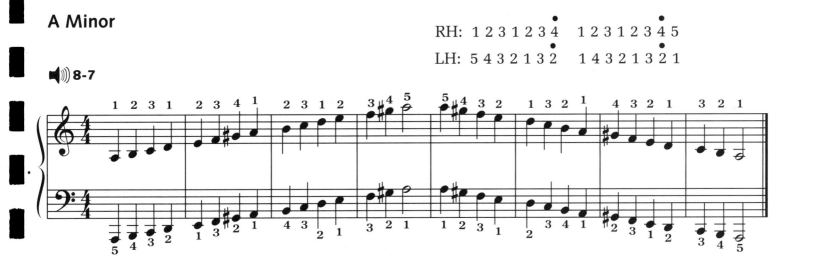

RH: 1 2 3 1 2 3 5
LH: 5 4 2 1 4 2 1

🔊 8-8

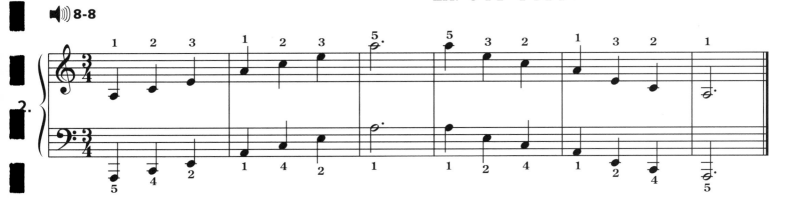

Playing Harmonic Minor
Scales and Arpeggios (continued)

E Minor

RH: 1 2 3 1 2 3 4   1 2 3 1 2 3 4 5
LH: 5 4 3 2 1 3 2   1 4 3 2 1 3 2 1

🔊 8-9

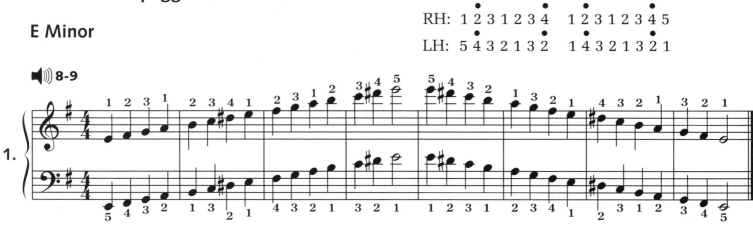

1.

RH: 1 2 3   1 2 3 5
LH: 5 4 2   1 4 2 1

🔊 8-10

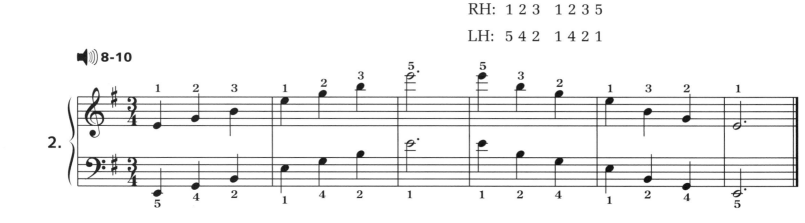

2.

D Minor

RH: 1 2 3 1 2 3 4   1 2 3 1 2 3 4 5
LH: 5 4 3 2 1 3 2   1 4 3 2 1 3 2 1

🔊 8-11

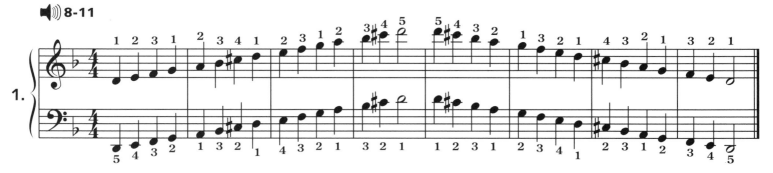

1.

RH: 1 2 3   1 2 3 5
LH: 5 4 2   1 4 2 1

🔊 8-12

2.

G Minor

RH: 1 2 3 1 2 3 4   1 2 3 1 2 3 4 5
LH: 5 4 3 2 1 3 2   1 4 3 2 1 3 2 1

🔊 8-13

1.

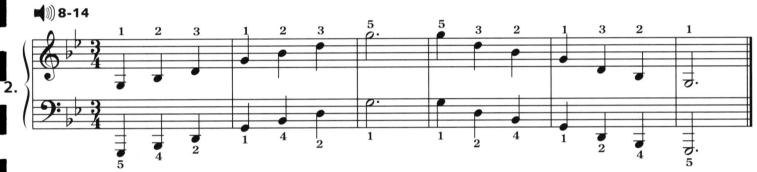

RH: 1 2 3   1 2 3 5
LH: 5 4 2   1 4 2 1

🔊 8-14

2.

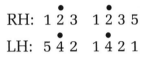

C Minor

RH: 1 2 3 1 2 3 4   1 2 3 1 2 3 4 5
LH: 5 4 3 2 1 3 2   1 4 3 2 1 3 2 1

🔊 8-15

1.

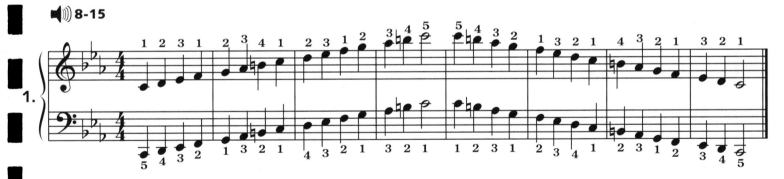

RH: 1 2 3   1 2 3 5
LH: 5 4 2   1 4 2 1

🔊 8-16

2.

𝒮olo Repertoire

Before playing:
- Find, identify and play each RH descending scale.
- Tap the rhythm hands together.

While playing:
- Lift hands for rests.

ALLEGRETTO

🔊 **8-17**

Cornelius Gurlitt (1820–1901)
Op. 82, No. 52

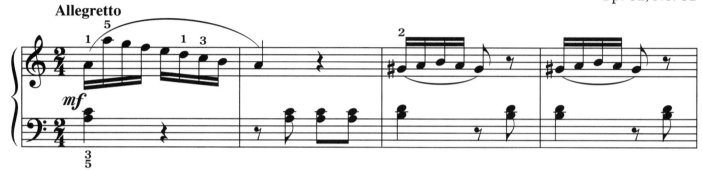

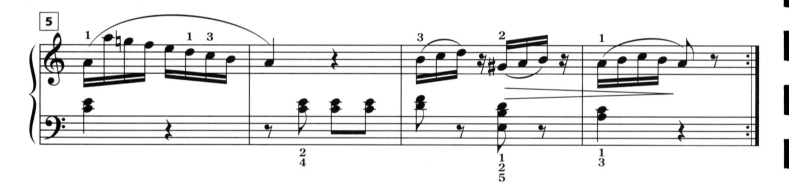

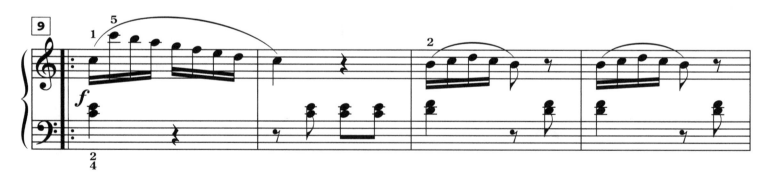

Harmonization

Harmonize each melody below using the root of the indicated triads.

◀))) 8-18

► Transpose to D minor.

◀))) 8-19

► Transpose to G minor.

◀))) 8-20

► Transpose to A minor.

Reading

Identify the key of each example. Use the indicated tempo, dynamics and articulation as you play these exercises.

Use the following practice directions:

1. Tap RH and count aloud; then LH.
2. Play hands separately and count aloud.
3. Tap hands together and count aloud.
4. Play hands together and count aloud.

ETUDE

🔊 8-21

Cornelius Gurlitt (1820–1901)
Op. 117, No. 21

🔊 8-22

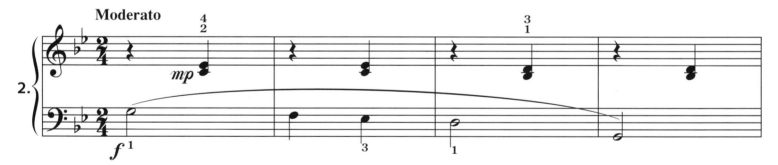

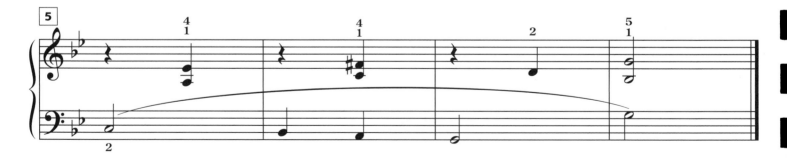

ETUDE

Cornelius Gurlitt (1820–1901)
Op. 82, No. 33

 8-23

Con moto

 8-24

Allegro moderato

Improvisation from Chord Symbols

Improvise a RH melody in A natural minor for the chord progression below while the LH plays the root of the indicated chords. Begin and end each phrase with the given notes. You can use the suggested rhythm for your improvisation or create your own rhythm to complement the accompaniment. Notate your favorite improvisation.

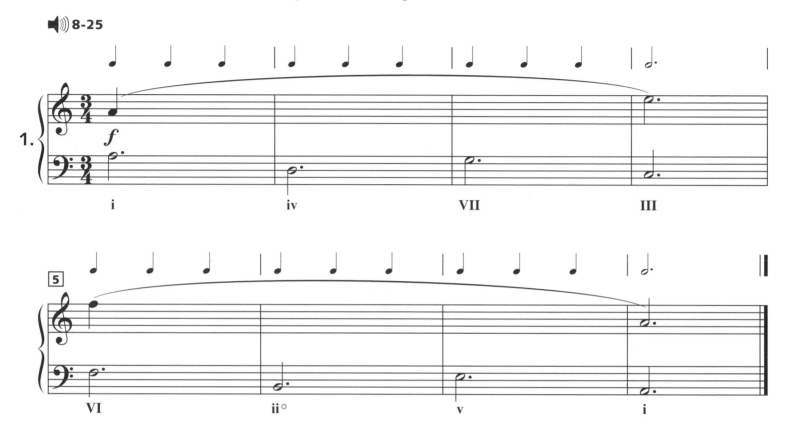

Continue the RH melodic sequence in A natural minor for the chord progression below while the LH plays the root-position chords.

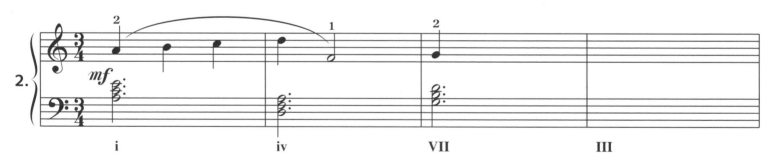

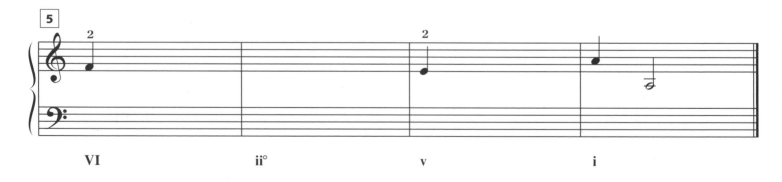

Review Worksheet

Name _____   *Date* _____

1. Identify each harmonic minor scale below by writing its name on the indicated line. Write the correct RH fingering on the lines above the staff and the correct LH fingering on the lines below the staff.

_____ Harmonic Minor Scale

_____ Harmonic Minor Scale

_____ Harmonic Minor Scale

_____ Harmonic Minor Scale

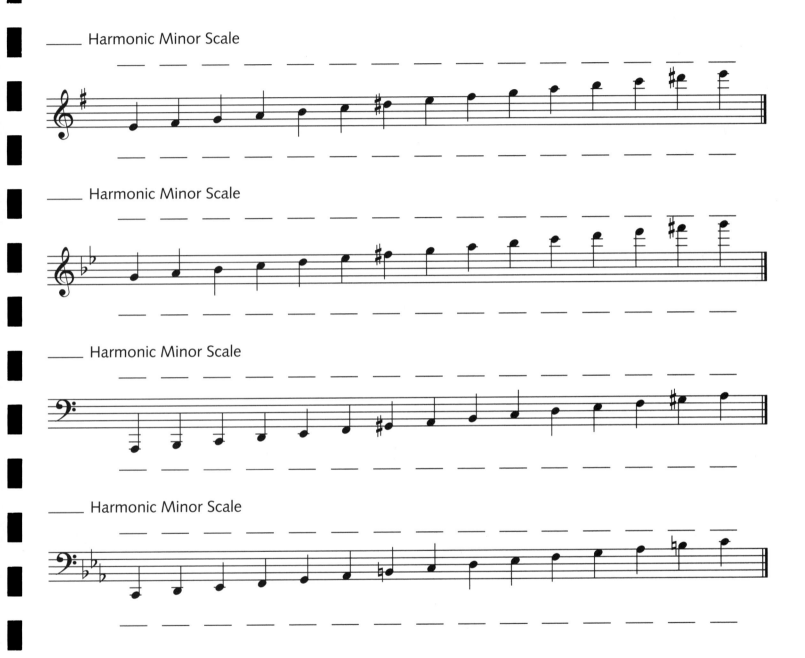

2. Identify each minor key by writing its name on the line above the staff. Write the Roman numeral name for each triad in that key on the line below the staff.

3. Identify each minor key signature below by writing its name
   in the blank. Following the key signature, write the notes for
   each harmonic minor scale on the staff, using whole notes.
   Write the sharps or flats from the key signature in front of the
   appropriate notes.

_____ Harmonic Minor Scale

_____ Harmonic Minor Scale

_____ Harmonic Minor Scale

_____ Harmonic Minor Scale

4. Identify each minor key by writing its name on the line above
   the staff. Using whole notes, write the triad in harmonic minor
   indicated by each Roman numeral.

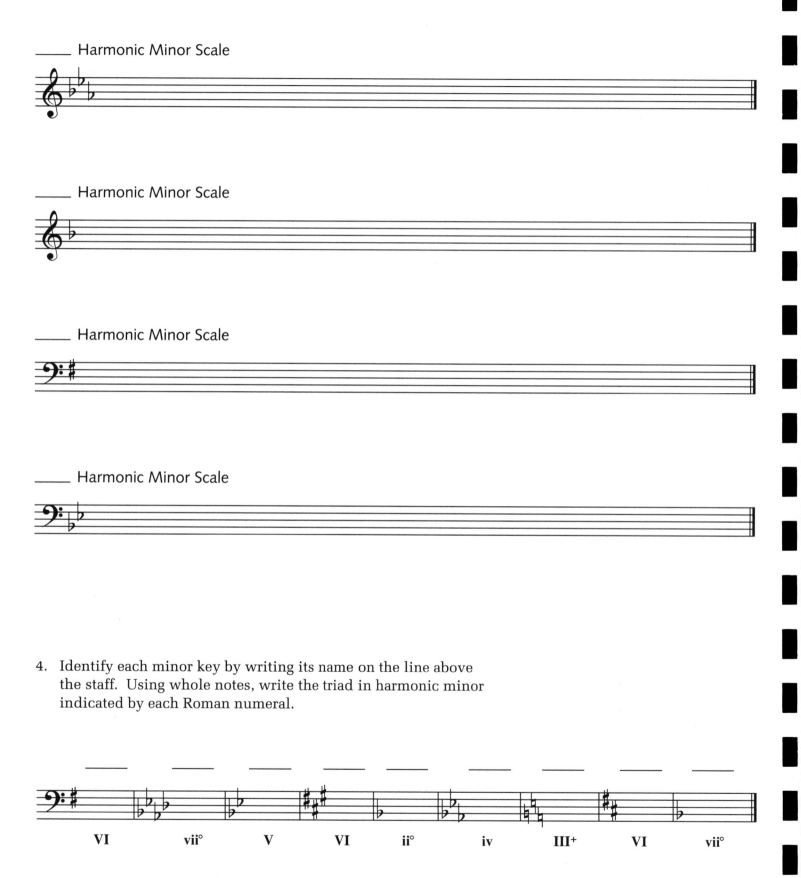

VI   vii°   V   VI   ii°   iv   III⁺   VI   vii°

Primary Chords in Minor Keys

Objectives

Upon completion of this unit the student will be able to:

1. Play i–iv$_4^6$–i–V$_5^6$–i chord progressions in all minor keys.

2. Perform solo repertoire that uses tonic, dominant and subdominant harmonies in minor keys.

3. Create ensemble parts to accompany solo repertoire.

4. Sight-read and transpose music that uses tonic, dominant and subdominant chords in minor keys.

5. Harmonize and transpose melodies with tonic, dominant and subdominant chords in minor keys.

6. Create two-hand accompaniments from chord symbols.

7. Improvise melodies over tonic, dominant and subdominant chords in minor keys.

Assignments

Week of _____

Write your assignments for the week in the space below.

Playing the i–iv⁶₄–i–V⁶₅–i Chord Progression

Play the **i–iv⁶₄–i–V⁶₅–i** chord progression exercise:

🔊 **8-27**

Practice the above exercise in the following minor keys:

🔊 **8-28**   1. B   E   F♯   B

🔊 **8-30**   3. B♭   E♭   F   B♭

🔊 **8-29**   2. C   F   G   C

🔊 **8-31**   4. C♯   F♯   G♯   C♯

Playing the i–iv–i–V⁷–i Chord Progression

Play the **i–iv–i–V⁷–i** chord progression exercise. The RH of the exercise is the same as above, but the LH plays only the root of each chord.

🔊 **8-32**

$\int$olo Repertoire

Before playing:
- Block the chords, first with the RH, then with the LH.
- Play the blocked chords, alternating hands.

While playing:
- Play legato so that the notes divided between the hands sound like one line.
- Listen for clear pedal changes.

ETUDE

🔊 8-33

Ludvig Schytte
(1848–1909)

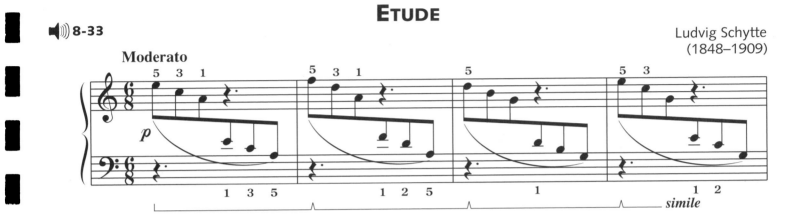

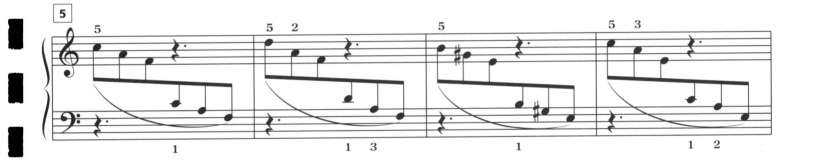

*E*nsemble Repertoire

Play the four-part ensemble using the indicated chords to complete parts 2, 3 and 4.

Part 1: Schytte *Etude* (page 211)

Part 2: Descending five-finger patterns (one octave higher than written throughout)

Part 3: Broken chords

Part 4: Roots of chords (one octave lower than written throughout)

🔊 8-34

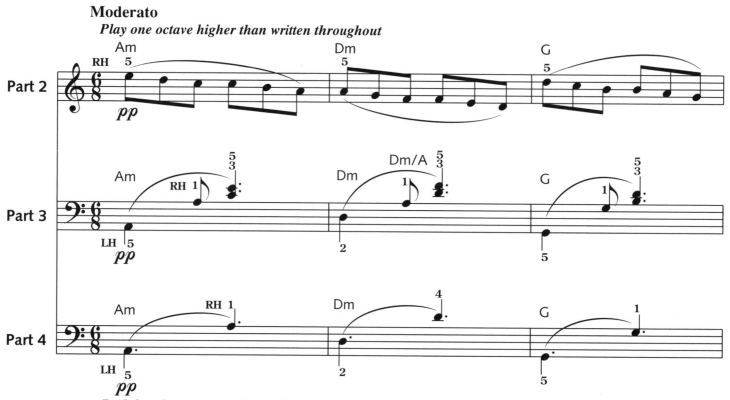

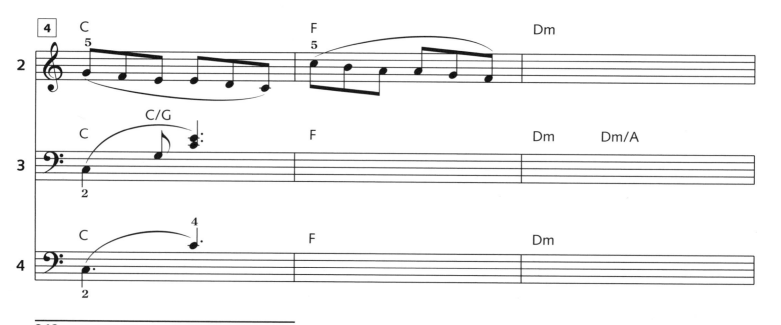

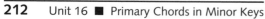

Reading

Identify the key of each example. Use the indicated tempo, dynamics and articulation as you play these exercises.

Use the following practice directions:
1. Tap RH and count aloud; then LH.
2. Play hands separately and count aloud.
3. Tap hands together and count aloud.
4. Play hands together and count aloud.

🔊 8-35

1.

▶ Transpose to E minor.

🔊 8-36

2.

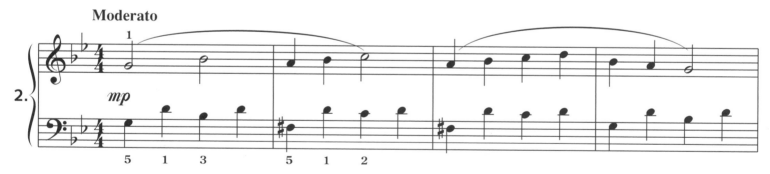

▶ Transpose to A minor.

🔊 8-37

Adagio moderato

3.

🔊 8-38

Allegro

4.

▶ Transpose to G minor.

▶ Transpose to D minor.

Harmonization

1. Harmonize with a broken chord accompaniment.

Broken Chord Accompaniment

🔊 8-39

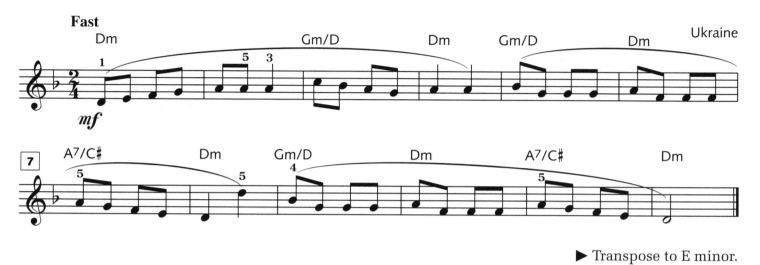

▶ Transpose to E minor.

2. Using i, iv$^6_4$ and V$^6_5$ chords, harmonize with a block chord accompaniment. Write the Roman numeral name of each chord on the line below the staff.

Block Chord Accompaniment

🔊 8-40

GO DOWN, MOSES

▶ Transpose to G minor.

3. Harmonize with a block chord accompaniment.

Block Chord Accompaniment

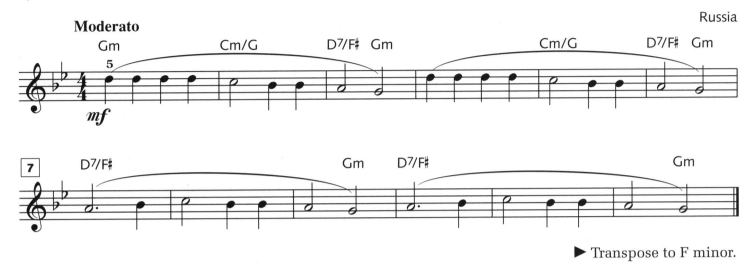

8-41

Moderato

Russia

► Transpose to F minor.

4. Using i, iv$_4^6$ and V$_5^6$ chords, harmonize with a waltz style accompaniment. Write the Roman numeral name of each chord on the line below the staff.

Waltz Style Accompaniment

RAISINS AND ALMONDS

8-42

Allegro moderato

Israel

Harmonization with Two-Hand Accompaniment

Using the indicated chords, create a two-hand accompaniment for the following melody by continuing the pattern given in the first measure.

JOSHUA FOUGHT THE BATTLE OF JERICHO

Key of E harmonic minor

8-43

Lively

Spiritual

i   i   V7   i

waltz, block chord, broken

i   i   V7   i

► Transpose to D minor.

Improvisation from Chord Symbols

Using the chord progressions below, improvise RH melodies while the LH plays appropriate accompaniment styles. (First play the LH chord progression using the suggested accompaniment style and observing the indicated meter.) You can use the suggested rhythm for your improvisation or create your own rhythm to complement the accompaniment. Notate your favorite improvisation.

Rules for Improvisation:

1. When the tonic chord is used, play mostly scale tones 1, 3 and 5 in the melody.
2. When the dominant chord is used, play mostly scale tones 2, 4, 5 and 7 in the melody.
3. When the subdominant chord is used, play mostly scale tones 1, 4 and 6 in the melody.
4. Most improvisations begin and end on tonic.
5. The ear should always be the final guide in determining which melody notes to play.

Minor Scales (Group 2) and Triads of the Key

Objectives

Upon completion of this unit the student will be able to:

1. Build a triad of the key on any note of the harmonic minor scale.

2. Play Group 2 minor scales and minor arpeggios using traditional fingerings.

3. Perform solo repertoire in a minor key.

4. Sight-read and transpose music that uses scale patterns and primary chords in minor keys.

5. Harmonize and transpose melodies with primary chords in minor keys.

6. Create two-hand accompaniments from chord symbols.

7. Improvise melodies over primary chords in minor keys.

Assignments

Week of _____

Write your assignments for the week in the space below.

_____

_____

_____

_____

_____

_____

_____

_____

_____

_____

_____

_____

_____

_____

_____

_____

_____

_____

_____

Playing Triads of the Key in Harmonic Minor

Play triads of the key in B harmonic minor. Note the quality of each chord.

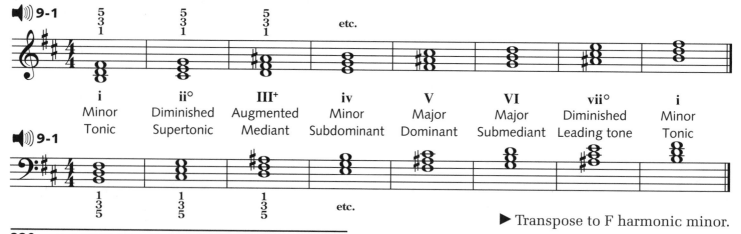

▶ Transpose to F harmonic minor.

Technique

◀))) 9-2

◀))) 9-3

◀))) 9-4

◀))) 9-4

◀))) 9-5

◀))) 9-5 Moderato

Practicing Minor Scales (Group 2 Keys): B and F

The following principles will help you remember the fingering for the Group 2 minor scales:

1. The RH fingering for B minor is the same as the Group 1 minor keys.
   RH: 1 2 3   1 2 3 4   1 2 3   1 2 3 4 5
2. The LH fingering for F minor is the same as the Group 1 minor keys.
   LH: 5 4 3 2 1   3 2 1   4 3 2 1   3 2 1
3. The fourth finger plays only once per octave in each scale (except for the first note of B minor in the LH and the last note of F minor in the RH).

Practice Suggestions (Note: If you are just beginning minor scales, you and your teacher may choose to practice the scale for one octave rather than two.)

1. Build each scale in tetrachord position.
2. Play the scale hands separately using the correct fingering. (See page 223.)

See page 122 for additional scale practice suggestions and challenges.

Practicing Minor Arpeggios (Group 2 Keys): B and F

The following principle will help you remember the fingering for the Group 2 minor arpeggios:

The fingering for both hands is the same as the Group 1 minor arpeggios.
   RH: 1 2 3   1 2 3 5
   LH: 5 4 2   1 4 2 1

Practice Suggestions (Note: If you are just beginning minor arpeggios, you and your teacher may choose to practice the arpeggio for one octave rather than two.)

See page 123 for additional arpeggio practice suggestions and challenges.

Playing Harmonic Minor Scales and Arpeggios

B Minor

RH: 1 2 3 1 2 3 4   1 2 3 1 2 3 4 5
LH: 4 3 2 1 4 3 2   1 3 2 1 4 3 2 1

RH: 1 2 3   1 2 3 5
LH: 5 4 2   1 4 2 1

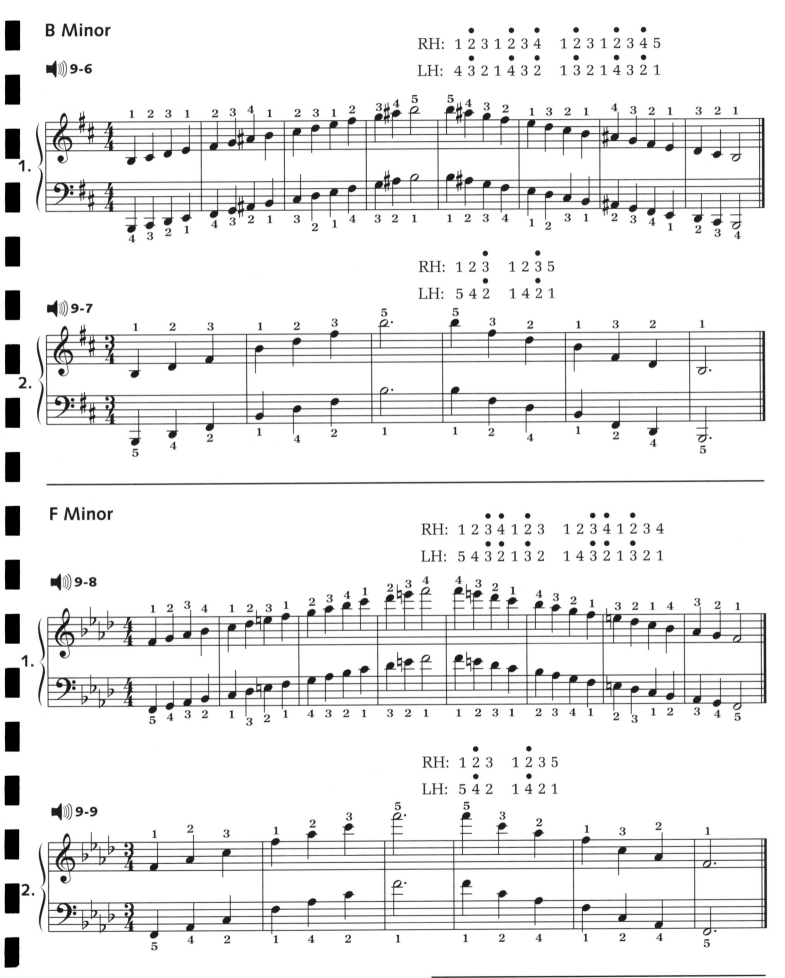

F Minor

RH: 1 2 3 4 1 2 3   1 2 3 4 1 2 3 4
LH: 5 4 3 2 1 3 2   1 4 3 2 1 3 2 1

RH: 1 2 3   1 2 3 5
LH: 5 4 2   1 4 2 1

♪olo Repertoire

Before playing:
- Write the counts below each measure.
- Tap the rhythm hands together.
- Find the places where each hand moves.

While playing:
- Make sure that beat 3 of each measure moves to beat 1 of the following measure in tempo.
- Listen to achieve a balance between the hands.

THE CUCKOO

François Couperin
(1668–1733)

◀))) 9-10

Moderato

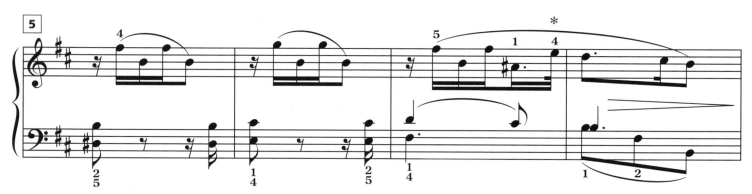

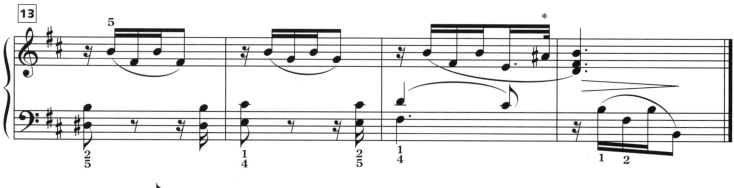

*Thirty-second note (♬) Four thirty-second notes are played in the time of one eighth note.

Reading

Identify the key of each example. Use the indicated tempo, dynamics and articulation as you play these exercises.

Use the following practice directions:

1. Tap RH and count aloud; then LH.
2. Play hands separately and count aloud.
3. Tap hands together and count aloud.
4. Play hands together and count aloud.

 9-11

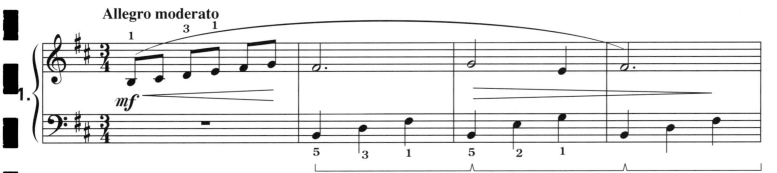

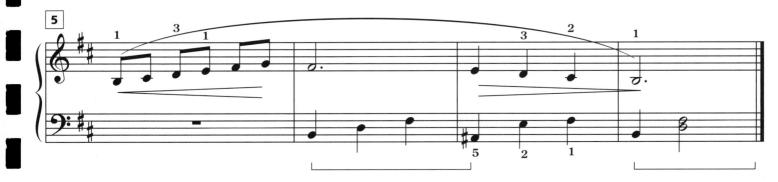

► Transpose to C minor.

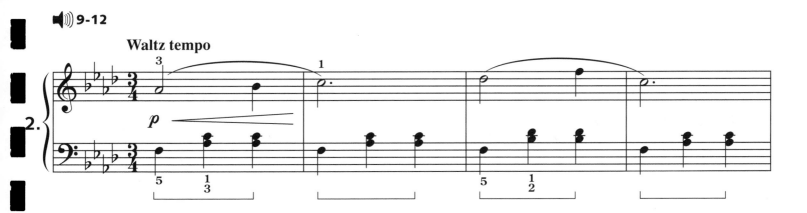 9-12

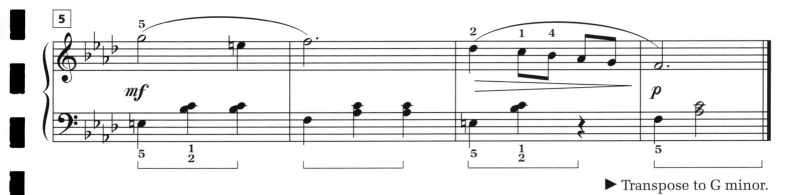

► Transpose to G minor.

Harmonization

1. Harmonize with a broken chord accompaniment.

Broken Chord Accompaniment

ALL THE PRETTY LITTLE HORSES

🔊 9-13

Tenderly

United States

2. Using i, iv$^6_4$ and V$^6_5$ chords, harmonize with a block chord accompaniment. Write the Roman numeral name of each chord on the line below the staff.

Block Chord Accompaniment

🔊 9-14

PAT-A-PAN

France

Briskly

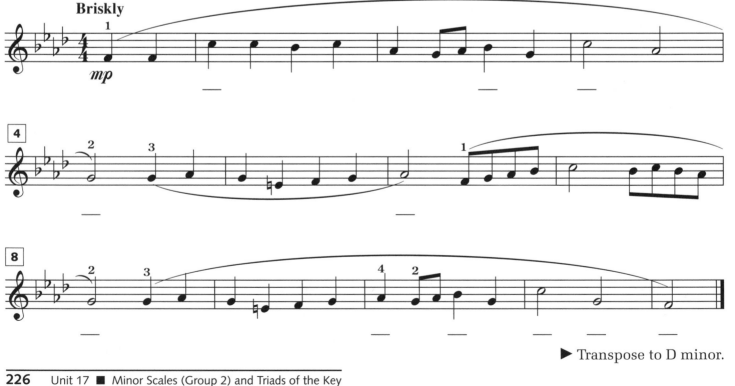

▶ Transpose to D minor.

3. Using i and iv$^6_4$ chords, harmonize with a block chord accompaniment. Write the Roman numeral name of each chord on the line below the staff.

Block Chord Accompaniment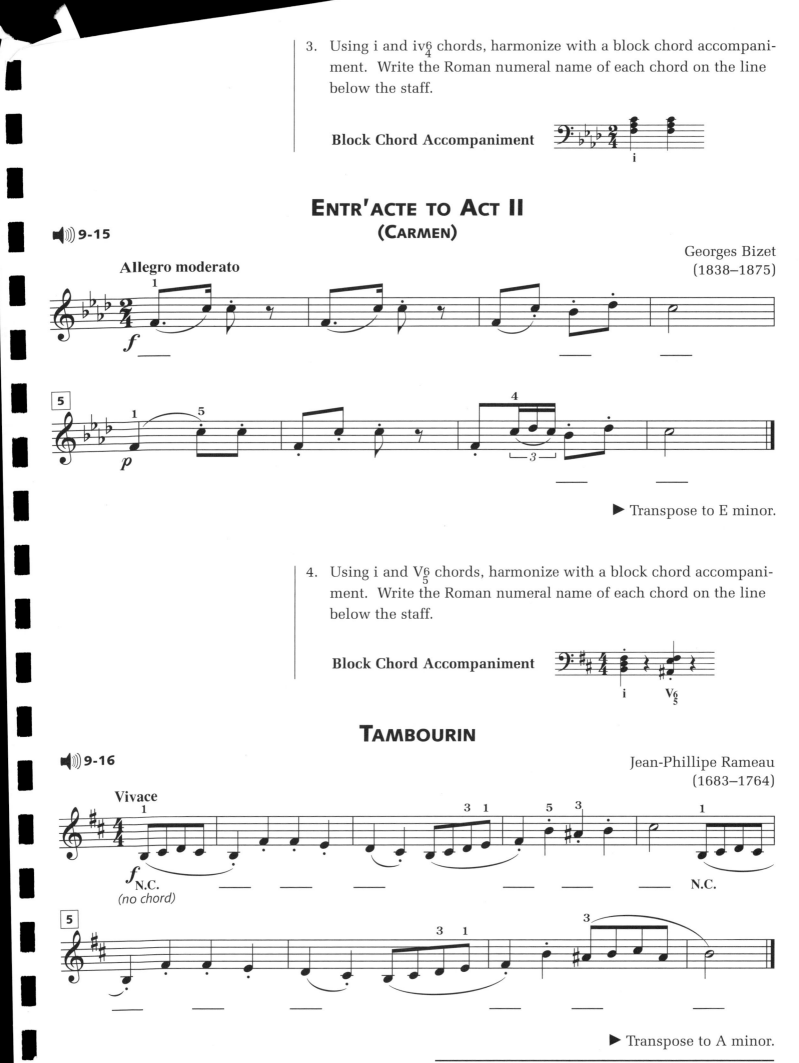

ENTR'ACTE TO ACT II
(CARMEN)

🔊 9-15

Georges Bizet
(1838–1875)

Allegro moderato

▶ Transpose to E minor.

4. Using i and V$^6_5$ chords, harmonize with a block chord accompaniment. Write the Roman numeral name of each chord on the line below the staff.

Block Chord Accompaniment

i   V$^6_5$

TAMBOURIN

🔊 9-16

Jean-Phillipe Rameau
(1683–1764)

Vivace

N.C.
(no chord)

▶ Transpose to A minor.

Harmonization with Two-Hand Accompaniment

Using the indicated chords, create a two-hand accompaniment the following melody by continuing the pattern given in the first two measures.

WAVES OF THE DANUBE

🔊 9-17

Ion Ivanovici
(1845–1902)

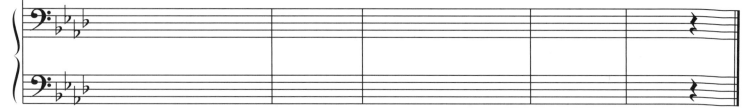

Improvisation from Chord Symbols

Using the chord progressions below, improvise RH melodies while the LH plays the suggested accompaniment style. (First play the LH chord progression using the suggested accompaniment style and observing the indicated meter.) You can use the suggested rhythm for your improvisation or create your own rhythm to complement the accompaniment. Notate your favorite improvisation.

Rules for improvisation:

1. When the tonic chord is used, play mostly scale tones 1, 3 and 5 in the melody.
2. When the subdominant chord is used, play mostly scale tones 1, 4 and 6 in the melody.
3. When the dominant chord is used, play mostly scale tones 2, 4, 5 and 7 in the melody.
4. Most improvisations begin and end on tonic.
5. The ear should always be the final guide in determining which melody notes to play.

🔊 9-18

Key of F minor

1. **Broken Chord Accompaniment**

🔊 9-19

Key of B minor

2. **Block Chord Accompaniment**

Major Scales (Group 3) and Triads of the Key

Objectives

Upon completion of this unit the student will be able to:

1. Build a triad on any note of the scale.
2. Play Group 3 major scales and arpeggios using traditional fingerings.
3. Sight-read and transpose music that uses scale patterns and primary chords in major keys.
4. Harmonize and transpose melodies that use primary chords in major keys.
5. Perform solo repertoire that uses primary chords.

Assignments

Week of _____

Write your assignments for the week in the space below.

_____

_____

_____

_____

_____

_____

_____

_____

_____

_____

_____

_____

_____

_____

_____

_____

_____

_____

Playing Triads of the Key

Triads may be built on any note of any scale. The sharps or flats in the key signature must be used when playing these triads. Triads of the key are identified by Roman numerals.

Play triads of the key in B♭ major. Note the quality of each chord.

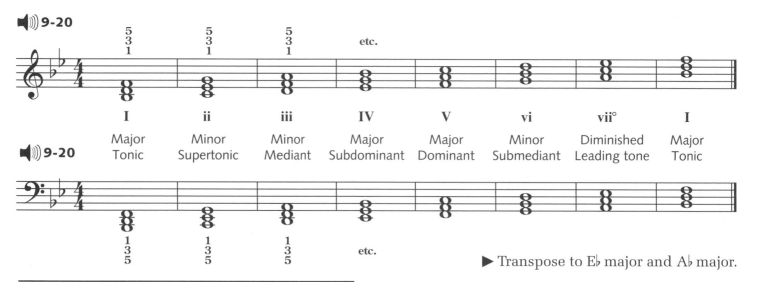

9-20

I	ii	iii	IV	V	vi	vii°	I
Major Tonic	Minor Supertonic	Minor Mediant	Major Subdominant	Major Dominant	Minor Submediant	Diminished Leading tone	Major Tonic

9-20

▶ Transpose to E♭ major and A♭ major.

Practicing Major Scales (Group 3 Keys): B♭, E♭ and A♭

The following principles will help you remember the fingering for the Group 3 major scales:

1. All three scales use the same LH fingering.
   LH: 3 2 1 4 3 2 1 3 2 1 4 3 2 1 3
2. The fourth finger in the RH always plays B♭.

See page 122 for scale practice suggestions and challenges.

Practicing Major Arpeggios (Group 3 Keys): B♭, E♭ and A♭

The following principles will help you remember the fingering for the Group 3 major arpeggios:

1. For the E♭ and A♭ major arpeggios (same as D♭ from Group 2):
   - Thumbs play the white keys. In addition to the thumbs, only fingers 2 and 4 are used.
   - In the right hand, the fourth finger plays the root.
     RH: 4 1 2   4 1 2 4
   - In the left hand, the second finger plays the root.
     LH: 2 1 4   2 1 4 2

2. For the B♭ major arpeggios:
   - The right hand fingering is the same as D♭, A♭ and E♭.
     RH: 4 1 2   4 1 2 4
   - The left hand has its own unique fingering.
     LH: 3 2 1   3 2 1 3

See page 122 for arpeggio practice suggestions and challenges.

Playing Major Scales and Arpeggios

B♭ Major

RH: 4 1 2 3 1 2 3   4 1 2 3 1 2 3 4
LH: 3 2 1 4 3 2 1   3 2 1 4 3 2 1 3

◀))) 9-21

RH: 4 1 2   4 1 2 4
LH: 3 2 1   3 2 1 3

◀))) 9-22

Playing Major Scales and Arpeggios (continued)

E♭ Major

RH: 3 1 2 3 4 1 2   3 1 2 3 4 1 2 3
LH: 3 2 1 4 3 2 1   3 2 1 4 3 2 1 3

🔊 9-23

1.

🔊 9-24

RH: 4 1 2   4 1 2 4
LH: 2 1 4   2 1 4 2

2.

A♭ Major

RH: 3 4 1 2 3 1 2   3 4 1 2 3 1 2 3
LH: 3 2 1 4 3 2 1   3 2 1 4 3 2 1 3

🔊 9-25

1.

RH: 4 1 2   4 1 2 4
LH: 2 1 4   2 1 4 2

🔊 9-26

2.

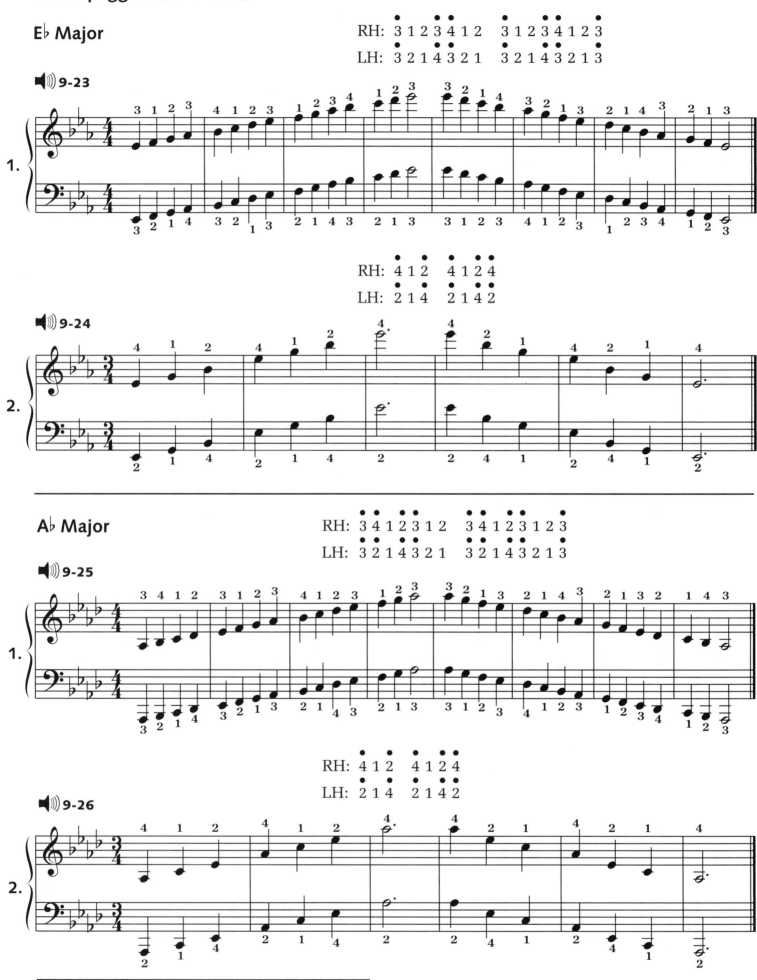

Technique

1.

▶ Transpose to A♭ major.

2.

▶ Transpose to E♭ major.

3.

▶ Transpose to B♭ major.

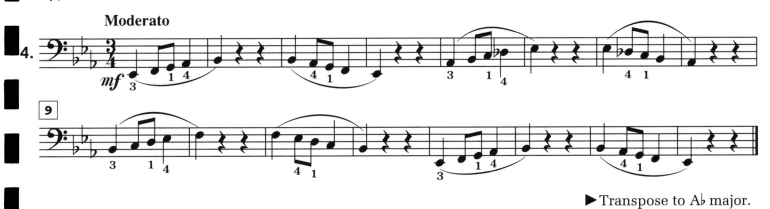

4.

▶ Transpose to A♭ major.

Reading

Identify the key of each example. Use the indicated tempo, dynamics and articulation as you play these exercises.

Use the following practice directions:

1. Tap RH and count aloud; then LH.
2. Play hands separately and count aloud.
3. Tap hands together and count aloud.
4. Play hands together and count aloud.

🔊 9-29

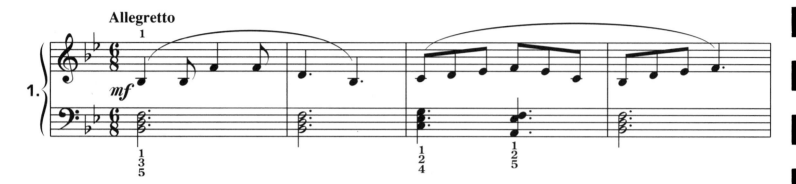

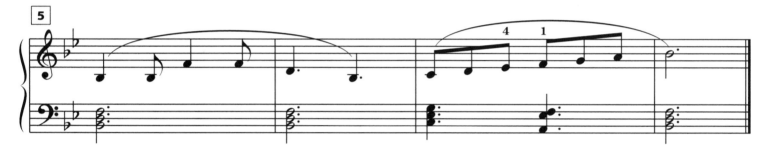

▶ Transpose to C major.

🔊 9-30

▶ Transpose to D major.

🔊 **9-31**

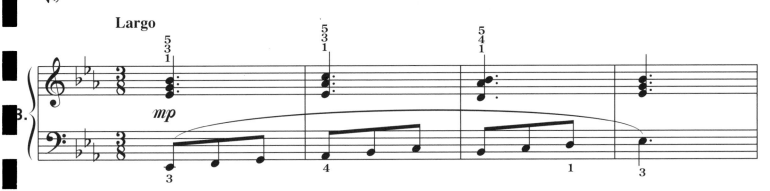

► Transpose to D major.

🔊 **9-32**

► Transpose to G major.

Harmonization

Using tonic (I), dominant (V^7 or V^6_5) or subdominant (IV or IV^6_4) chords, harmonize the following melodies with the indicated accompaniment style.

1. **Block Chord Accompaniment**

POLOVETSIAN DANCE

Alexander Borodin
(1833–1887)

🔊 9-33

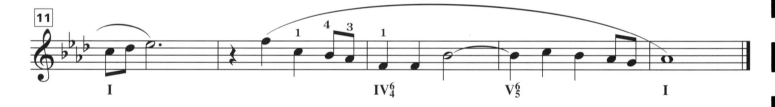

2. **Block Chord Accompaniment**

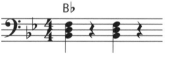

HUMORESQUE

Antonin Dvořák
(1841–1904)

🔊 9-34

Write the Roman numeral name of each chord on the line below the staff.

3. **Broken Chord Accompaniment**

FOR HE'S A JOLLY GOOD FELLOW

🔊 9-35

Traditional

▶ Transpose to F major.

4. **Alberti Bass Accompaniment**

UP ON THE HOUSETOP

🔊 9-36

Benjamin R. Hanby
(1833–1867)

▶ Transpose to D major.

♩olo Repertoire

Before playing:
- Note the clef changes in the LH at measures 9 and 13.
- Label the I, IV and V⁷ chords.

While playing:
- Play the RH a little louder than the LH.
- Slightly emphasize the downbeat of each measure to create the rhythmic feel of a dance.

DANCE

🔊 9-37

Christian Gottlob Neefe
(1748–1798)

Allegretto scherzando

Review Worksheet

Name _____   *Date* _____

1. Identify each major scale below by writing its name on the indicated
   line. Write the correct RH fingering on the lines above the staff and
   the correct LH fingering on the lines below the staff.

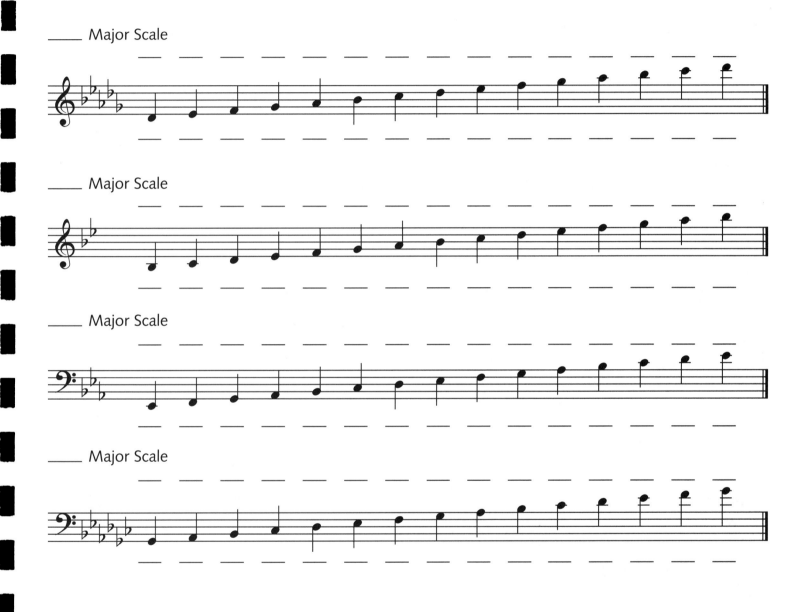

____ Major Scale

____ Major Scale

____ Major Scale

____ Major Scale

2. Identify each major key by writing its name on the line above the staff.
   Using whole notes, write a V chord on the staff. Write the letter name
   for each chord on the line below the staff.

3. Identify each major arpeggio below by writing its name on the indicated line. Write the correct RH fingering on the lines above the staff and the correct LH fingering on the lines below the staff.

_____ Major Arpeggio

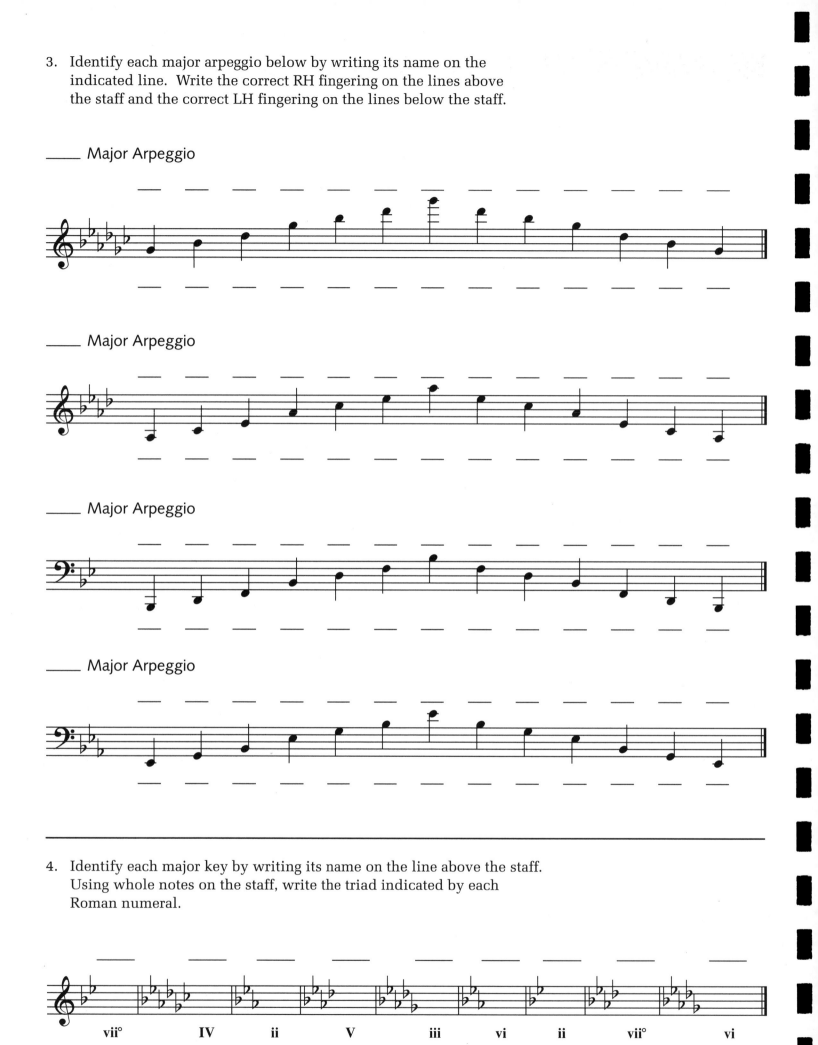

_____ Major Arpeggio

_____ Major Arpeggio

_____ Major Arpeggio

4. Identify each major key by writing its name on the line above the staff. Using whole notes on the staff, write the triad indicated by each Roman numeral.

vii°   IV   ii   V   iii   vi   ii   vii°   vi

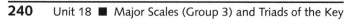

The ii Chord

Objectives

Upon completion of this unit the student will be able to:

1. Play I–ii_6–I^6_4–V^7–I chord progressions in all major and minor keys.

2. Perform solo repertoire that uses supertonic harmonies.

3. Create a three-part ensemble to accompany repertoire.

4. Sight-read and transpose music that uses supertonic chords.

5. Harmonize and transpose melodies with supertonic chords.

6. Create two-hand accompaniments from chord symbols.

Assignments

Week of _____

Write your assignments for the week in the space below.

_____

_____

_____

_____

_____

_____

_____

_____

_____

_____

_____

_____

_____

_____

The ii Chord

The ii chord (supertonic) is often substituted for the IV chord since they have two notes in common. It is frequently used in the first inversion (ii_6).

Key of C major:

In major keys, the ii chord is a minor triad.

Key of C major:

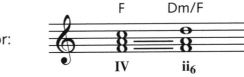

In natural and harmonic minor keys, the ii° chord is a diminished triad.

Key of A minor:

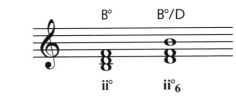

Playing Chord Progressions with the ii Chord

Play the following chord progressions hands separately.

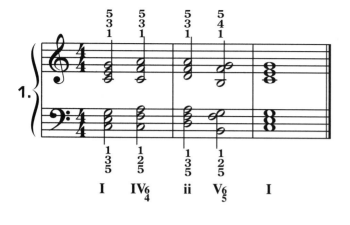

1.

$$\text{I} \qquad \text{IV}^6_4 \qquad \text{ii} \qquad \text{V}^6_5 \qquad \text{I}$$

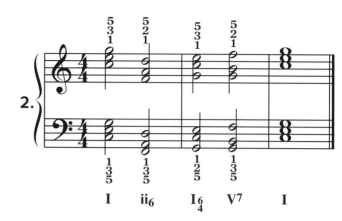

2.

$$\text{I} \qquad \text{ii}_6 \qquad \text{I}^6_4 \qquad \text{V}^7 \qquad \text{I}$$

▶ Transpose each progression to G major, F major, A harmonic minor and C harmonic minor.

Playing the I–ii₆–I⁶₄–V⁷–I Chord Progression

Play the $\text{I}–\text{ii}_6–\text{I}^6_4–\text{V}^7–\text{I}$ chord progression exercise:

◀)) 10-1

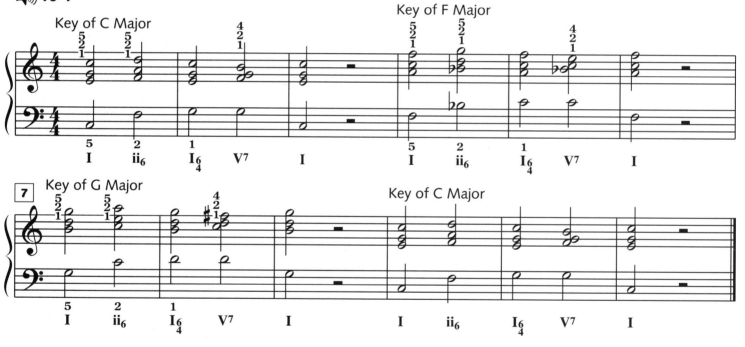

Practice the above exercise in the following keys:

◀)) 10-2	1.	D	G	A	D	major
◀)) 10-3	2.	E	A	B	E	major
◀)) 10-4	3.	D♭	G♭	A♭	D♭	major
◀)) 10-5	4.	E♭	A♭	B♭	E♭	major
◀)) 10-6	5.	A	D	E	A	harmonic minor
◀)) 10-7	6.	B	E	F♯	B	harmonic minor
◀)) 10-8	7.	C	F	G	C	harmonic minor
◀)) 10-9	8.	B♭	E♭	F	B♭	harmonic minor
◀)) 10-10	9.	C♯	F♯	G♯	C♯	harmonic minor

♪olo Repertoire

Before playing:
- Find the ii chords.
- Label the ii^6–V^7–I chord progression.

While playing:
- Play the RH a little louder than the LH.
- Use subtle *crescendos* and *diminuendos* to shape each phrase.

WALTZ

🔊 **10-11**

Anton Diabelli
(1781–1858)

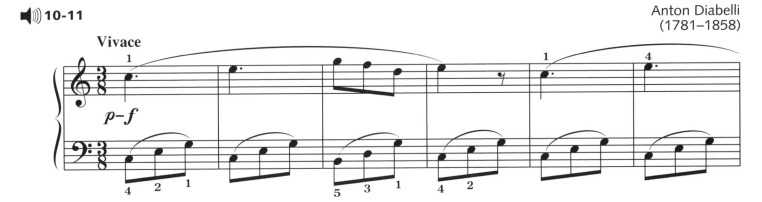

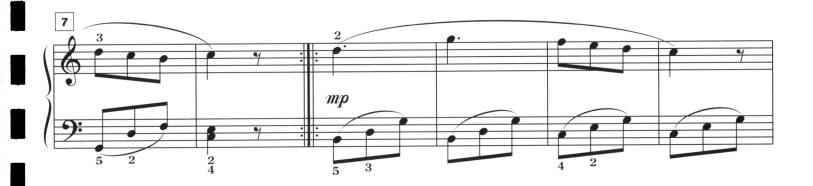

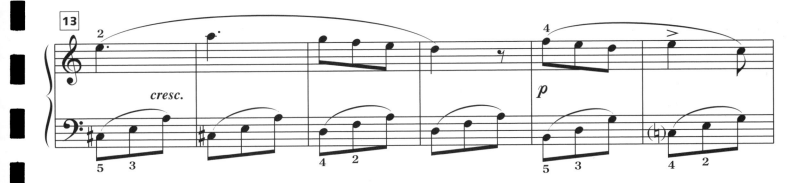

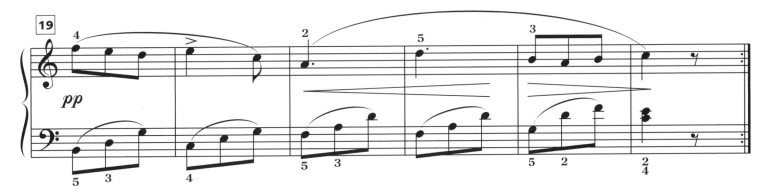

ℰnsemble Repertoire

Play the four-part ensemble using the indicated chords to complete parts 3 and 4.

Part 1: Diabelli *Waltz* (page 243)
Part 2: Countermelody
Part 3: Broken chords
Part 4: Waltz bass with bottom notes of triads and inversions in LH

🔊 10-12

Reading

Identify the key of each example. Use the indicated tempo, dynamics and articulation as you play these exercises.

Use the following practice directions:

1. Tap RH and count aloud; then LH.
2. Play hands separately and count aloud.
3. Tap hands together and count aloud.
4. Play hands together and count aloud.

🔊 **10-13**

▶ Transpose to G major.

DANCE

🔊 **10-14**

Ludvig Schytte (1848–1909)
Op. 108, No. 1

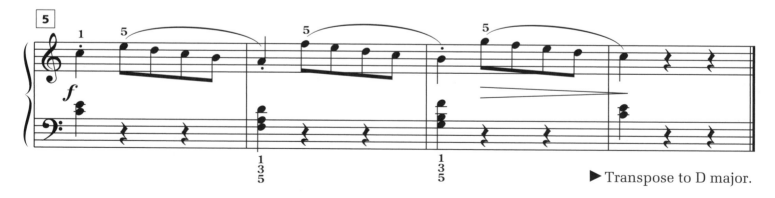

▶ Transpose to D major.

ETUDE

Cornelius Gurlitt (1820–1901)
Op. 82, No. 43

🔊 10-15

▶ Transpose to A minor.

STUDY

Ferdinand Beyer (1803–1863)
Op. 101, No. 62

🔊 10-16

▶ Transpose to D major.

Harmonization

1. Harmonize with a block chord accompaniment.

Block Chord Accompaniment

HANUKKAH

🔊 10-17

Moderately slow

Israel

▶ Transpose to C major.

2. Using I, V7 and ii₆ chords, harmonize with a waltz style accompaniment. Write the Roman numeral name of each chord on the line below the staff.

Waltz Style Accompaniment

🔊 10-18

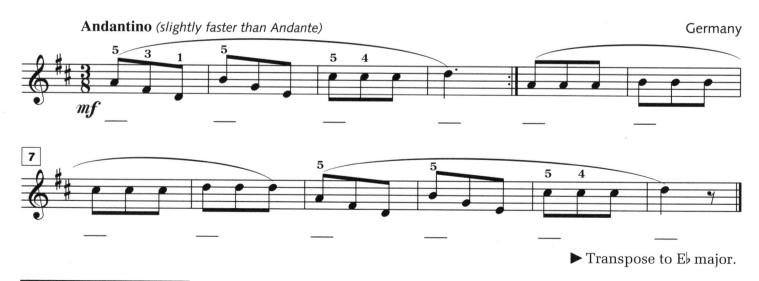

Andantino *(slightly faster than Andante)*

Germany

▶ Transpose to E♭ major.

3. Harmonize with a block chord accompaniment.

Block Chord Accompaniment

🔊 **10-19**

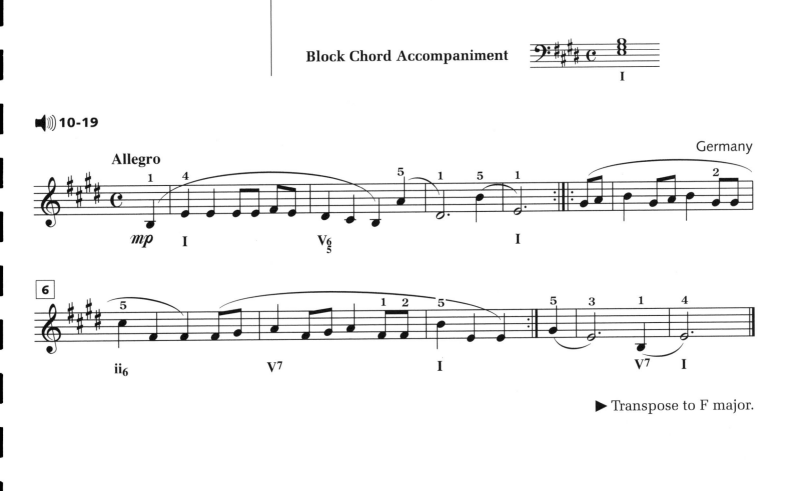

Germany

Allegro

I   V⁶₅   I

6

ii₆   V⁷   I   V⁷   I

▶ Transpose to F major.

4. Using i, i₆, iv⁶₄, V⁷ and ii°₆ chords, harmonize with a broken chord accompaniment. Write the Roman numeral name of each chord on the line below the staff.

Broken Chord Accompaniment

🔊 **10-20**

Andantino

Mexico

5

▶ Transpose to A minor.

Harmonization with Two-Hand Accompaniment

Using the indicated chords, create a two-hand accompaniment for the following melodies by continuing the pattern given in the first two measures.

🔊 10-21

OVER THE WAVES

Jurentino Rosas
(1868–1894)

Moderato

1.

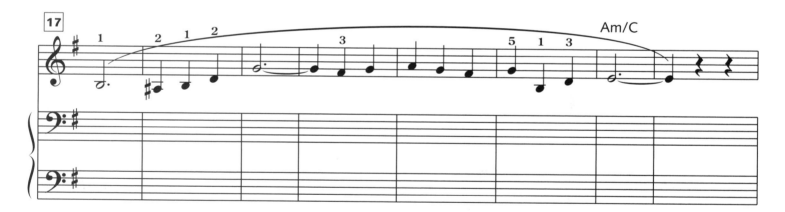

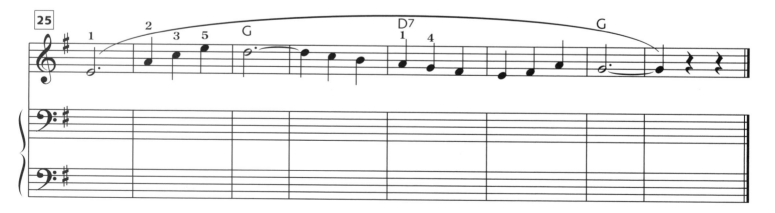

🔊 **10-22**

Allegretto

United States

2.

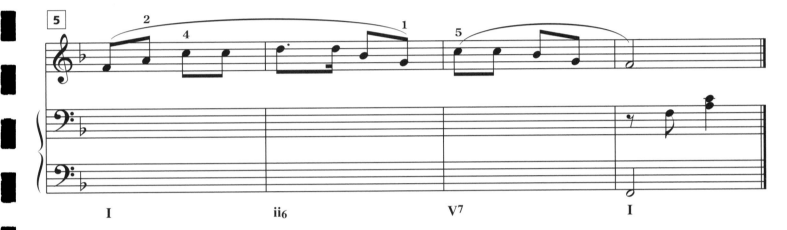

I   ii₆   V⁷   I

5

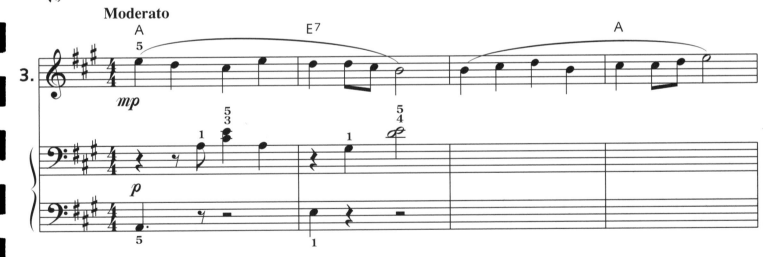

I   ii₆   V⁷   I

🔊 **10-23**

Moderato

3.

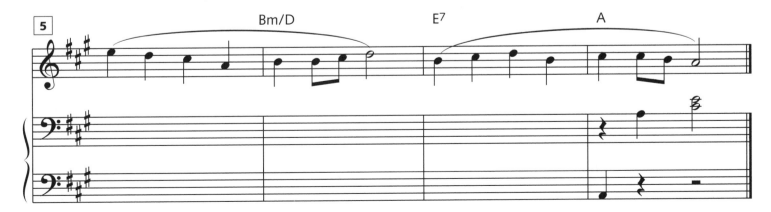

5

The vi Chord

Objectives

Upon completion of this unit the student will be able to:

1. Play $I–vi–IV–ii6–I^6_4–V^7–I$ chord progressions in all major and minor keys.
2. Perform solo repertoire that uses submediant harmonies.
3. Improvise melodies over primary and secondary chords in major and minor keys.
4. Sight-read and transpose music that uses submediant chords.
5. Harmonize and transpose melodies with submediant chords.
6. Create two-hand accompaniments from chord symbols.

Assignments

Week of _____

Write your assignments for the week in the space below.

_____

_____

_____

_____

_____

_____

_____

_____

_____

_____

_____

_____

_____

_____

_____

_____

_____

The vi Chord

The vi chord (submediant) is often substituted for the I chord, since the chords have two notes in common.

Key of C Major:

In major keys, the vi chord is a minor triad.

Key of C Major:

In natural and harmonic minor keys, the VI chord is a major triad.

Key of A Minor:

Playing a Chord Progression with the vi Chord

Play the following chord progression hands separately.

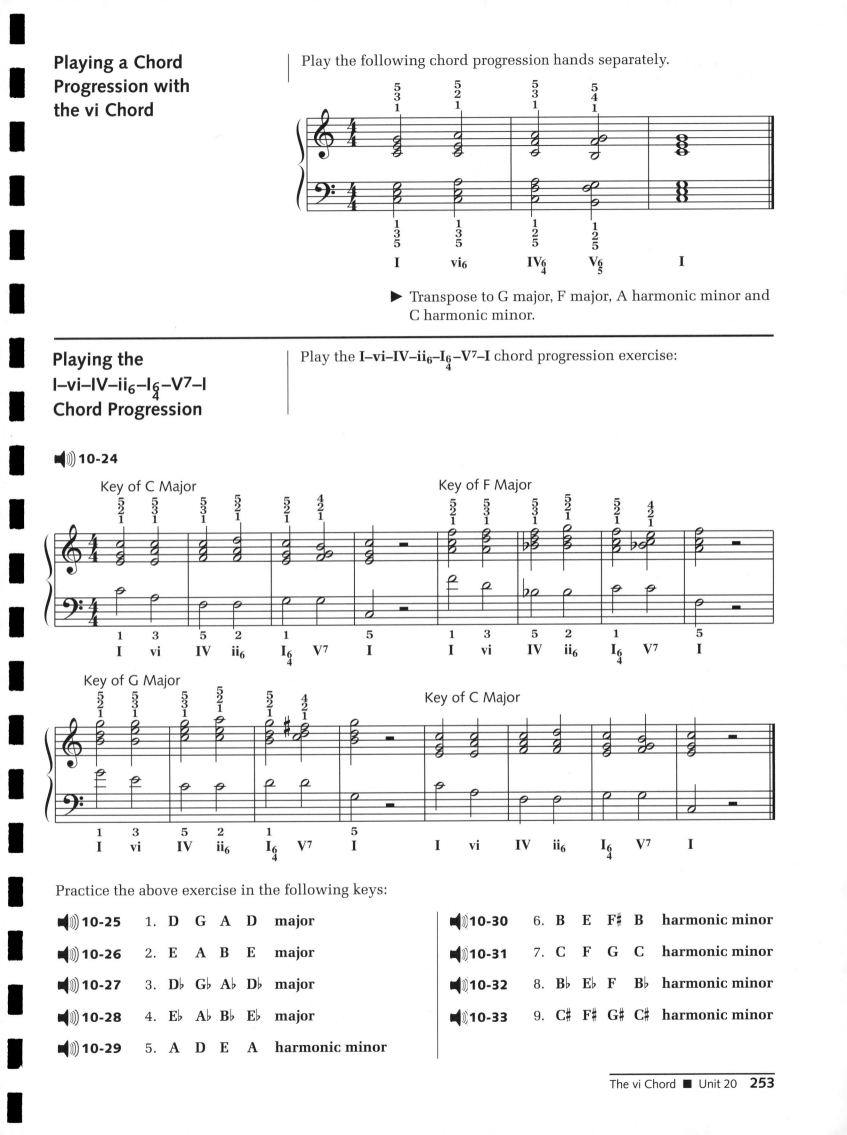

▶ Transpose to G major, F major, A harmonic minor and C harmonic minor.

Playing the I–vi–IV–ii₆–I₆₄–V⁷–I Chord Progression

Play the **I–vi–IV–ii₆–I₆₄–V⁷–I** chord progression exercise:

🔊 **10-24**

Practice the above exercise in the following keys:

🔊 **10-25**	1.	D G A D	major			
🔊 **10-26**	2.	E A B E	major			
🔊 **10-27**	3.	D♭ G♭ A♭ D♭	major			
🔊 **10-28**	4.	E♭ A♭ B♭ E♭	major			
🔊 **10-29**	5.	A D E A	harmonic minor			

🔊 **10-30**	6.	B E F♯ B	harmonic minor
🔊 **10-31**	7.	C F G C	harmonic minor
🔊 **10-32**	8.	B♭ E♭ F B♭	harmonic minor
🔊 **10-33**	9.	C♯ F♯ G♯ C♯	harmonic minor

$\int$olo Repertoire

Before playing:
- Notice the clef changes in the LH at measures 9 and 13.
- Find the vi chord.

While playing:
- Play the RH a little louder than the LH.

🔊 **10-34**

ECOSSAISE

Allegretto

Franz Schubert
(1797–1828)

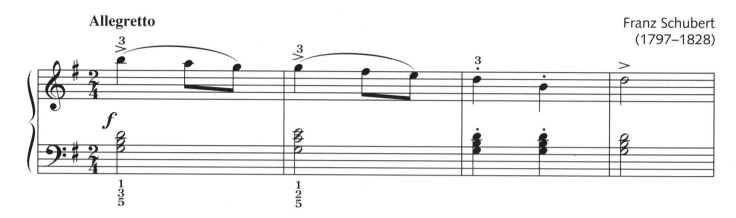

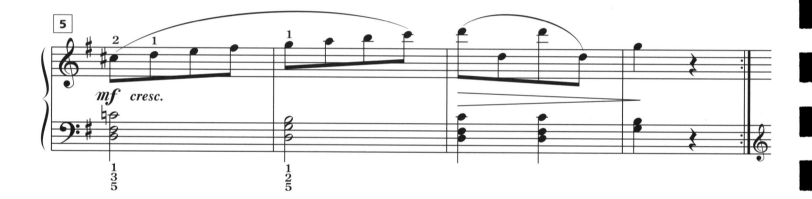

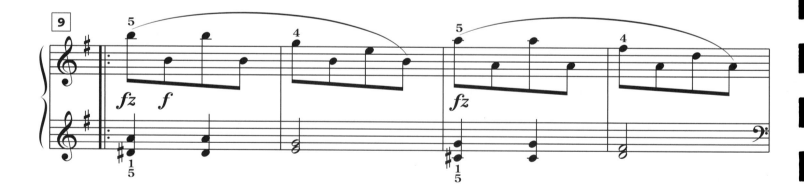

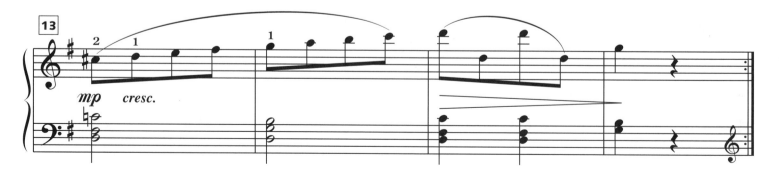

Improvisation from Chord Symbols

Using the chord progressions below, improvise RH melodies while the LH plays the suggested accompaniment style. (First play the LH chord progression using the suggested accompaniment style and observing the indicated meter.) You can use the suggested rhythm for your improvisation or create your own rhythm to complement the accompaniment. Notate your favorite improvisation.

Rules for Improvisation:

1. When the tonic chord is used, play mostly scale tones 1, 3 and 5 in the melody.
2. When the dominant chord is used, play mostly scale tones 2, 4, 5 and 7 in the melody.
3. When the subdominant chord is used, play mostly scale tones 1, 4 and 6 in the melody.
4. When the supertonic chord is used, play mostly scale tones 2, 4 and 6 in the melody.
5. When the submediant chord is used, play mostly scale tones 1, 3 and 6 in the melody.
6. Most improvisations begin and end on tonic.
7. The ear should always be the final guide in determining which melody notes to play.

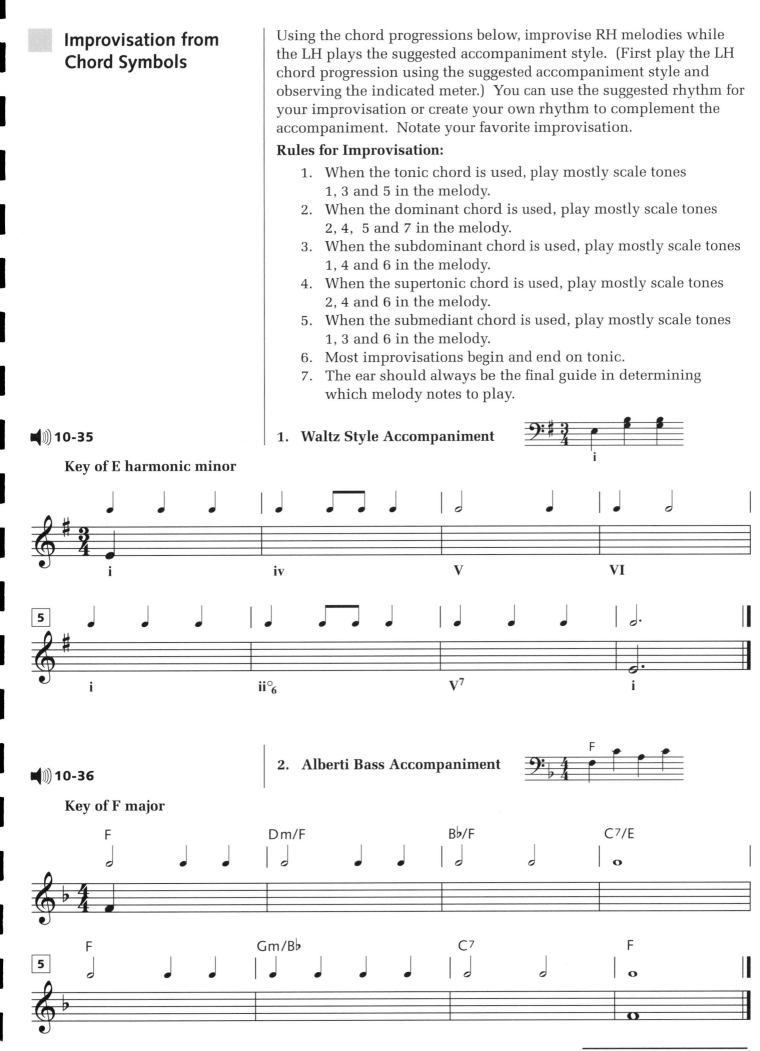

◄))) 10-35

Key of E harmonic minor

1. **Waltz Style Accompaniment**

◄))) 10-36

Key of F major

2. **Alberti Bass Accompaniment**

Reading

Identify the key of each example. Use the indicated tempo, dynamics and articulation as you play these exercises.

Use the following practice directions:

1. Tap RH and count aloud; then LH.
2. Play hands separately and count aloud.
3. Tap hands together and count aloud.
4. Play hands together and count aloud.

◀))) 10-37

1.

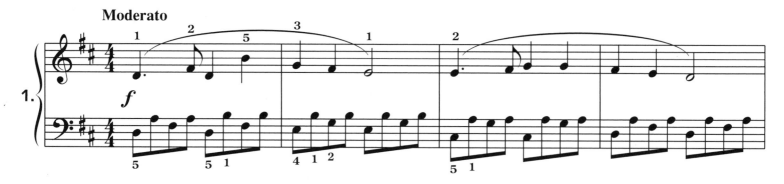

▶ Transpose to C major.

◀))) 10-38

2.

▶ Transpose to G major.

10-39

Moderato

▶ Transpose to G major.

ETUDE

10-40

Cornelius Gurlitt (1820–1901)
Op. 82, No. 35

Andante

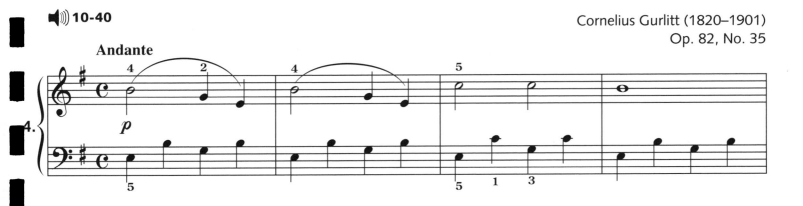

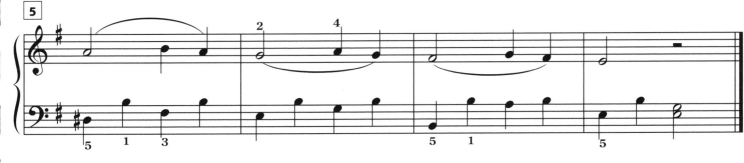

▶ Transpose to D minor.

Harmonization

Harmonize the following melodies with the indicated accompaniment style.

1. **Broken Chord Accompaniment**

🔊 10-41

ECOSSAISE

Allegro con brio (quickly with vigor)

Ludwig van Beethoven
(1770–1827)

▶ Transpose to D major.

2. **Broken Chord Accompaniment**

🔊 10-42

CONCERTO FOR HORN

Allegro

Wolfgang Amadeus Mozart (1756–1791)
K. 417

▶ Transpose to D major.

3. **Block Chord Accompaniment**

🔊 10-43

SIMPLE GIFTS

Shaker Hymn

Andante

▶ Transpose to G major.

Using I, V7, IV, vi and ii chords, harmonize with a block chord accompaniment. Use inversions to improve sound and for ease in performance. Write the Roman numeral name of each chord on the line below the staff.

4. **Block Chord Accompaniment**

VIVE L'AMOUR

🔊 10-44

France

Allegro

▶ Transpose to C major.

5. **Block Chord Accompaniment**

BINGO

🔊 10-45

Scotland

Moderato

▶ Transpose to F major.

Harmonization with Two-Hand Accompaniment

Using the indicated chords, create a two-hand accompaniment for the following melody by continuing the pattern given in the first two measures.

🔊 10-46

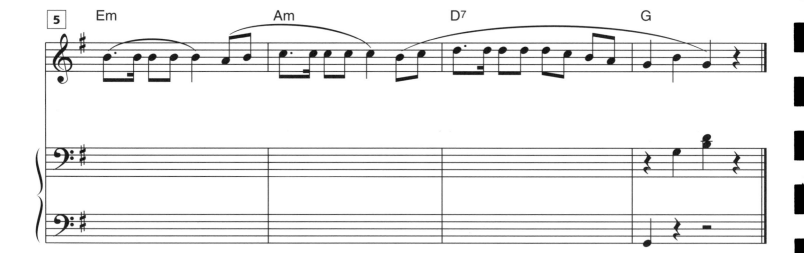

▶ Transpose to F major.

The iii Chord

Objectives

Upon completion of this unit the student will be able to:

1. Play I–IV–vii°–iii–vi–ii–V–I chord progressions in all major and minor keys.

2. Perform solo repertoire that uses mediant harmonies.

3. Sight-read and transpose music that uses mediant chords.

4. Harmonize and transpose melodies with mediant chords.

5. Create two-hand accompaniments from chord symbols.

6. Improvise melodies over primary and secondary chords in major and minor keys.

7. Perform duet repertoire with a partner.

Assignments

Week of _____

Write your assignments for the week in the space below.

_____

_____

_____

_____

_____

_____

_____

_____

_____

_____

_____

_____

_____

_____

_____

_____

_____

_____

_____

The iii Chord

The iii chord (mediant) is sometimes substituted for the V chord since the chords have two notes in common.

Key of C Major
Em   G
iii   V

In major keys, the iii chord is a minor triad.

Key of C Major
Em
iii

In natural minor keys, the III chord is a major triad.

Key of A Natural Minor
C
III

In harmonic minor keys, the III chord is an augmented triad.

Key of A Harmonic Minor
C+
III+

Playing a Chord Progression with the iii Chord

Play the following chord progression hands separately.

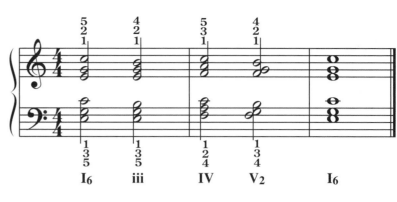

I_6 iii   IV V_2 I_6

▶ Transpose to G major, F major, A harmonic minor and C harmonic minor.

Playing the I–IV–vii°–iii–vi–ii–V–I Chord Progression

🔊 **11-1**

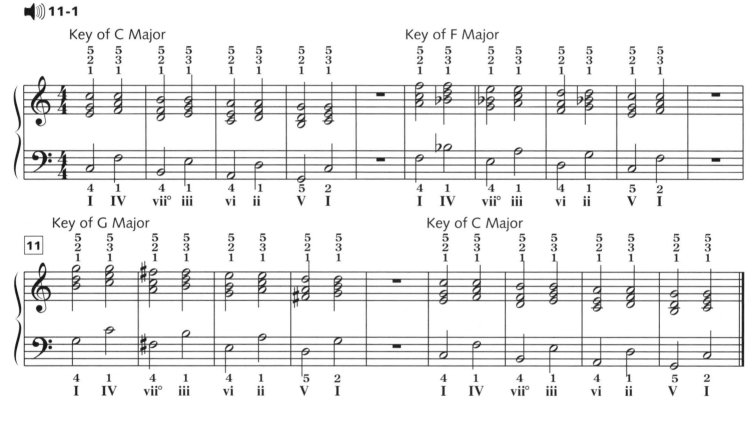

🔊 **11-2**	1.	D	G	A	D	major
🔊 **11-3**	2.	E	A	B	E	major
🔊 **11-4**	3.	D♭	G♭	A♭	D♭	major
🔊 **11-5**	4.	E♭	A♭	B♭	E♭	major
🔊 **11-6**	5.	A	D	E	A	natural minor
🔊 **11-7**	6.	B	E	F♯	B	natural minor
🔊 **11-8**	7.	C	F	G	C	natural minor
🔊 **11-9**	8.	B♭	E♭	F	B♭	natural minor
🔊 **11-10**	9.	C♯	F♯	G♯	C♯	natural minor

Practice the above exercise in the following keys:

Solo Repertoire

Before playing:
- Find the iii chords.
- Identify and play the interval between the first two notes of each measure in the RH.

While playing:
- Play the RH a little louder than the LH.
- Lift hands for rests.
- Shape the motive in each measure of the RH.

ETUDE IN C MAJOR

🔊 11-11

Ludwig Schytte (1848–1909)
Op. 160, No. 14

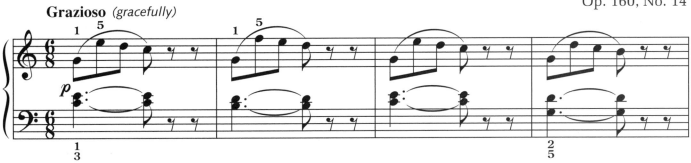

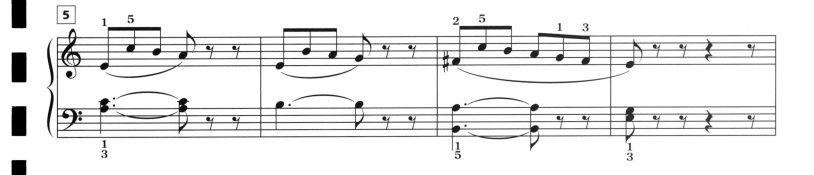

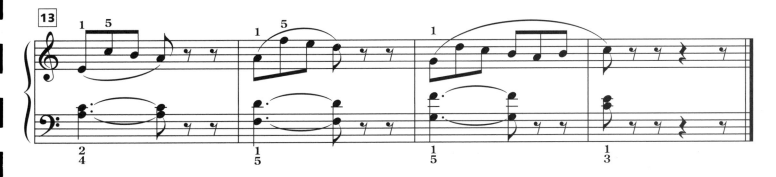

Reading

Identify the key of each example. Use the indicated tempo, dynamics and articulation as you play these exercises.

Use the following practice directions:
1. Tap RH and count aloud; then LH.
2. Play hands separately and count aloud.
3. Tap hands together and count aloud.
4. Play hands together and count aloud.

ETUDE

🔊 11-12

Ludwig Schytte (1848–1909)
Op. 160, No. 15

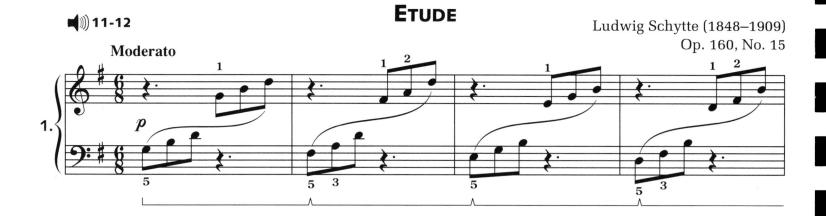

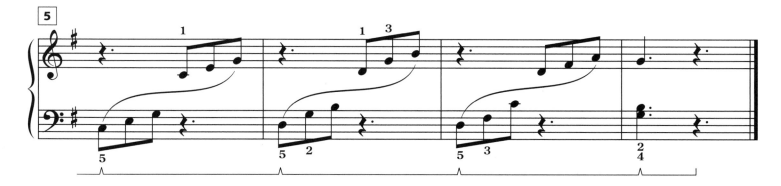

ETUDE

🔊 11-13

Ludwig Schytte (1848–1909)
Op. 160, No. 16

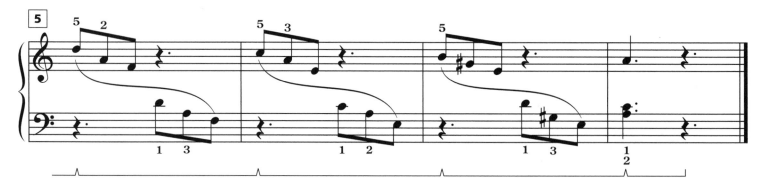

▶ Transpose to G minor.

🔊 11-14

Lento

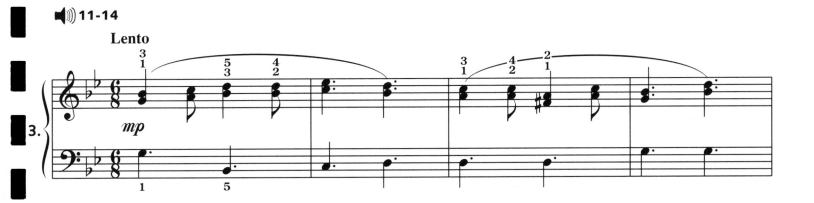

3.

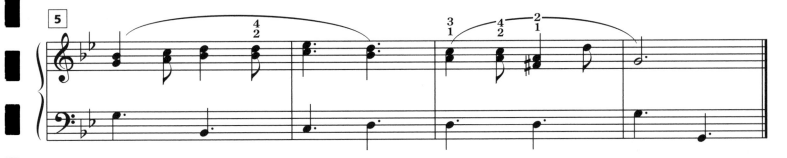

5

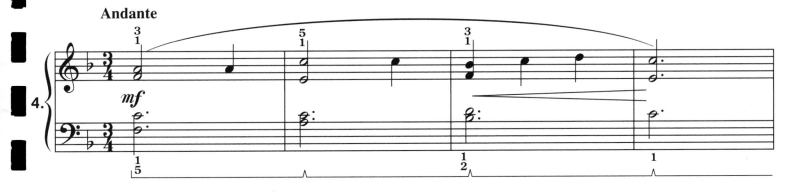

▶ Transpose to A minor.

🔊 11-15

Andante

4.

5

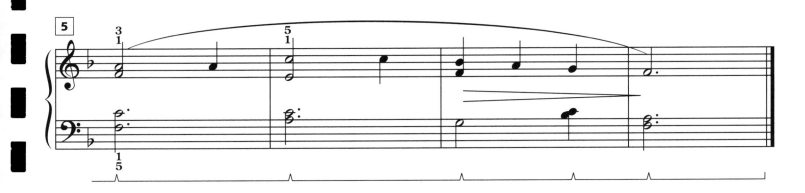

Harmonization

1. Harmonize with a broken chord accompaniment.

Broken Chord Accompaniment

REUBEN, RACHEL

🔊 11-16

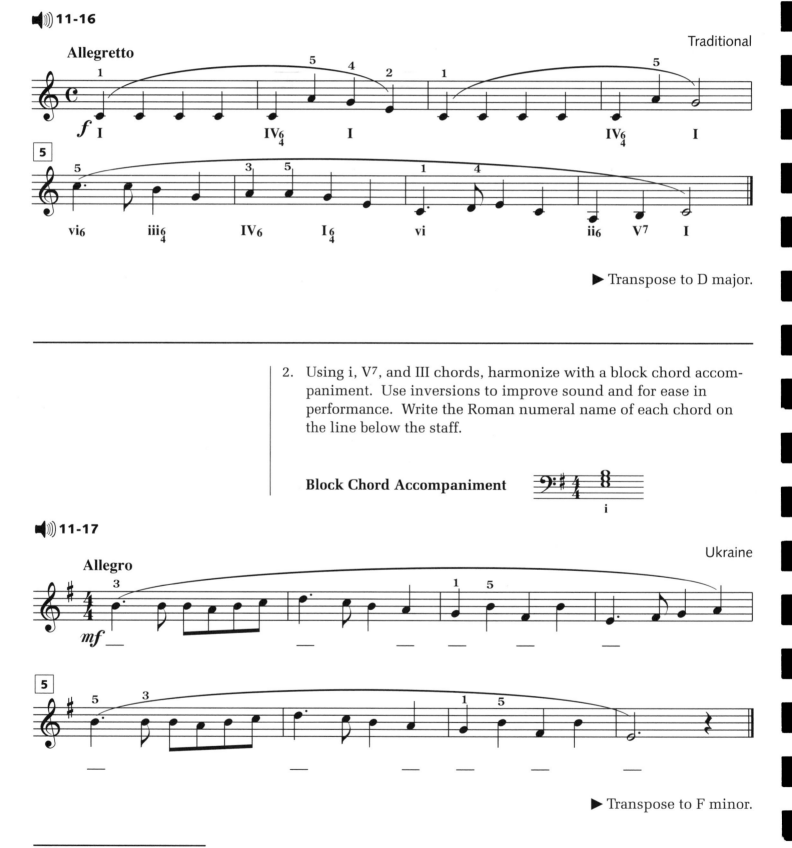

Traditional

Allegretto

▶ Transpose to D major.

2. Using i, V7, and III chords, harmonize with a block chord accompaniment. Use inversions to improve sound and for ease in performance. Write the Roman numeral name of each chord on the line below the staff.

Block Chord Accompaniment

🔊 11-17

Allegro

Ukraine

mf

▶ Transpose to F minor.

Harmonize each melody below in two ways:
- Using the bottom note of each indicated triad and inversion.
- Using the indicated triads and inversions.

SHENANDOAH

United States

ANGELS WE HAVE HEARD ON HIGH

French Carol

Harmonization with Two-Hand Accompaniment

Using the indicated chords, create a two-hand accompaniment for the following melody by continuing the pattern given in the first two measures.

E minor scale

GREENSLEEVES

🔊 11-20

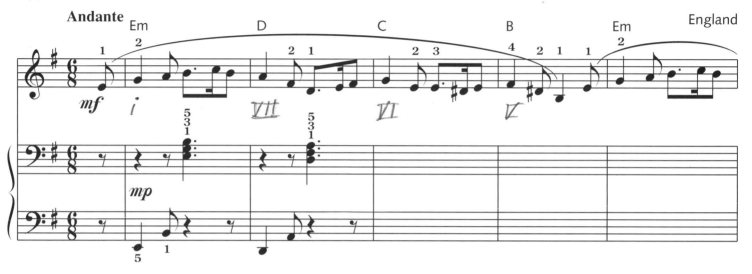

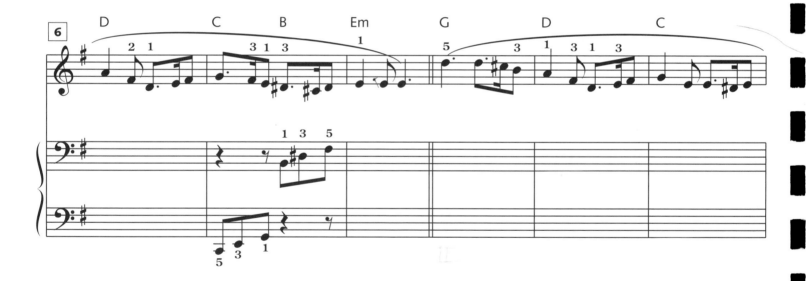

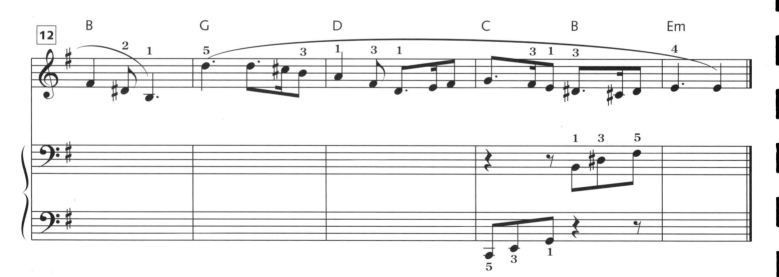

Improvisation from Chord Symbols

Using the chord progressions below, improvise RH melodies while the LH plays the suggested accompaniment style. (First play the LH chord progression using the suggested accompaniment style and observing the indicated meter.) You can use the suggested rhythm for your improvisation or create your own rhythm to complement the accompaniment. Notate your favorite improvisation.

Rules for improvisation:

1. When the tonic chord is used, play mostly scale tones 1, 3 and 5 in the melody.
2. When the dominant chord is used, play mostly scale tones 2, 4, 5 and 7 in the melody.
3. When the subdominant chord is used, play mostly scale tones 1, 4 and 6 in the melody.
4. When the supertonic chord is used, play mostly scale tones 2, 4 and 6 in the melody.
5. When the submediant chord is used, play mostly scale tones 1, 3 and 6 in the melody.
6. When the mediant chord is used, play mostly scale tones 3, 5 and 7 in the melody.
7. Most improvisations begin and end on tonic.
8. The ear should always be the final guide in determining which melody notes to play.

11-21

Key of A harmonic minor

1. **Broken Chord Accompaniment**

2. **Alberti Bass Accompaniment**

11-22

Key of G major

DANCE
Secondo

Daniel Gottlob Türk
(1756–1813)

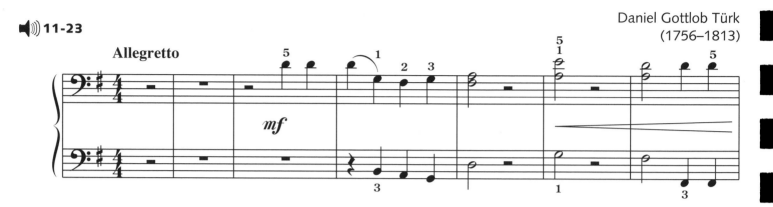

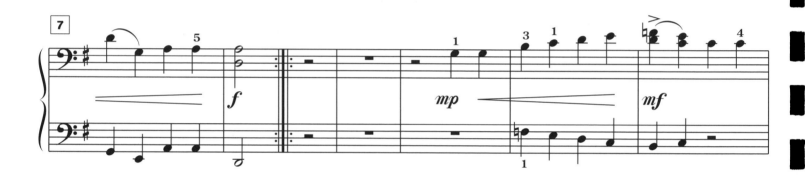

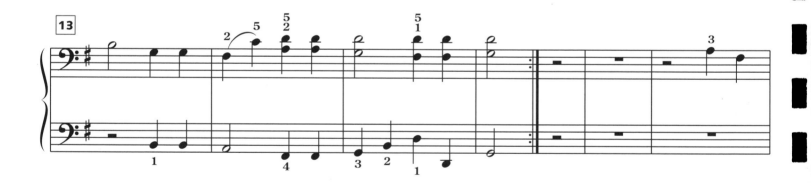

DANCE

Primo

 11-23

Daniel Gottlob Türk
(1756–1813)

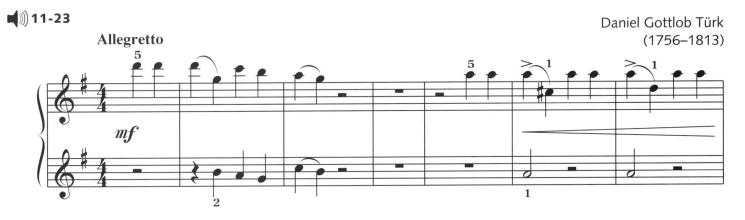

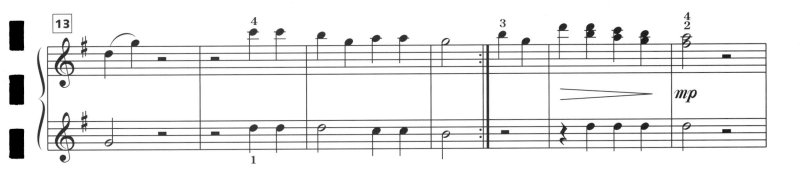

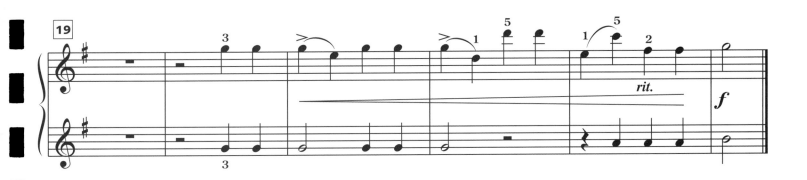

Minor Scales (Group 3) and Triads of the Key

Objectives

Upon completion of this unit the student will be able to:

1. Build a triad of the key on any note of the harmonic minor scale.
2. Play Group 3 minor scales and minor arpeggios, using traditional fingerings.
3. Perform solo repertoire in a minor key.
4. Sight-read and transpose music that uses primary and secondary chords in minor keys.
5. Harmonize and transpose melodies with primary and secondary chords.

Assignments

Week of _____

Write your assignments for the week in the space below.

_____
_____
_____
_____
_____
_____
_____
_____
_____
_____
_____
_____
_____
_____
_____

Playing Triads of the Key in Harmonic Minor

Play triads of the key in C♯ harmonic minor. Note the quality of each chord.

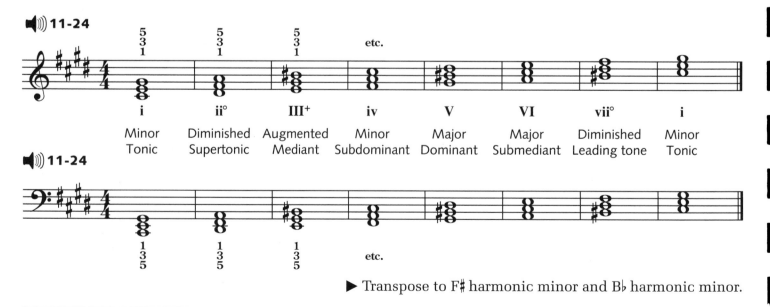

◀))) 11-24

i	ii°	III⁺	iv	V	VI	vii°	i
Minor Tonic	Diminished Supertonic	Augmented Mediant	Minor Subdominant	Major Dominant	Major Submediant	Diminished Leading tone	Minor Tonic

▶ Transpose to F♯ harmonic minor and B♭ harmonic minor.

Practicing Minor Scales (Group 3 Keys): F♯, C♯, G♯, B♭ and E♭

The following principles will help you remember the fingering for the Group 3 minor scales:

1. Use fingers 2, 3 and 4 on black keys.
2. F♯, C♯ and G♯ harmonic minor scales use the same fingering in the RH.
   RH: 3 4 1 2 3 1 2 3 4 1 2 3 1 2 3
3. C♯ and G♯ harmonic minor scales use the same fingering in the LH.
   LH: 3 2 1 4 3 2 1 3 2 1 4 3 2 1 3
4. The right hand fingering of B♭ minor is the same as B♭ major.
   RH: 4 1 2 3 1 2 3 4 1 2 3 1 2 3 4
5. The right hand fingering of E♭ minor is the same as E♭ major.
   RH: 3 1 2 3 4 1 2 3 1 2 3 4 1 2 3

See page 122 for scale practice suggestions and challenges.

Practicing Minor Arpeggios (Group 3 Keys): F♯, C♯, G♯, B♭ and E♭

The following principles will help you remember the fingering for the Group 3 minor arpeggios:

1. For the F♯, C♯ and G♯ minor arpeggios
   • Thumbs play the white keys. In addition to the thumbs, only fingers 2 and 4 are used.
   • All three arpeggios use the same fingering.
   RH: 4 1 2 4 1 2 4
   LH: 2 1 4 2 1 4 2
2. For the B♭ minor arpeggio
   • The left hand fingering is the same as B♭ major.
   LH: 3 2 1 3 2 1 3
   • The right hand has its own unique fingering.
   RH: 2 3 1 2 3 1 2
3. For the E♭ minor arpeggio
   The fingering is the same as E major.
   RH: 1 2 3 1 2 3 5
   RH: 5 3 2 1 3 2 1

See page 123 for arpeggio practice suggestions and challenges.

Playing Harmonic Minor Scales and Arpeggios

F♯ Minor

RH: 3 4 1 2 3 1 2   3 4 1 2 3 1 2 3
LH: 4 3 2 1 3 2 1   4 3 2 1 3 2 1 4

🔊 11-25

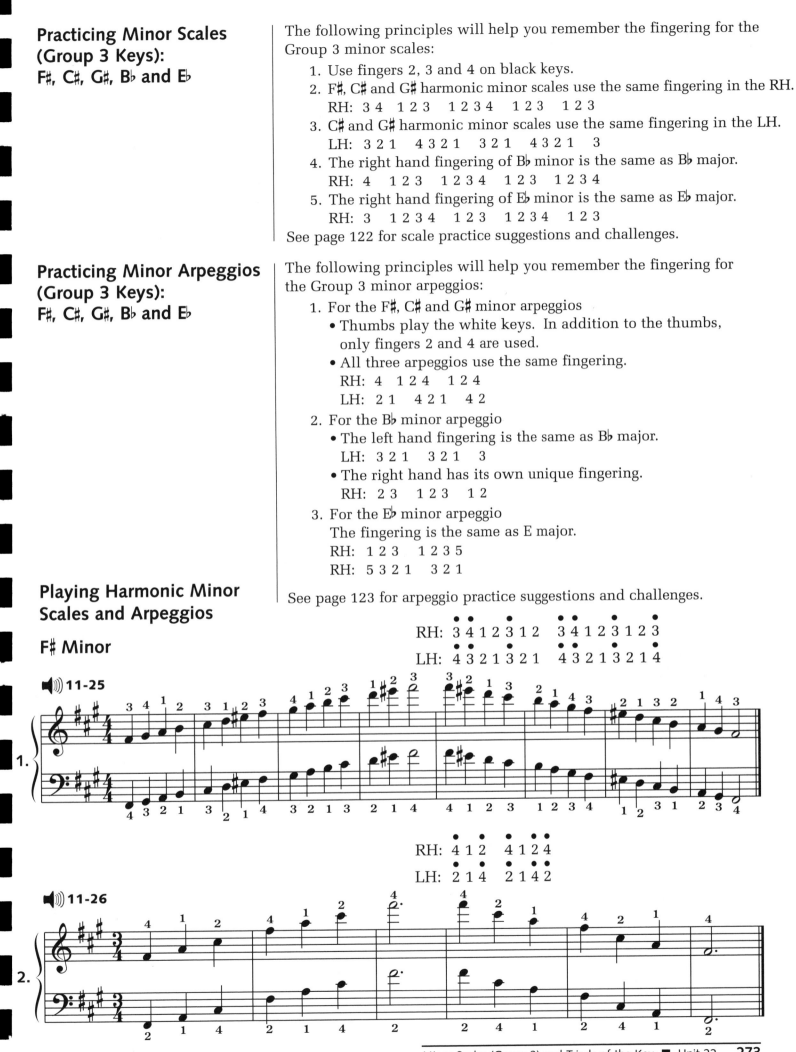

RH: 4 1 2   4 1 2 4
LH: 2 1 4   2 1 4 2

🔊 11-26

Playing Harmonic Minor
Scales and Arpeggios (continued)

C# Minor

RH: 3 4 1 2 3 1 2   3 4 1 2 3 1 2 3
LH: 3 2 1 4 3 2 1   3 2 1 4 3 2 1 3

🔊 11-27

RH: 4 1 2   4 1 2 4
LH: 2 1 4   2 1 4 2

🔊 11-28

G# Minor

RH: 3 4 1 2 3 1 2   3 4 1 2 3 1 2 3
LH: 3 2 1 4 3 2 1   3 2 1 4 3 2 1 3

🔊 11-29

RH: 4 1 2   4 1 2 4
LH: 2 1 4   2 1 4 2

🔊 11-30

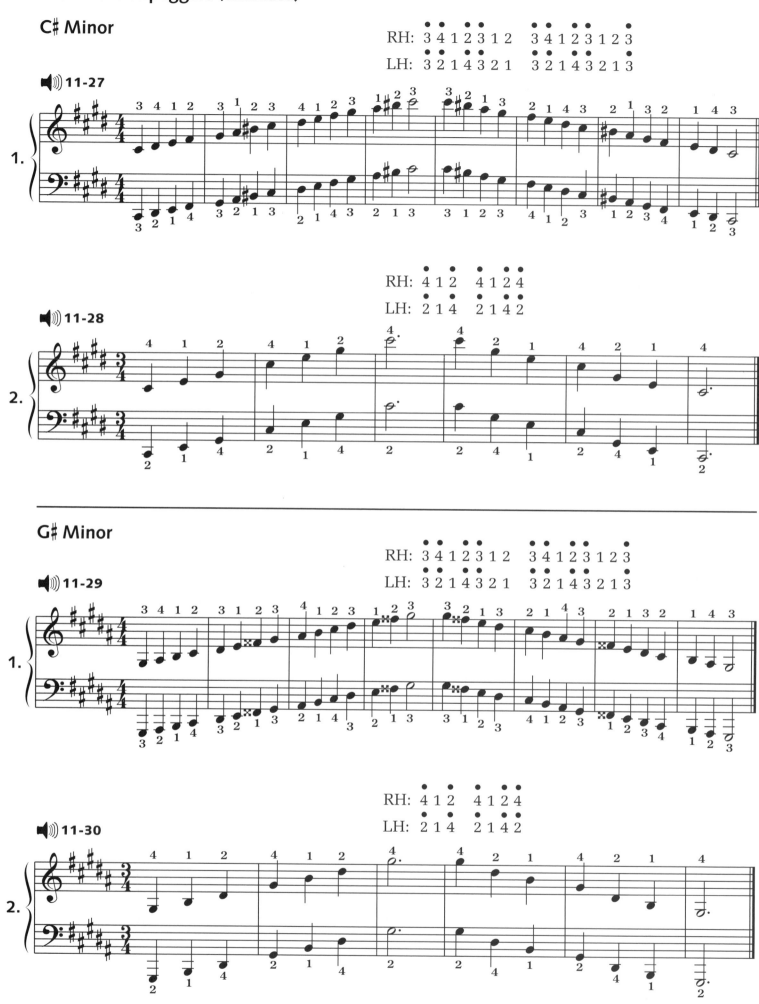

B♭ Minor

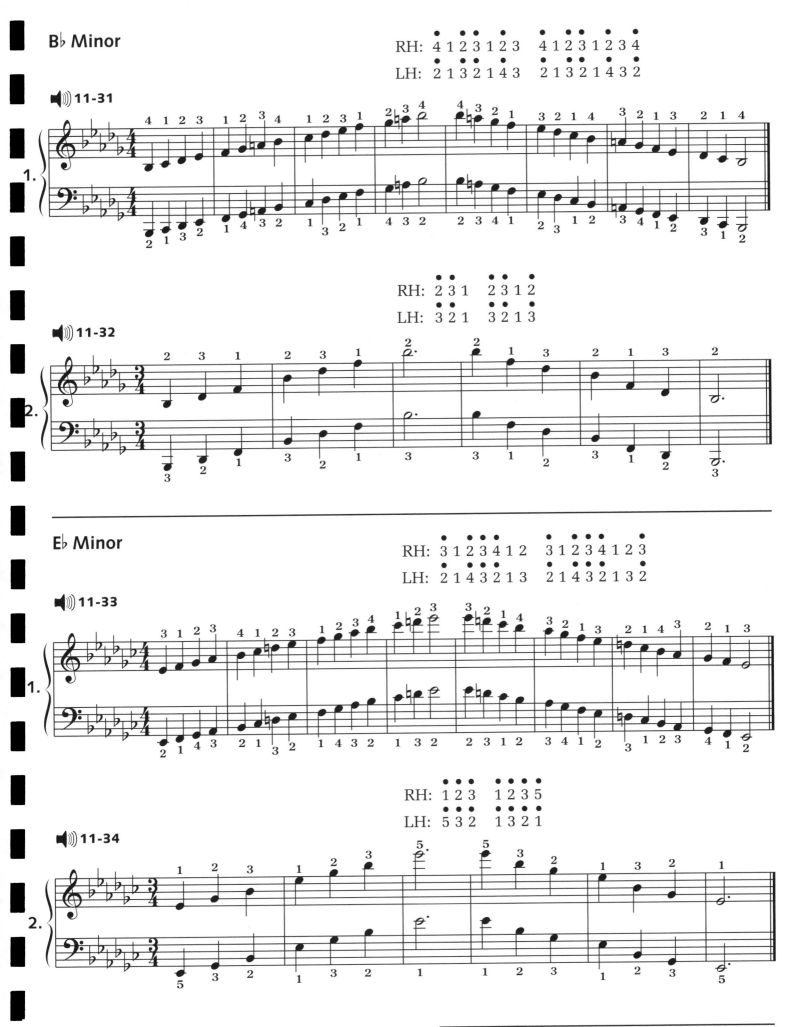

RH: 4 1 2 3 1 2 3   4 1 2 3 1 2 3 4
LH: 2 1 3 2 1 4 3   2 1 3 2 1 4 3 2

🔊 11-31

1.

RH: 2 3 1   2 3 1 2
LH: 3 2 1   3 2 1 3

🔊 11-32

2.

E♭ Minor

RH: 3 1 2 3 4 1 2   3 1 2 3 4 1 2 3
LH: 2 1 4 3 2 1 3   2 1 4 3 2 1 3 2

🔊 11-33

1.

RH: 1 2 3   1 2 3 5
LH: 5 3 2   1 3 2 1

🔊 11-34

2.

Solo Repertoire

Before playing:
- Block the broken chords (triplets).
- Tap the rhythm of measures 5–7 and 23–26 hands together.
- Practice the C♯ minor arpeggio in the RH of measures 27–28.

While playing:
- Project the RH melody over the LH broken chords.
- Listen for clear pedal changes.

THEME FROM THE
MOONLIGHT SONATA

11-35

Ludwig van Beethoven (1770–1827)
arr. Kenon D. Renfrow
Op. 27, No. 2

Adagio sostenuto
(Slow and sustained)

Technique

11-36

Moderato

1.

▶ Transpose to F# minor.

11-36

Moderato

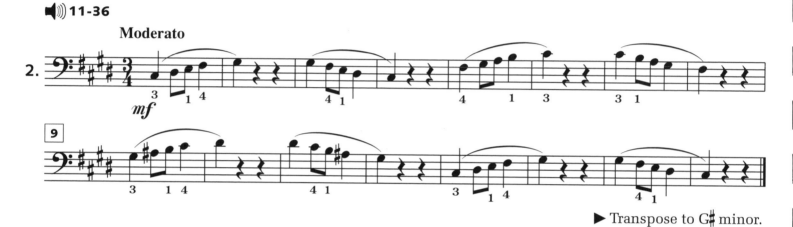

2.

▶ Transpose to G# minor.

11-37

Moderato

3.

▶ Transpose to E♭ minor.

11-37

Moderato

4.

▶ Transpose to E♭ minor.

Reading

Identify the key of each example. Use the indicated tempo, dynamics and articulation as you play these exercises.

Use the following practice directions:

1. Tap RH and count aloud; then LH.
2. Play hands separately and count aloud.
3. Tap hands together and count aloud.
4. Play hands together and count aloud.

🔊 11-38

Andante

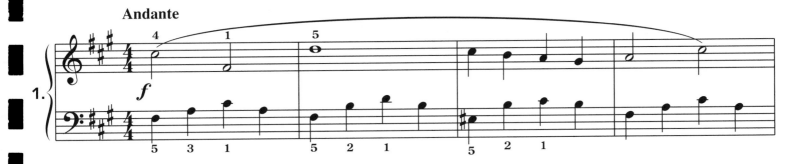

1.

▶ Transpose to G minor.

🔊 11-39

Adagio

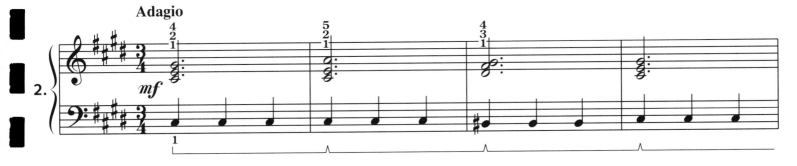

2.

Harmonization

Harmonize each melody below in two ways:
- Using the bottom note of each indicated triad and inversion.
- Using the indicated triads and inversions.

🔊 11-40

1.

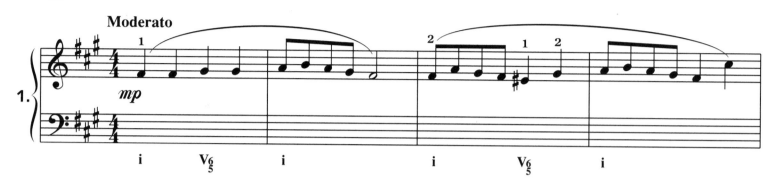

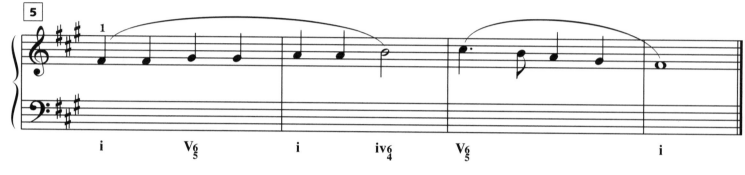

▶ Transpose to G minor.

🔊 11-41

2.

Review Worksheet

Name _____   *Date* _____

1. Identify each harmonic minor scale below by writing its name on the
   indicated line. Write the correct RH fingering on the lines above the
   staff and the correct LH fingering on the lines below the staff.

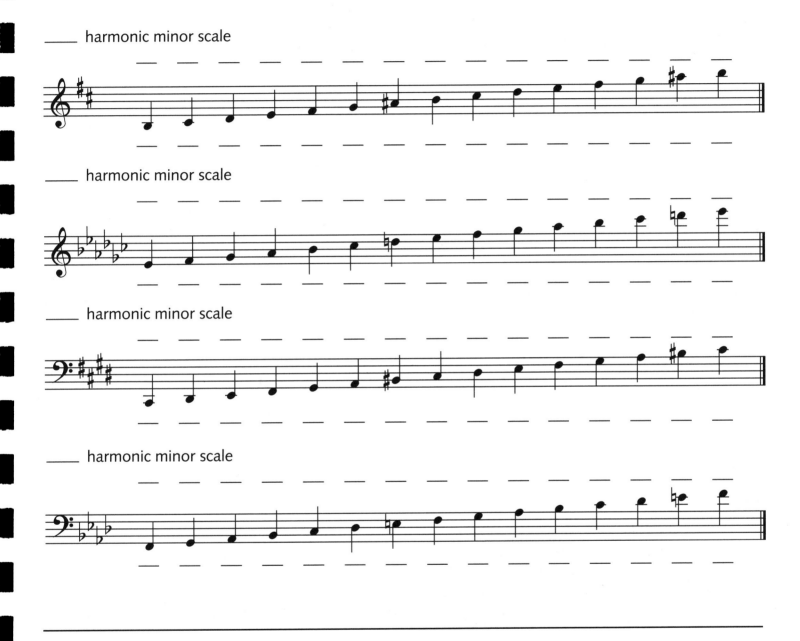

____ harmonic minor scale

____ harmonic minor scale

____ harmonic minor scale

____ harmonic minor scale

2. Identify each harmonic minor key by writing its name on the line
   above the staff. Using whole notes, write a VI chord on the staff.
   Write the letter name for each chord on the line below the staff.

3. Identify each minor arpeggio by writing its name on the indicated line. Write the correct RH fingering on the lines above the staff and the correct LH fingering on the lines below the staff.

_____ minor arpeggio

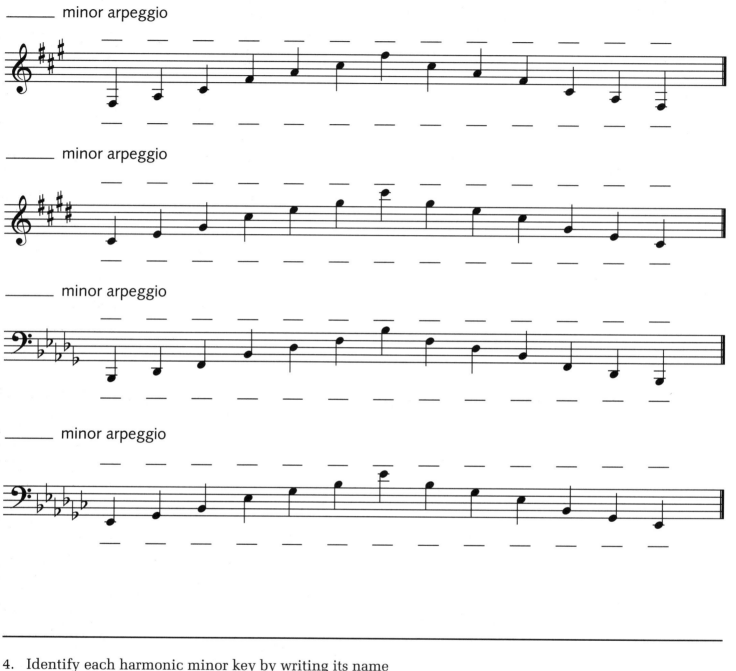

_____ minor arpeggio

_____ minor arpeggio

_____ minor arpeggio

4. Identify each harmonic minor key by writing its name on the line above the staff. Using whole notes, write the triad indicated by each Roman numeral on the staff.

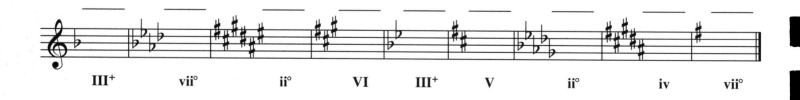

III⁺   vii°   ii°   VI   III⁺   V   ii°   iv   vii°

Seventh Chords

Objectives

Upon completion of this unit the student will be able to:

1. Play five types of seventh chords and inversions.
2. Sight-read music that uses seventh chords.
3. Perform solo repertoire that uses seventh chords.
4. Harmonize melodies with seventh chords.
5. Create two-hand accompaniments from chord symbols.
6. Improvise melodies over seventh chords.

Assignments

Week of _____

Write your assignments for the week in the space below.

Seventh Chords

To form a seventh chord from a root position triad, a note that is a seventh above the root is added. Seventh chords in root position look like this:

LINE ——	7th
LINE ——	5th
LINE ——	3rd
LINE ——	ROOT

OR

SPACE ——	7th
SPACE ——	5th
SPACE ——	3rd
SPACE ——	ROOT

Five Types of Seventh Chords

There are five types of seventh chords:

Play the seventh-chord exercises with the RH as written. Then play with the LH one octave lower than written.

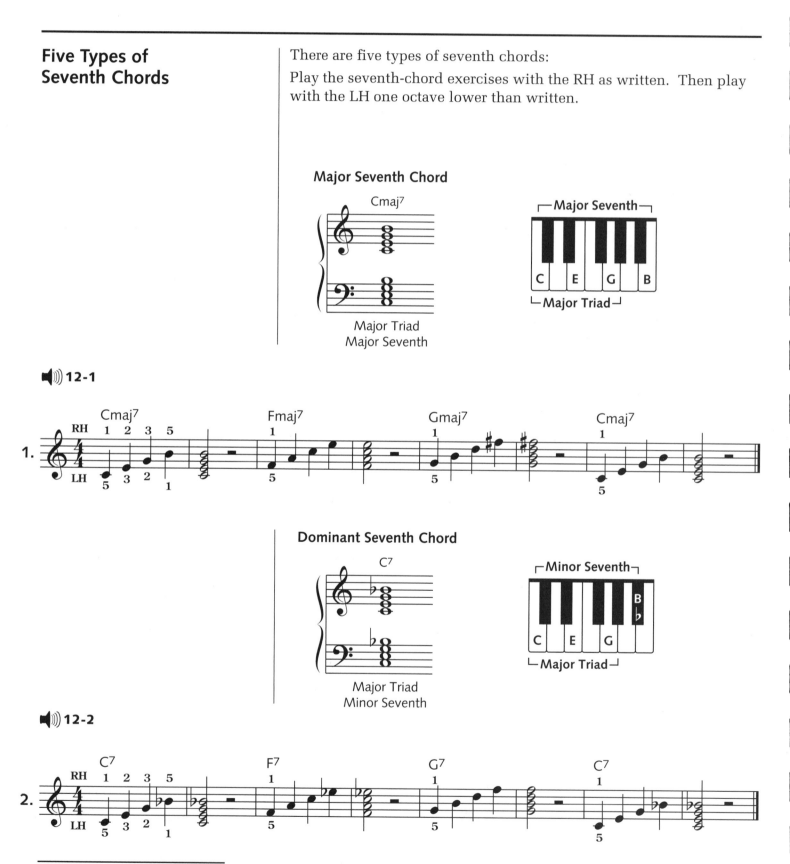

Major Seventh Chord

Cmaj⁷

Major Triad
Major Seventh

┌─ Major Seventh ─┐
C   E   G   B
└─ Major Triad ─┘

12-1

1. Cmaj⁷   RH 1 2 3 5   Fmaj⁷   Gmaj⁷   Cmaj⁷
   LH 5 3 2 1

Dominant Seventh Chord

C⁷

Major Triad
Minor Seventh

┌─ Minor Seventh ─┐
C   E   G   B♭
└─ Major Triad ─┘

12-2

2. C⁷   RH 1 2 3 5   F⁷   G⁷   C⁷
   LH 5 3 2 1

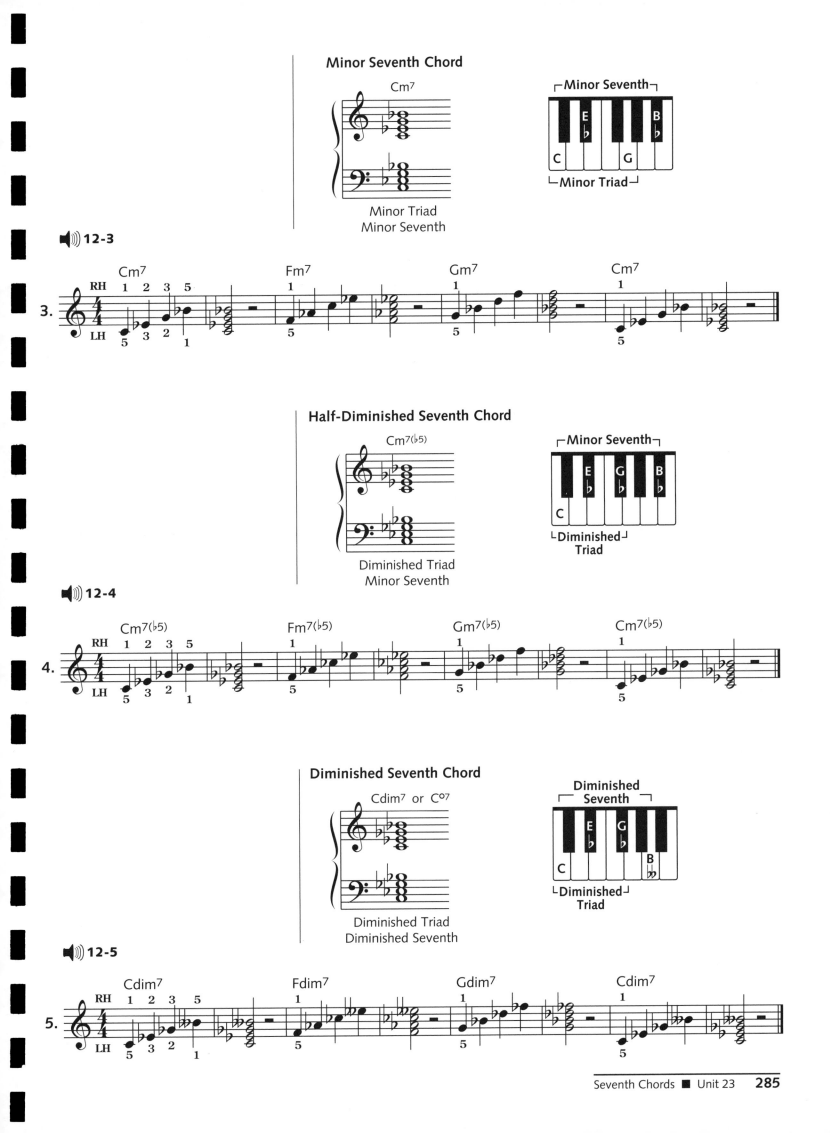

Playing Seventh Chords

Play the following seventh chord exercise hands separately.
Use fingers 5 3 2 1 for the LH.
Use fingers 1 2 3 5 for the RH and play one octave higher than written.

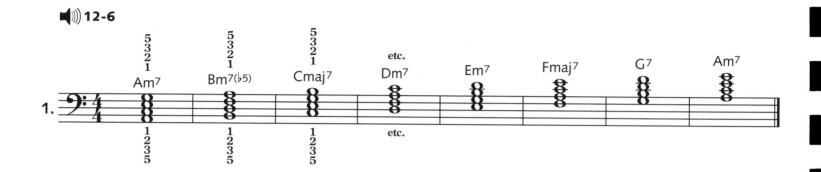

The 5th is often omitted from the seventh chord. This makes it easier to play with one hand. Play the following exercise with the LH.

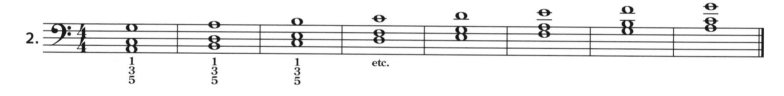

The 3rd is sometimes omitted from the seventh chord. Play the following exercise with the LH.

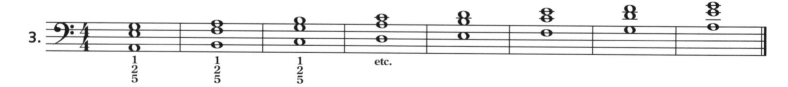

Playing Five Types of Seventh Chords

Play the following seventh chord exercise hands separately. Use fingers 1 2 3 5 for the RH and fingers 5 3 2 1 for the LH.

🔊 12-7

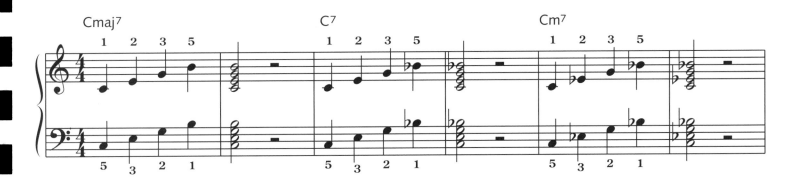

Continue downward
by half steps until. . .

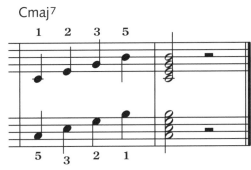

Both hands 8ᵛᵃ lower - - - - ⌐

Inversions of Seventh Chords

Four-note seventh chords may be played in the following positions. All note names are the same in each position, but in a different order!

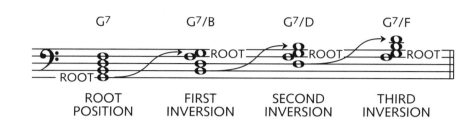

ROOT POSITION   FIRST INVERSION   SECOND INVERSION   THIRD INVERSION

The first, second and third inversions are easily recognized by the interval of a 2nd in each chord. The top note of the 2nd is always the root!

Play the G7 chord and its inversions.

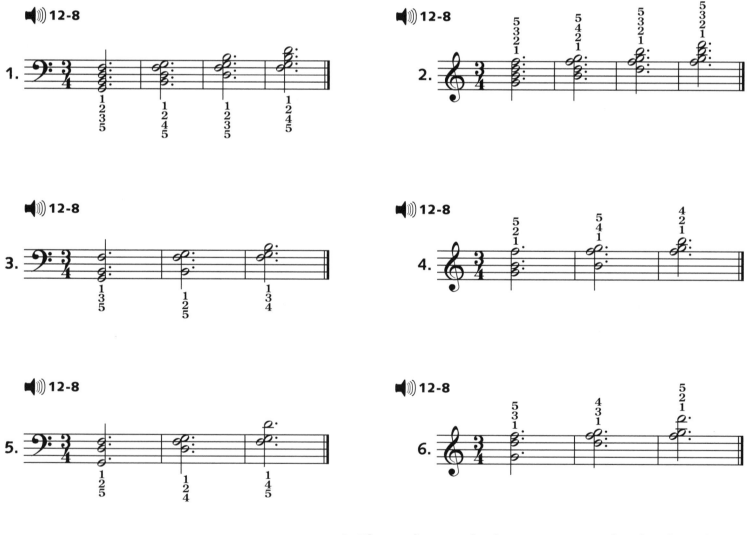

▶ Play each example above using a D7 chord and C7 chord.

Reading

Identify the key of each example. Use the indicated tempo, dynamics and articulation as you play these exercises.

Use the following practice directions:

1. Tap RH and count aloud; then LH.
2. Play hands separately and count aloud.
3. Tap hands together and count aloud.
4. Play hands together and count aloud.

🔊 12-9

Freely

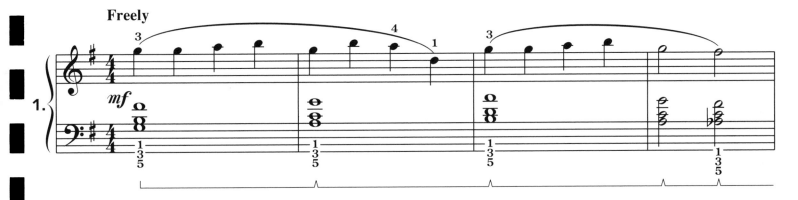

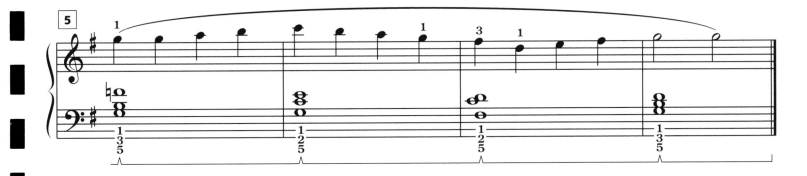

🔊 12-10

Misterioso *(mysteriously)*

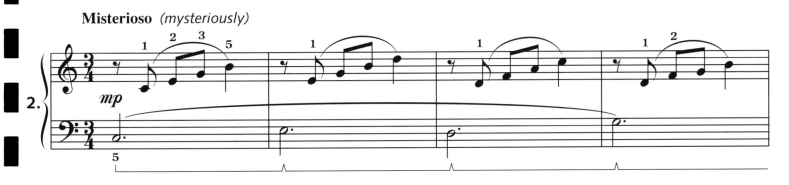

𝒮olo Repertoire

Before playing:
- Practice the LH moves.
- Practice LH alone with pedal.

While playing:
- Play the RH a little louder than the LH.
- Listen for clear pedal changes.
- Hold the top notes in the RH of measures 19–20 for the entire measure.

🔊 **12-11**

FULL MOON RISING

Dennis Alexander

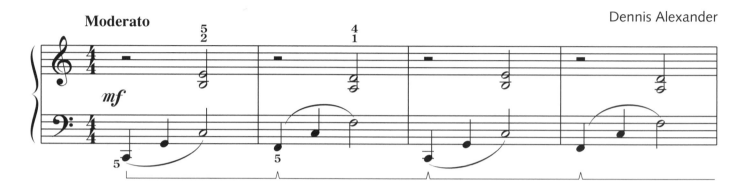

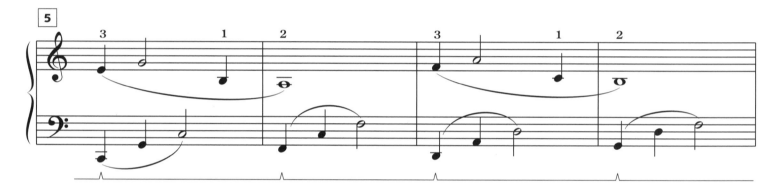

"Full Moon Rising" from SIMPLY SENSATIONAL, Book 1, by Dennis Alexander
Copyright © MCMXCI by Alfred Publishing Co., Inc.

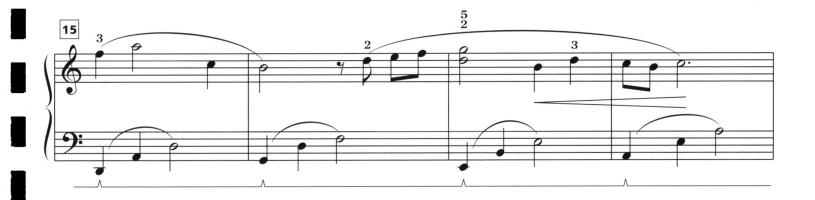

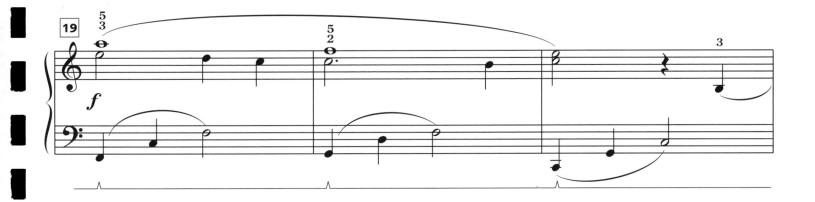

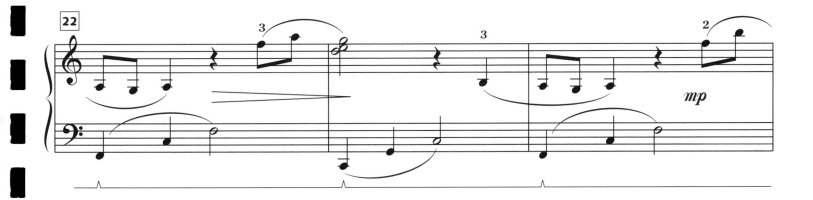

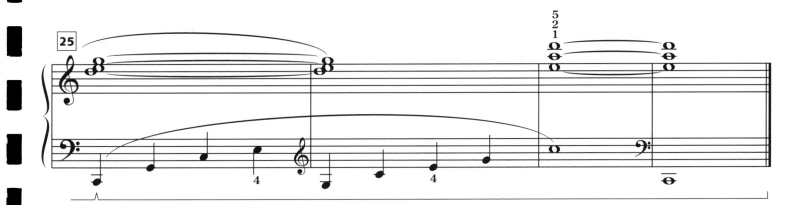

Harmonization

Harmonize each melody below in two ways:
- • Using the bottom note of each indicated seventh chord.
- • Using the indicated root-position seventh chords.

🔊 **12-12**

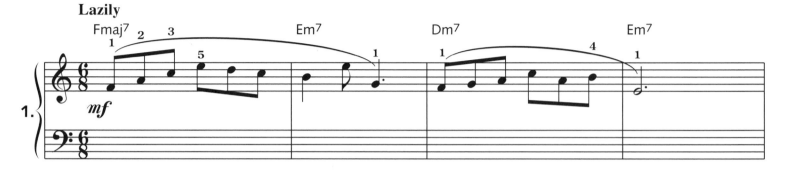

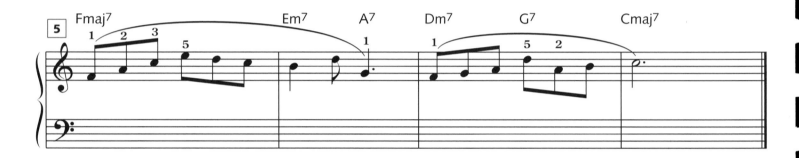

🔊 **12-13**

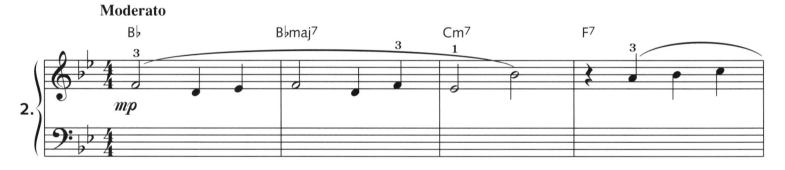

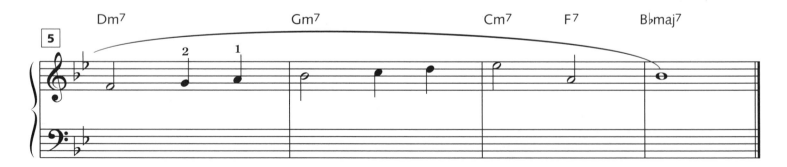

◀))) 12-14

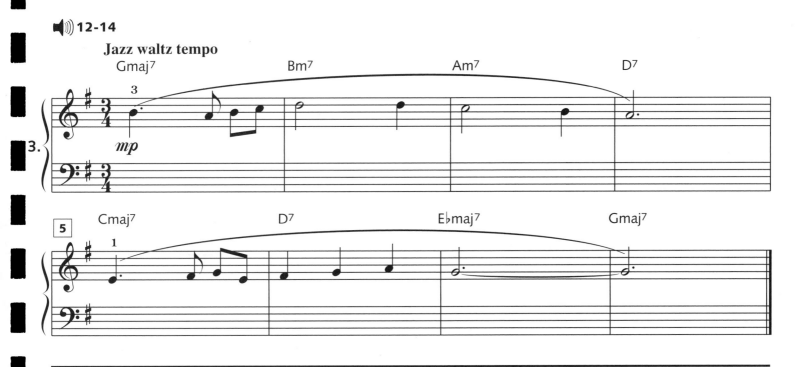

3.

Harmonization with Two-Hand Accompaniment

Using the indicated chords, create a two-hand accompaniment for the following melody by continuing the pattern given in the first measure.

THE MOLDAU

Bedrich Smetana
(1824–1884)

◀))) 12-15

Ensemble Repertoire

Play the four-part ensemble using the indicated chords to complete parts 3 and 4.

Part 1: Melody
Part 2: Countermelody
Part 3: Two-hand accompaniment
Part 4: Bass line (root–5th–root)

🔊 12-16

PRELUDE IN SEVENTHS

E. L. Lancaster

Improvisation from Chord Symbols

Using the chord progressions below, improvise RH melodies while the LH plays the suggested accompaniment style. (First play the LH chord progressions using the suggested accompaniment style and observing the indicated meter.) You can use the suggested rhythm for your improvisation or create your own rhythm to complement the accompaniment. Notate your favorite improvisation.

Rules for Improvisation:

1. Use mostly chord tones and passing tones in the melody.
2. Most improvisations begin and end on tonic.
3. The ear should always be the final guide in determining which melody notes to play.

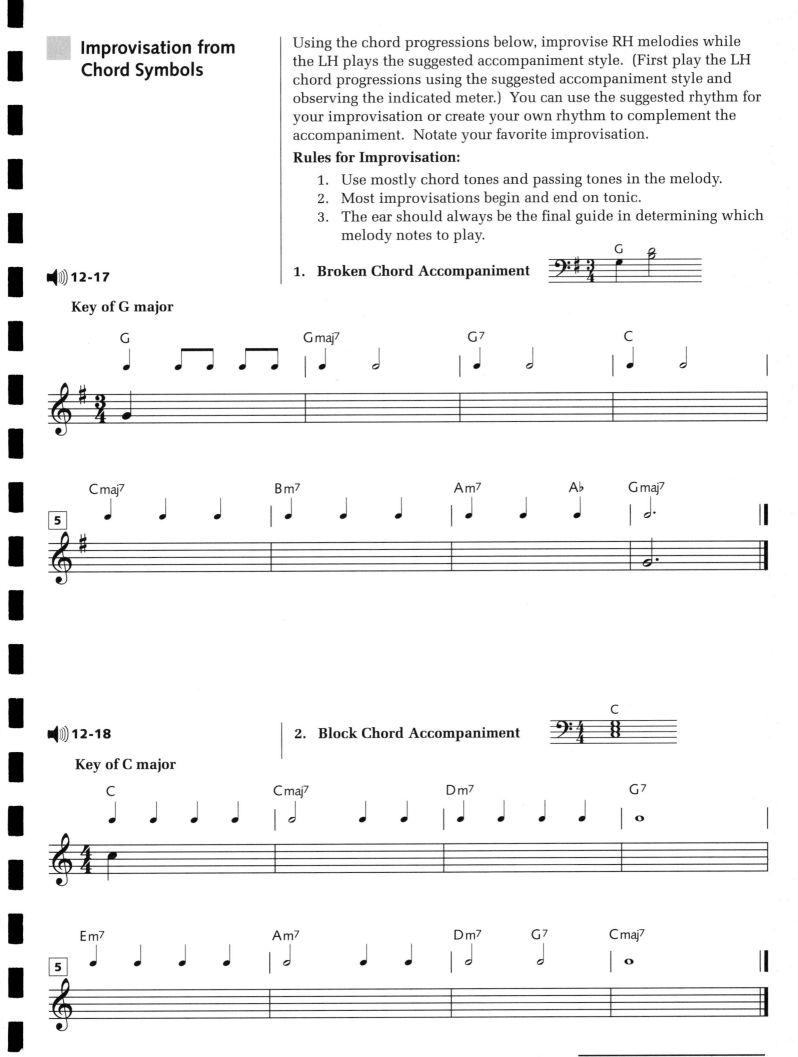

🔊 12-17

Key of G major

1. **Broken Chord Accompaniment**

🔊 12-18

Key of C major

2. **Block Chord Accompaniment**

Other Scale Structures

Objectives

Upon completion of this unit the student will be able to:

1. Play chromatic, whole tone and blues scales.

2. Sight-read music that uses chromatic, whole tone and blues scales.

3. Perform solo repertoire that uses chromatic scales and whole tone scales.

4. Improvise melodies over a 12-bar blues accompaniment.

Assignments

Week of _____

Write your assignments for the week in the space below.

_____
_____
_____
_____
_____
_____
_____
_____
_____
_____
_____
_____
_____
_____
_____
_____
_____
_____
_____
_____
_____
_____
_____
_____
_____
_____
_____
_____
_____

The Chromatic Scale

The **chromatic scale** is made up entirely of half steps. It goes up and down, using every key, black and white. It may begin on any note.

The fingering rules are:

- Use 3 on each black key.
- Use 1 on each white key, except when two white keys are together (no black key between), then use 1 2, or 2 1.

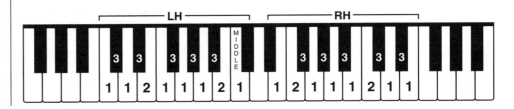

Play the one-octave chromatic scale hands separately. Then play hands together in contrary motion.

Reading

Practice Suggestions: See page 289.

🔊 12-19

Solo Repertoire

Before playing:
- Practice each chromatic scale passage with the correct fingering.
- Analyze and block the LH chords.
- Map the piece using D.C. al Fine, first ending, repeat, and second ending.

While playing:
- Be careful not to play fast.
- Observe the 8va in the RH of measures 9–16.
- Listen for steady eighth notes throughout.

CHROMATIC RAG

Willard A. Palmer
Morton Manus
Amanda Vick Lethco

◀))) 12-20

"Chromatic Rag" from Alfred's Basic Piano Library FUN BOOK, Level 3, by Willard Palmer, Morton Manus and Amanda Vick Lethco
Copyright © MCMLXXXVI by Alfred Publishing Co., Inc.

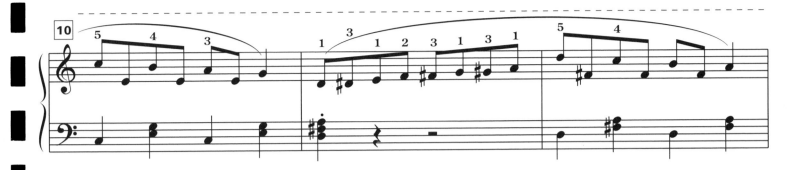

The Whole-Tone Scale

The **whole-tone scale** is made up entirely of whole steps. From the twelve tones of the chromatic scale, two whole tone scales can be built, each consisting of six whole tones within an octave. Usually, the ascending scale is written with sharps and the descending scale is written with flats.

Play the one-octave whole-tone scales hands separately.

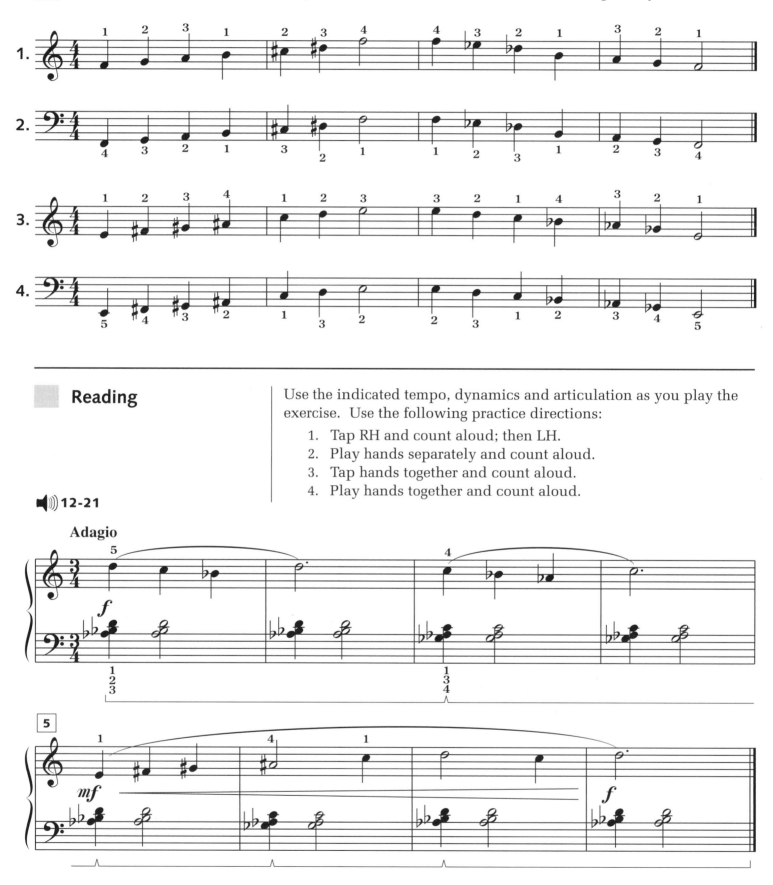

Reading

Use the indicated tempo, dynamics and articulation as you play the exercise. Use the following practice directions:
1. Tap RH and count aloud; then LH.
2. Play hands separately and count aloud.
3. Tap hands together and count aloud.
4. Play hands together and count aloud.

🔊 12-21

Adagio

♩olo Repertoire

Before playing:
- Identify the scale used in the RH.

While playing:
- Listen for steady eighth notes throughout.
- Play the RH louder than the LH.

🔊 12-22

THE BEAR

Vladimir Rebikov
(1866–1920)

pesante (heavy, with emphasis)

The Blues Scale

The **blues scale** contains seven tones in the following order:

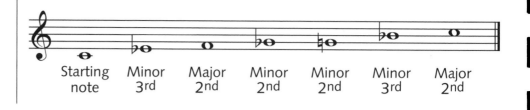

| Starting note | Minor 3rd | Major 2nd | Minor 2nd | Minor 2nd | Minor 3rd | Major 2nd |

Play the one-octave blues scales on C, G and F hands separately.

C Blues Scale

G Blues Scale

F Blues Scale

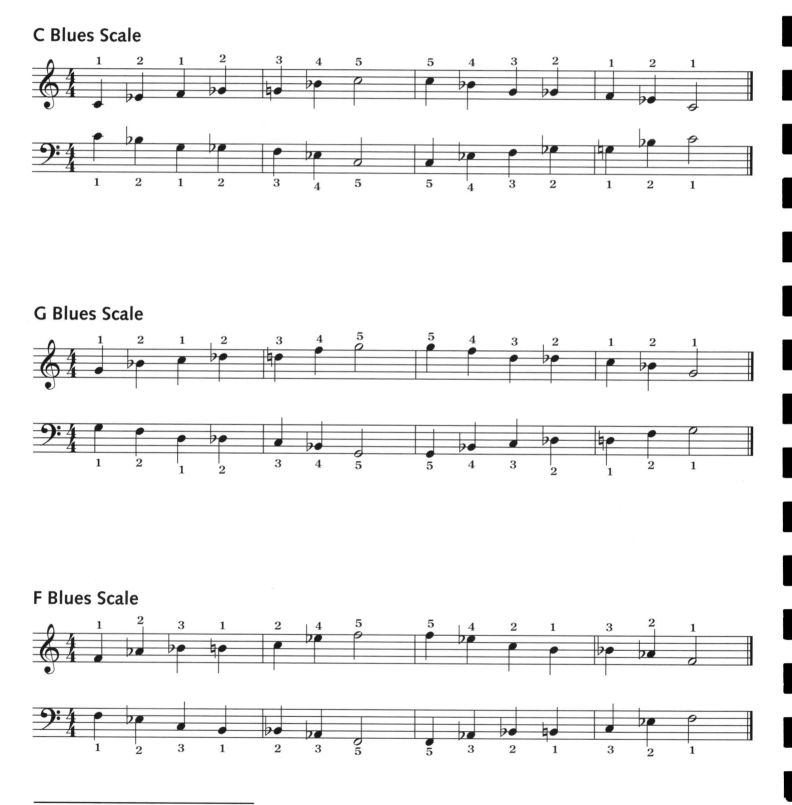

Reading

Use the indicated tempo, dynamics and articulation as you play the exercise.

Use the following practice directions:
1. Tap RH and count aloud; then LH.
2. Play hands separately and count aloud.
3. Tap hands together and count aloud.
4. Play hands together and count aloud.

🔊 12-23

Andante moderato

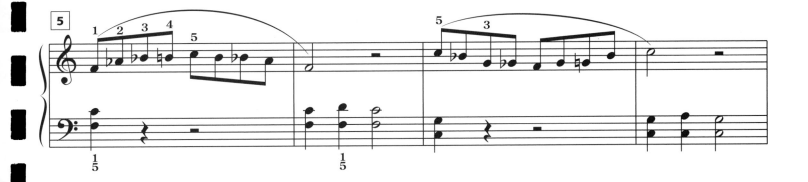

12-Bar Blues Improvisation

Improvise a 12-measure melody using the appropriate blues scale as your teacher plays each accompaniment. Listen to the 4-measure introduction to establish the tempo, mood and style before beginning the melody. You can use the suggested rhythm for your improvisation or create your own rhythm to complement the accompaniment.

C, F and G Blues Scales: Begin and end your melody on C.

🔊 12-24

TEACHER ACCOMPANIMENT

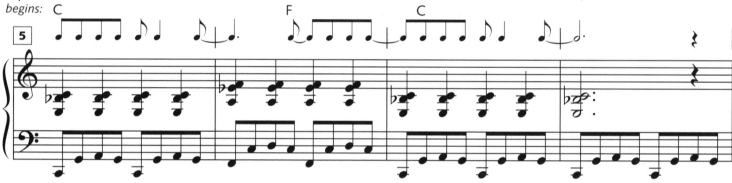

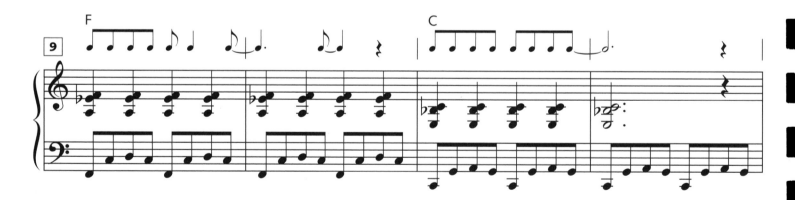

Modes

Objectives

Upon completion of this unit the student will be able to:

1. Play Lydian, Mixolydian, Dorian and Phrygian scales built on any note.

2. Play triads of the key in Lydian, Mixolydian, Dorian and Phrygian modes.

3. Sight-read music in Lydian, Mixolydian, Dorian and Phrygian modes.

4. Harmonize melodies in Lydian, Mixolydian, Dorian and Phrygian modes.

5. Improvise melodies in Lydian, Mixolydian, Dorian and Phrygian modes as the teacher plays an accompaniment.

6. Create a four-part ensemble from chord symbols.

Assignments

Week of _____

Write your assignments for the week in the space below.

_____

_____

_____

_____

_____

_____

_____

_____

_____

_____

_____

_____

_____

_____

_____

Ionian Mode

In ancient Greece, the early church used a system of music based on modes. Almost all music written before the 1500s was based on the various modes. Many well-known folk songs are modal. Recently, modal music has become more popular and modern composers use modal melodies and harmonies in their compositions.

Any scale of eight neighboring white keys is a **modal scale.** The scale using eight white keys beginning and ending on C, which we call the C major scale, may also be called the **Ionian scale.**

The melody for *Yankee Doodle* in Ionian (major) follows.

YANKEE DOODLE

🔊 13-1

Traditional

Lydian Mode

The scale using eight white keys, beginning and ending on F, is called the **Lydian scale.** The Lydian scale is like a major scale with the 4th tone raised one half-step.

Using tetrachord position, play the Lydian scale.

▶ Transpose to C Lydian, G Lydian, B♭ Lydian and E♭ Lydian.

Play triads of the key in F Lydian.

◀))) 13-2

I	II	iii	iv°	V	vi	vii	I
Major	Major	Minor	Diminished	Major	Minor	Minor	Major

◀))) 13-2

▶ Transpose to C Lydian and B♭ Lydian.

Reading in Lydian Mode

Use the indicated tempo, dynamics and articulation as you play the exercise. Use the following practice directions:

1. Tap RH and count aloud; then LH.
2. Play hands separately and count aloud.
3. Tap hands together and count aloud.
4. Play hands together and count aloud.

◀))) 13-3

Moderato

mf

Harmonization in Lydian Mode

Harmonize with a broken chord accompaniment.

Broken Chord Accompaniment

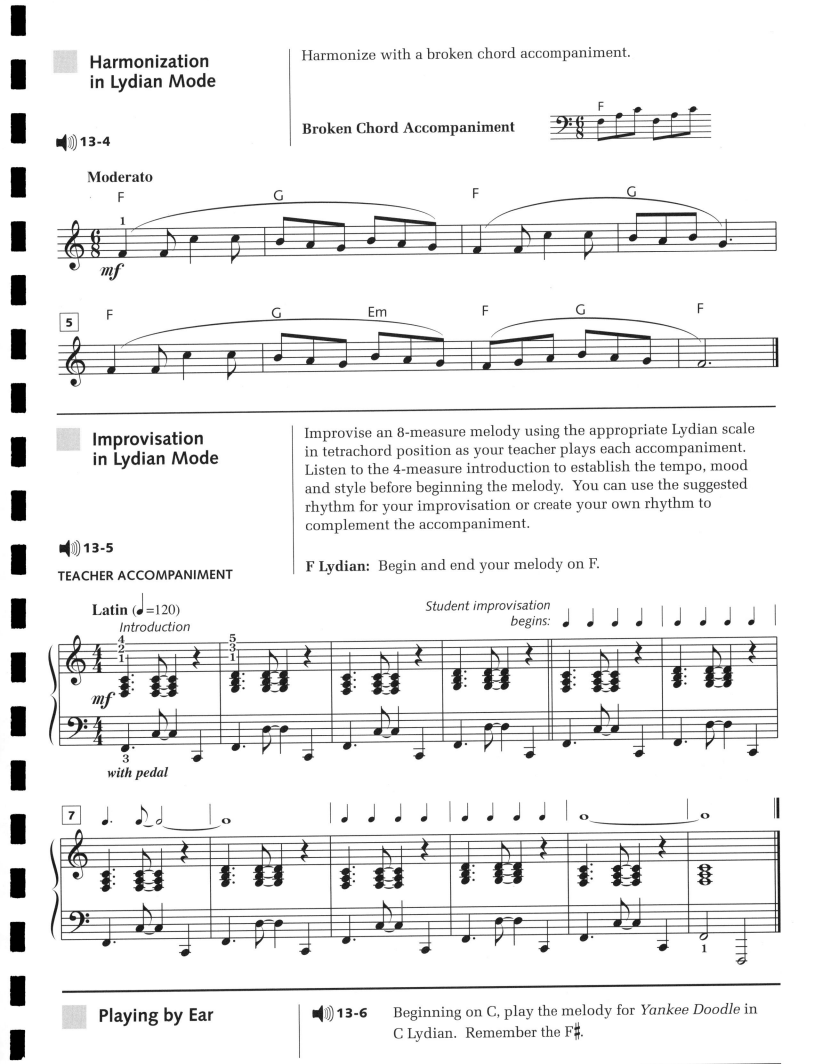

🔊 **13-4**

Improvisation in Lydian Mode

Improvise an 8-measure melody using the appropriate Lydian scale in tetrachord position as your teacher plays each accompaniment. Listen to the 4-measure introduction to establish the tempo, mood and style before beginning the melody. You can use the suggested rhythm for your improvisation or create your own rhythm to complement the accompaniment.

🔊 **13-5**

TEACHER ACCOMPANIMENT

F Lydian: Begin and end your melody on F.

Playing by Ear

🔊 **13-6** Beginning on C, play the melody for *Yankee Doodle* in C Lydian. Remember the F♯.

Mixolydian Mode

The scale using eight white keys, beginning and ending on G, is called the **Mixolydian scale**. The Mixolydian scale is like a major scale with the 7th tone lowered one half-step.

Using tetrachord position, play the Mixolydian scale.

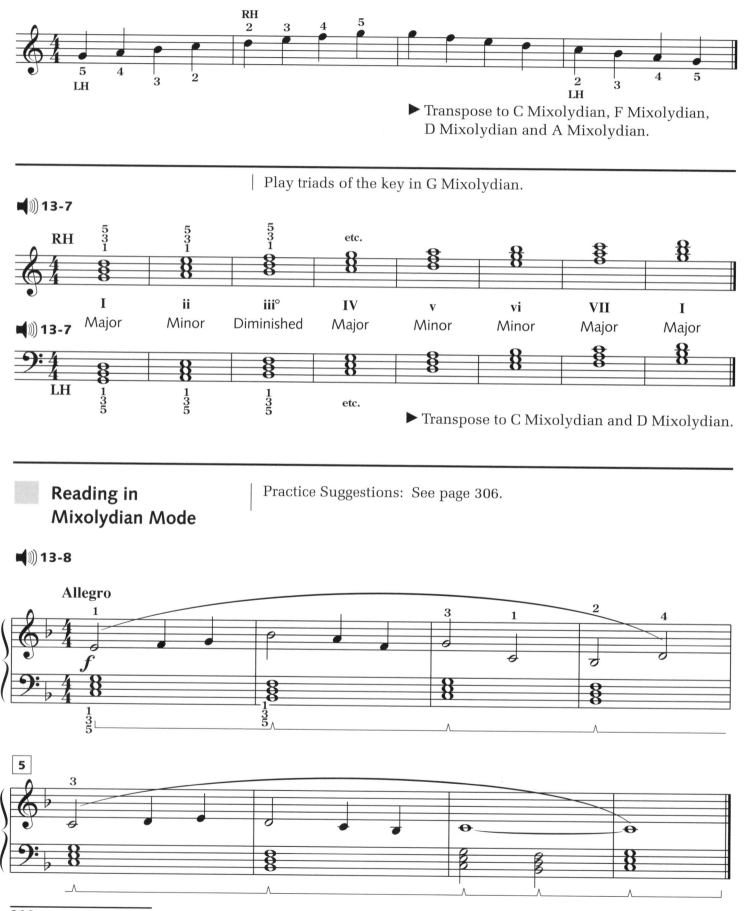

▶ Transpose to C Mixolydian, F Mixolydian, D Mixolydian and A Mixolydian.

Play triads of the key in G Mixolydian.

🔊 13-7

🔊 13-7

I	ii	iii°	IV	v	vi	VII	I
Major	Minor	Diminished	Major	Minor	Minor	Major	Major

▶ Transpose to C Mixolydian and D Mixolydian.

Reading in Mixolydian Mode

Practice Suggestions: See page 306.

🔊 13-8

Allegro

Harmonization in Mixolydian Mode

Harmonize with a waltz style accompaniment.

Waltz Style Accompaniment

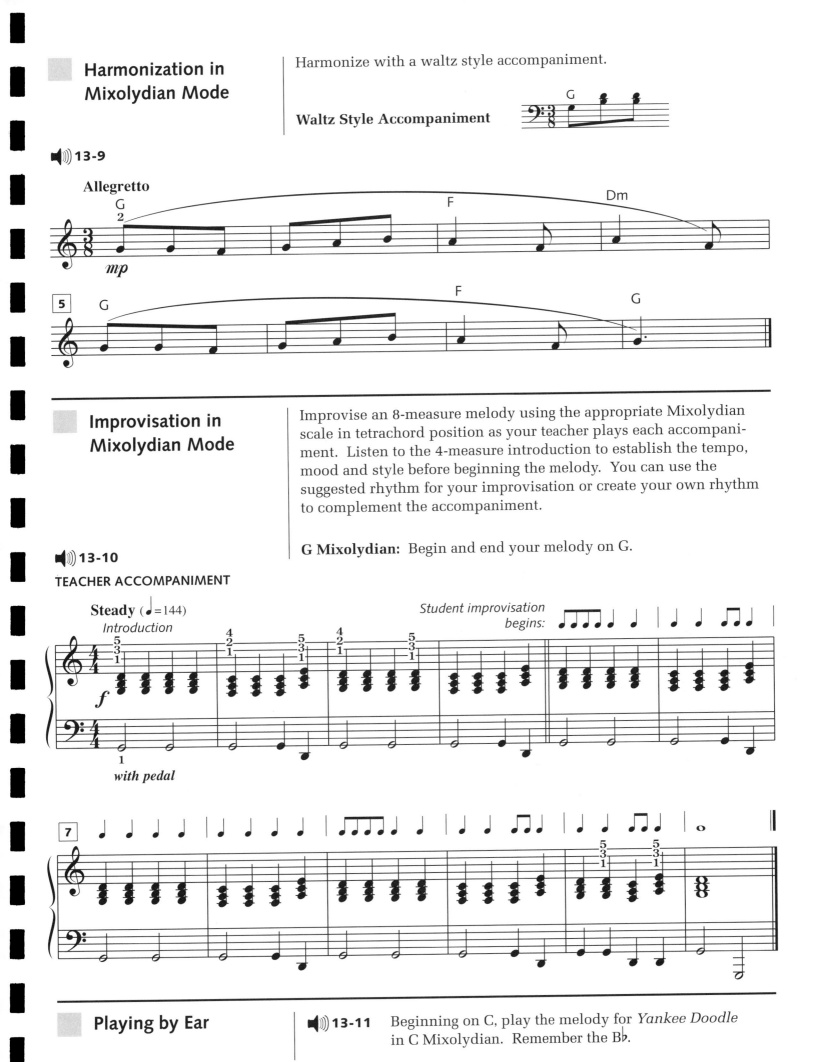

🔊 **13-9**

🔊 **13-10**
TEACHER ACCOMPANIMENT

Improvisation in Mixolydian Mode

Improvise an 8-measure melody using the appropriate Mixolydian scale in tetrachord position as your teacher plays each accompaniment. Listen to the 4-measure introduction to establish the tempo, mood and style before beginning the melody. You can use the suggested rhythm for your improvisation or create your own rhythm to complement the accompaniment.

G Mixolydian: Begin and end your melody on G.

Playing by Ear

🔊 **13-11** Beginning on C, play the melody for *Yankee Doodle* in C Mixolydian. Remember the B♭.

Aeolian Mode

The scale using eight white keys beginning and ending on A, which we call the A natural minor scale, may also be called the **Aeolian scale.**

Using tetrachord position, play the Aeolian scale.

▶ Transpose to C Aeolian, D Aeolian, E Aeolian and G Aeolian.

Dorian Mode

The scale using eight white keys, beginning and ending on D, is called the **Dorian scale.** The Dorian scale is like a natural minor scale with the 6th tone raised one half-step.

Using tetrachord position, play the Dorian scale.

▶ Transpose to A Dorian, E Dorian, G Dorian and C Dorian.

| Play triads of the key in D Dorian.

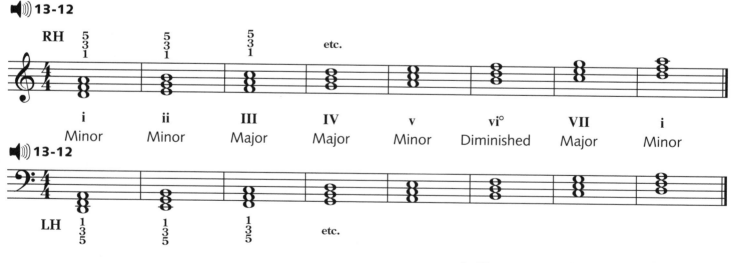

▶ Transpose to A Dorian and G Dorian.

Reading in Dorian Mode

Use the indicated tempo, dynamics and articulation as you play the exercise.

Use the following practice directions:

1. Tap RH and count aloud; then LH.
2. Play hands separately and count aloud.
3. Tap hands together and count aloud.
4. Play hands together and count aloud.

SCARBOROUGH FAIR

🔊 13-13

England

Andante moderato

Harmonization in Dorian Mode

Harmonize with a broken chord accompaniment.

Broken Chord Accompaniment

🔊 **13-14**

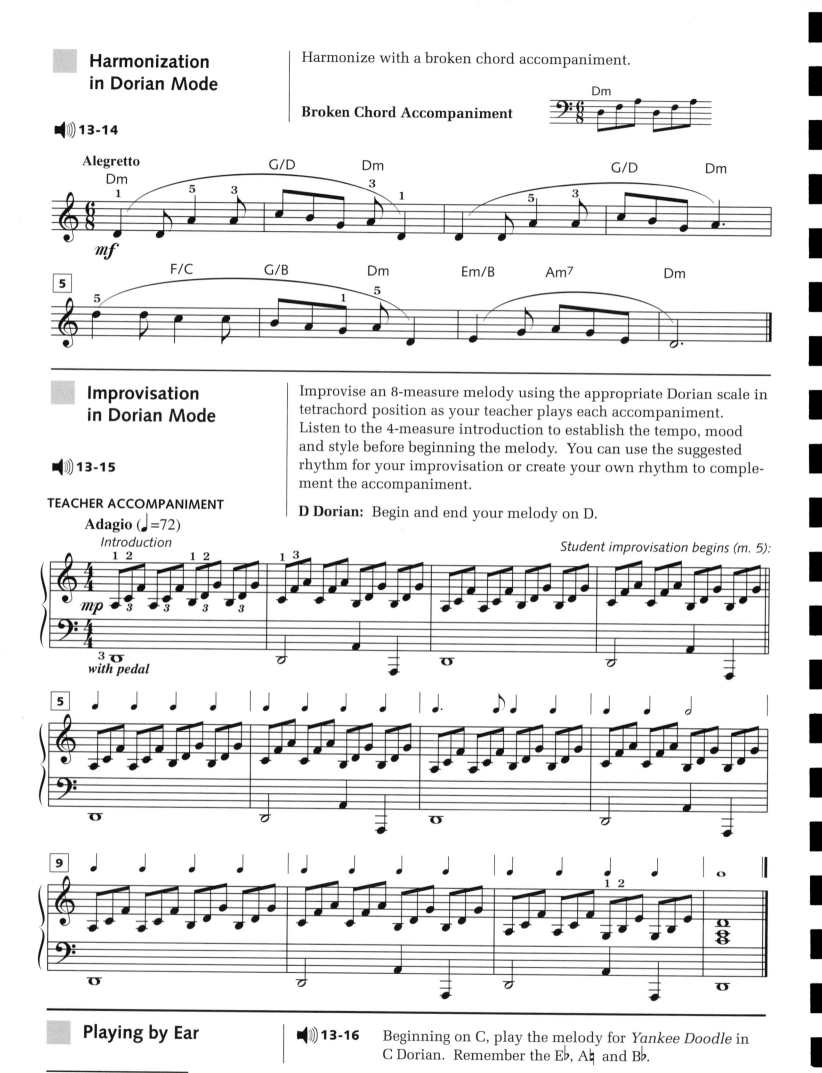

Improvisation in Dorian Mode

🔊 **13-15**

Improvise an 8-measure melody using the appropriate Dorian scale in tetrachord position as your teacher plays each accompaniment. Listen to the 4-measure introduction to establish the tempo, mood and style before beginning the melody. You can use the suggested rhythm for your improvisation or create your own rhythm to complement the accompaniment.

D Dorian: Begin and end your melody on D.

TEACHER ACCOMPANIMENT

Playing by Ear

🔊 **13-16** Beginning on C, play the melody for *Yankee Doodle* in C Dorian. Remember the E♭, A♮ and B♭.

Ensemble Repertoire

Play the four-part ensemble using the indicated chords to complete parts 2, 3 and 4.

Part 1: Melody
Part 2: Broken chords
Part 3: Two-hand accompaniment
Part 4: Roots of chords

JOHNNY HAS GONE FOR A SOLDIER

13-17

United States

Phrygian Mode

The scale using eight white keys, beginning and ending on E, is called the **Phrygian scale.** The Phrygian scale is like a natural minor scale with the 2nd tone lowered one half-step.

Using tetrachord position, play the Phrygian scale.

▶ Transpose to A Phrygian, D Phrygian, B Phrygian and F♯ Phrygian.

Play triads of the key in E Phrygian.

◀))) 13-18

i	II	III	iv	v°	VI	vii	i
Minor	Major	Major	Minor	Diminished	Major	Minor	Minor

◀))) 13-18

▶ Transpose to A Phrygian and B Phrygian.

Reading in Phrygian Mode

Practice Suggestions: See page 311.

◀))) 13-19

Adagio

Harmonization in Phrygian Mode

🔊 13-20

Harmonize with a broken chord accompaniment.

Broken Chord Accompaniment

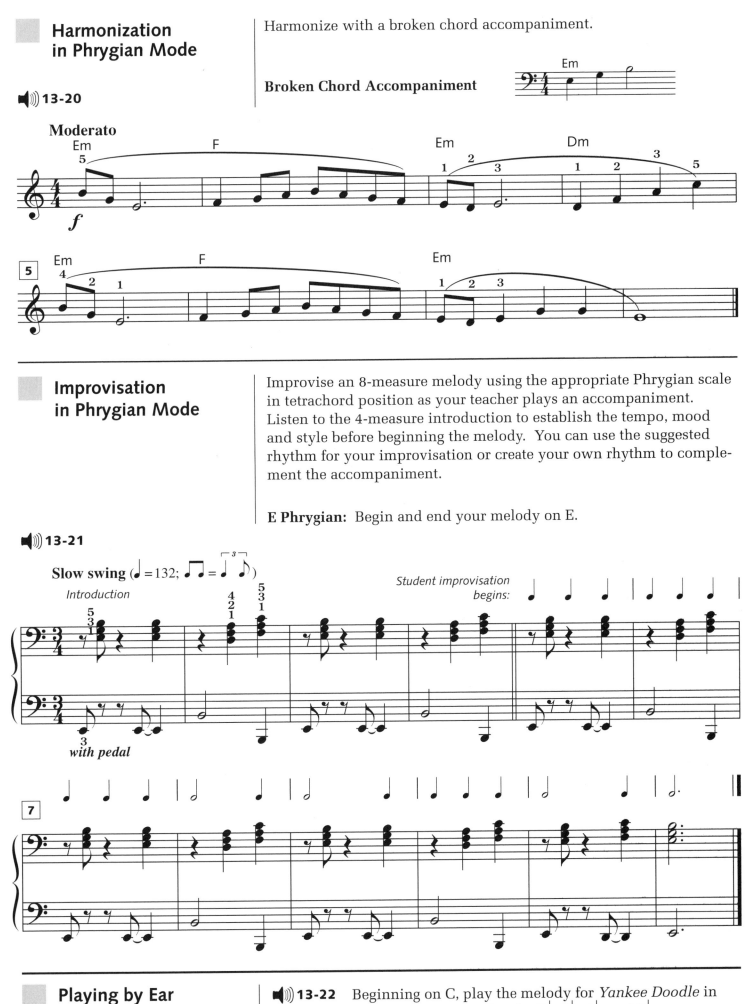

Improvisation in Phrygian Mode

Improvise an 8-measure melody using the appropriate Phrygian scale in tetrachord position as your teacher plays an accompaniment. Listen to the 4-measure introduction to establish the tempo, mood and style before beginning the melody. You can use the suggested rhythm for your improvisation or create your own rhythm to complement the accompaniment.

E Phrygian: Begin and end your melody on E.

🔊 13-21

Playing by Ear

🔊 13-22 Beginning on C, play the melody for *Yankee Doodle* in C Phrygian. Remember the D♭, E♭, A♭, and B♭.

Review

Objectives

Upon completion of this unit the student will be able to:

1. Play I–vi–IV–ii$_6$–I$_4^6$–V^7–I chord progressions in all major keys.

2. Perform solo repertoire that uses scale patterns and primary and secondary chords.

3. Sight-read and transpose music that uses primary and secondary chords.

4. Harmonize and transpose melodies with primary, secondary and seventh chords.

5. Create two-hand accompaniments from chord symbols.

6. Improvise melodies over primary, secondary and seventh chords.

Assignments

Week of _____

Write your assignments for the week in the space below.

_____

_____

_____

_____

_____

_____

_____

_____

_____

_____

_____

_____

_____

_____

_____

Playing the I–vi–IV–ii$_6$–I$_4^6$–V^7–I Chord Progression

Play the **I–vi–IV–ii$_6$–I$_4^6$–V^7–I** chord-progression exercise.

🔊 **13-23**

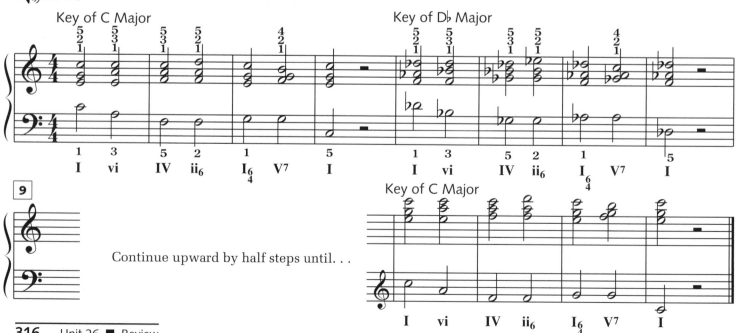

Continue upward by half steps until. . .

♪olo Repertoire

Before playing:
- Analyze the chords in the LH of measures 1–8.
- Practice the LH moves in measures 9–16.
- Map the piece observing the *D.C. al Fine* and repeats.

While playing:
- Play the RH a little louder than the LH.
- Take a little time to accent the second RH note in measures 2 and 6.

ECOSSAISE

🔊 13-24

Ludwig van Beethoven
(1770–1827)

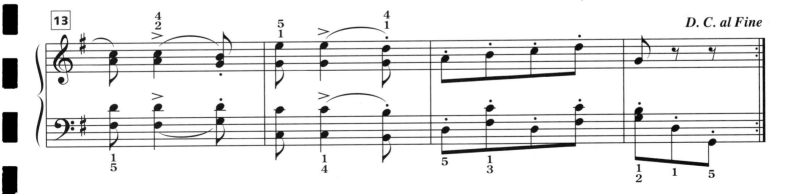

Reading

Identify the key of each example. Use the indicated tempo, dynamics and articulation as you play these exercises.

Use the following practice directions:
1. Tap RH and count aloud; then LH.
2. Play hands separately and count aloud.
3. Tap hands together and count aloud.
4. Play hands together and count aloud.

🔊 13-25

1.

Andante

▶ Transpose to D minor.

🔊 13-26

2.

Allegretto

▶ Transpose to C minor.

THE SCALE LADDER

🔊 13-27

Allegro non troppo

Daniel Gottlob Türk
(1756–1813)

mp

3.

5

▶ Transpose to C major.

ETUDE

🔊 13-28

Allegro

Louis Köhler (1820–1886)
Op. 190, No. 31

mf

4.

5

▶ Transpose to G minor.

Harmonization

1. Harmonize with a block chord accompaniment.

Block Chord Accompaniment

EINE KLEINE NACHTMUSIK

🔊 13-29

Wolfgang Amadeus Mozart (1756–1791)
K. 525

2. Using I, V⁷, IV, vi and ii chords, harmonize with a waltz style accompaniment. Use inversions to improve sound and for ease in performance. Write the Roman numeral name of each chord on the line below the staff.

Waltz Style Accompaniment

🔊 13-30

Germany

▶ Transpose to G major.

3. Harmonize the melody below in two ways:
   •Using the bottom note of each indicated seventh chord.
   •Using the indicated root-position seventh chords.

◀))) 13-31

Harmonization with Two-Hand Accompaniment

Using the indicated chords, create a two-hand accompaniment for the following melody by continuing the pattern given in the first measure.

STILL, STILL, STILL

◀))) 13-32

▶ Transpose to D major.

Improvisation from Chord Symbols

Using the chord progressions below, improvise RH melodies while the LH plays the suggested accompaniment style. (First play the LH chord progressions using the suggested accompaniment style and observing the indicated meter.) You can use the suggested rhythm for your improvisation or create your own rhythm to complement the accompaniment. Notate your favorite improvisation.

Rules for Improvisation:

1. Use mostly chord tones and passing tones in the melody.

2. Most improvisations begin and end on tonic.

3. The ear should always be the final guide in determining which melody notes to play.

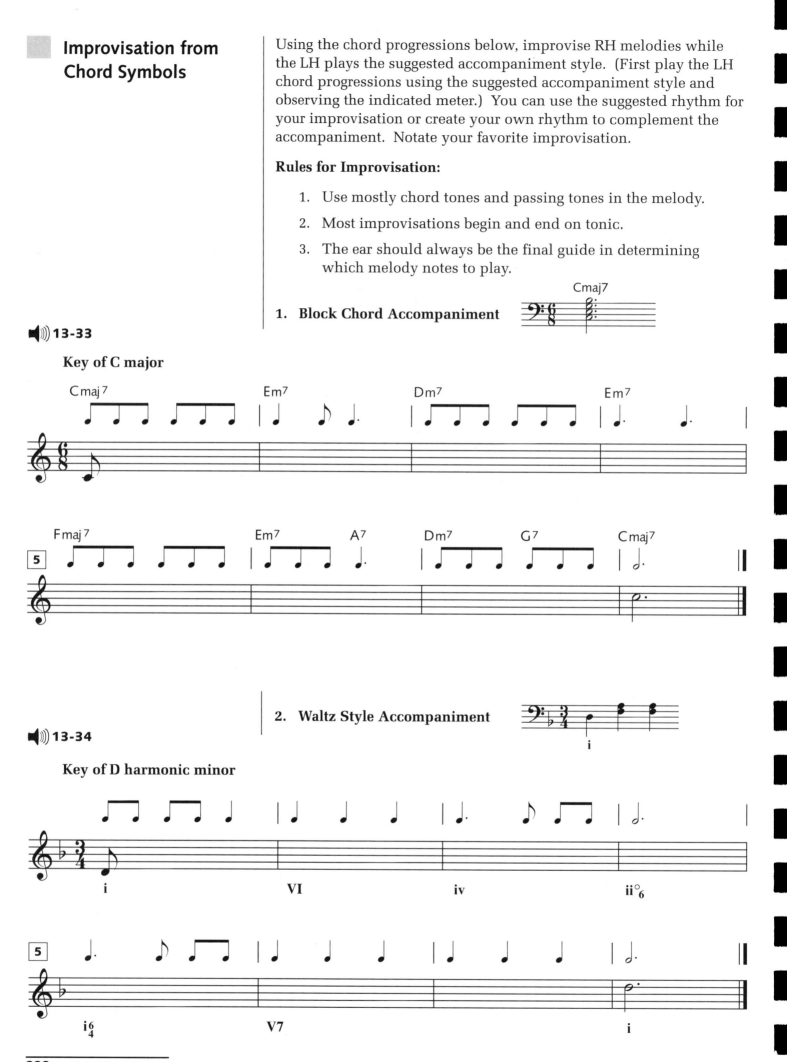

1. **Block Chord Accompaniment**

◀))) 13-33

Key of C major

2. **Waltz Style Accompaniment**

◀))) 13-34

Key of D harmonic minor

Review Worksheet

Name _____   *Date* _____

1. Identify each scale below by writing its name (Aeolian, Dorian, Phrygian, Lydian, Mixolydian, whole tone, chromatic or blues) on the line.

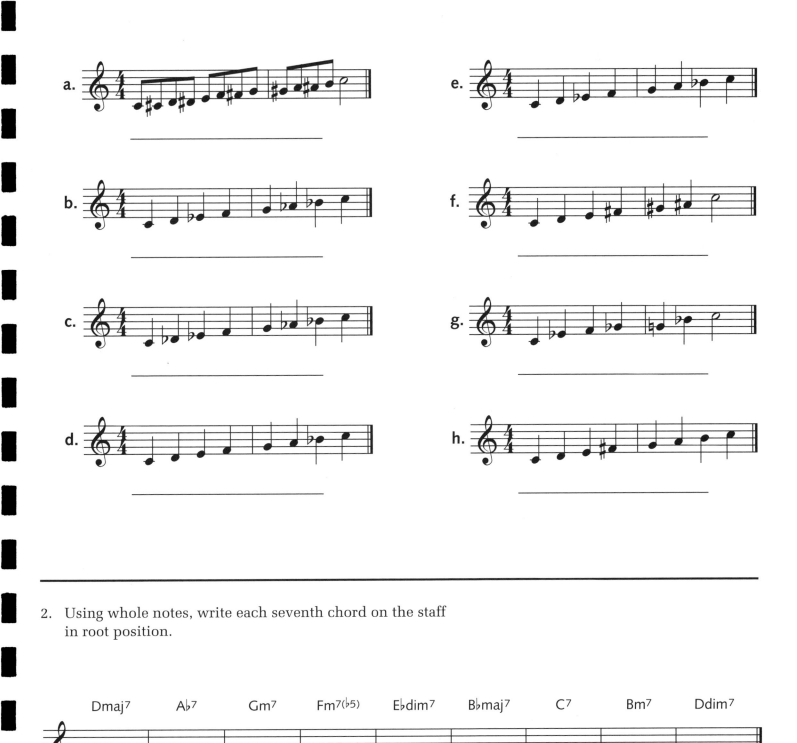

2. Using whole notes, write each seventh chord on the staff in root position.

3. Draw a line to connect the chord on the right with its key and
   Roman numeral on the left.

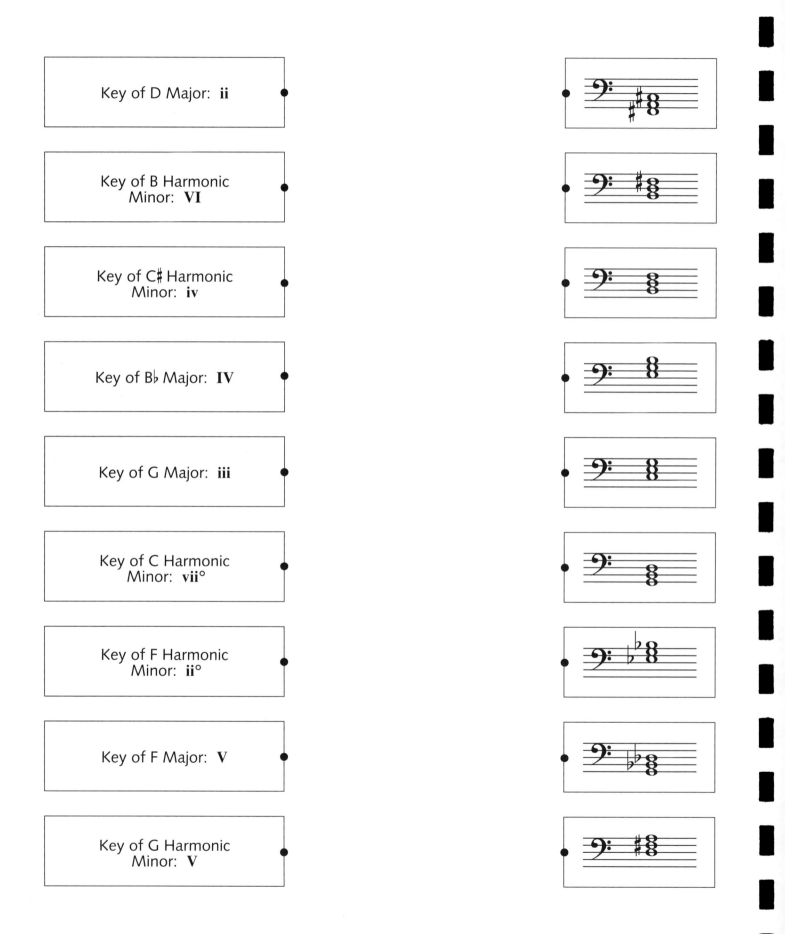

Key of D Major: **ii**

Key of B Harmonic Minor: **VI**

Key of C♯ Harmonic Minor: **iv**

Key of B♭ Major: **IV**

Key of G Major: **iii**

Key of C Harmonic Minor: **vii°**

Key of F Harmonic Minor: **ii°**

Key of F Major: **V**

Key of G Harmonic Minor: **V**

Supplementary Solo Repertoire

Before playing:
- Tap the rhythm first hands separately, then hands together, with the correct fingers.

While playing:
- Play the RH a little louder than the LH.
- Add small *crescendos* and *diminuendos* to follow the rise and fall of the melodic line within the phrases.

SONG
(THE FIRST TERM AT THE PIANO)

Béla Bartók
(1881–1945)

◀))) 14-1

Before playing:
- Notice that the RH is written in bass clef beginning in measure 9 and that both hands change to treble clef in the last measure.
- Tap the rhythm hands together.

While playing:
- Shape the RH line by carefully observing the *crescendos* and *diminuendos*.

THE SHEPHERD PIPES

Tat'iana Salutrinskaya
(dates unknown)

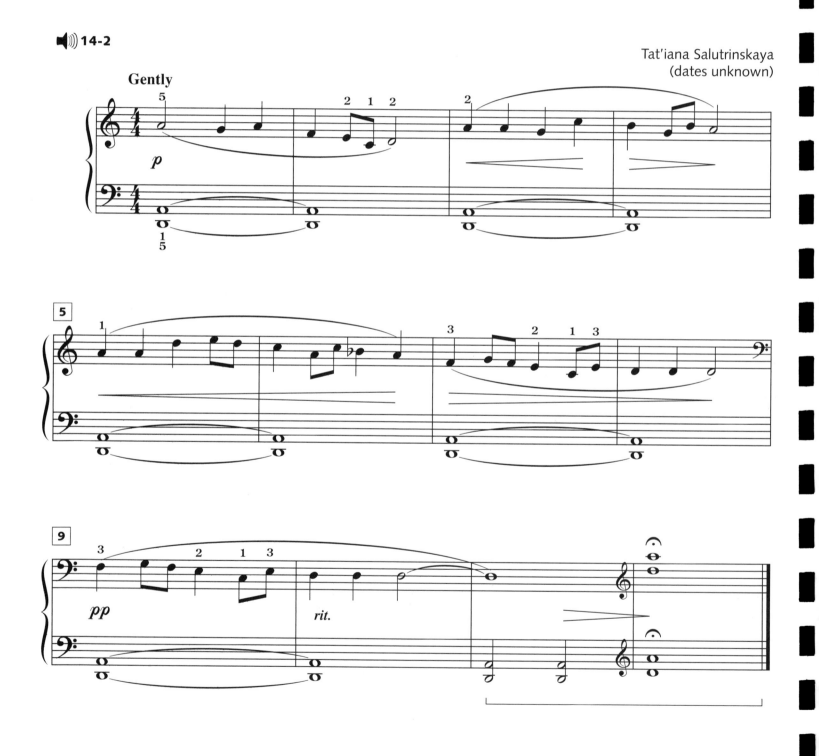

Before playing:
- Block the RH chords.

While playing:
- Listen for clear pedal changes.

CANON

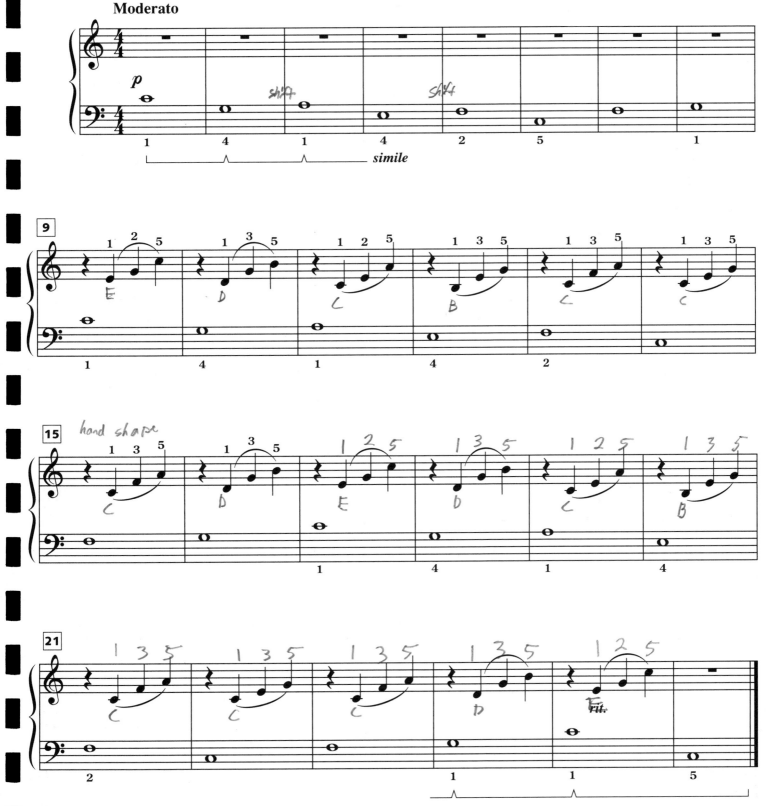

🔊 **14-3**

Johann Pachelbel (1653–1706)
arr. Kenon D. Renfrow

Before playing:
- Tap the rhythm hands together. Listen for the difference between the triplet figures and the pairs of eighth notes.

While playing:
- Play the RH a little louder than the LH.
- Clearly define the phrase structure in your performance.

SONATINA IN C MAJOR

🔊 14-4

William Duncombe
(18th century)

Before playing:
- Practice the RH alone, observing the contractions and expansions in the fingering.

While playing:
- Play the RH a little louder than the LH.
- Shape the RH line by carefully observing the *crescendos* and *diminuendos*.

BAGATELLE

14-5

Anton Diabelli
(1781–1858)

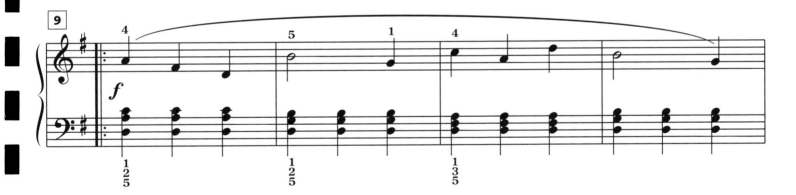

Before playing:
- Block the RH broken chords and inversions.
- Name the chords in measures 3–4, 7–8 and 15–16.

While playing:
- Shape the RH line by following the rise and fall of the line and observing the *crescendos* and *diminuendos*.

THE CHASE

🔊 14-6

Grazioso

Cornelius Gurlitt
(1820–1901)

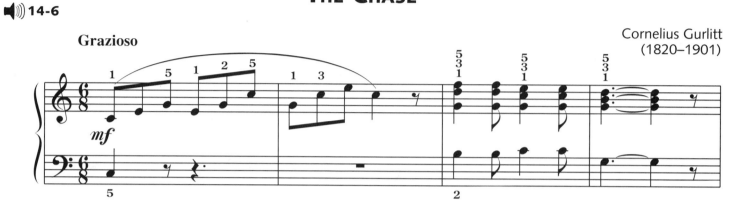

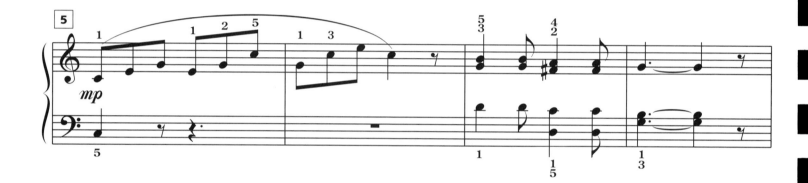

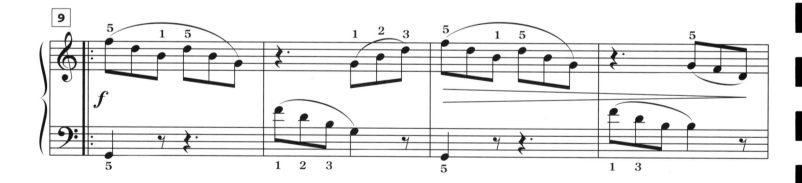

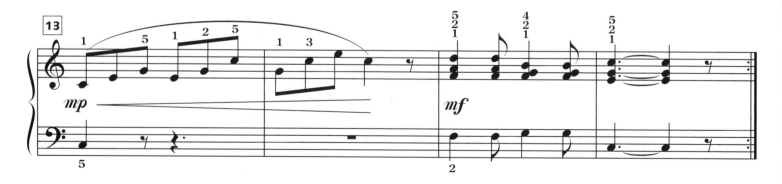

Before playing:
- Find the ii chords.
- Label the ii$_6$-V^7-I chord progressions.

While playing:
- Play the RH a little louder than the LH.
- Observe the repeats.

GERMAN DANCE

🔊 14-7

Franz Joseph Haydn
(1732–1809)

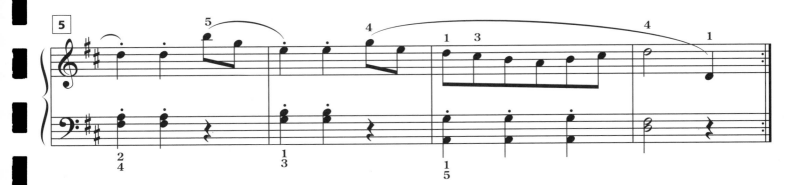

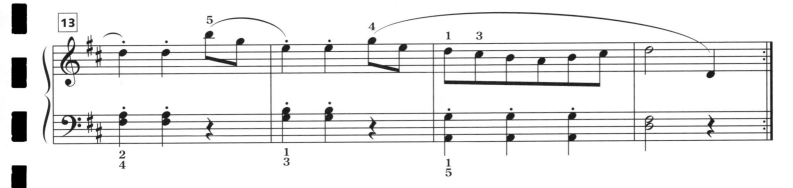

Before playing:
- Notice that both hands begin in treble clef.
- Circle each clef change.
- Play the first note of each sixteenth-note group with the correct finger.

While playing:
- Listen for an even sound on each five-finger pattern.
- Play the staccato notes short without sounding abrupt.

ETUDE

Felix LeCouppey (1811–1887)
Op. 17, No. 6

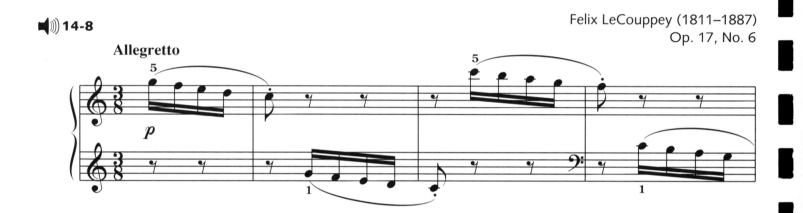

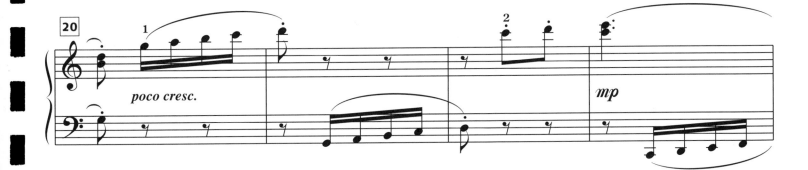

Before playing:
- Tap the rhythm hands together.
- Map the piece using the *D.C. al Fine* and *Fine.*

While playing:
- Play the RH a little louder than the LH.
- Add small *crescendos* and *diminuendos* to follow the rise and fall of the melodic line within the phrases.

RONDINO

🔊 14-9

Jean-Philippe Rameau
(1683–1764)

Before playing:
- Practice the RH alone, observing the contractions and expansions in the fingering.
- Observe the repeats.

While playing:
- Play the RH a little louder than the LH.

🔊 14-10

GERMAN DANCE

Franz Joseph Haydn
(1732–1809)

Allegretto

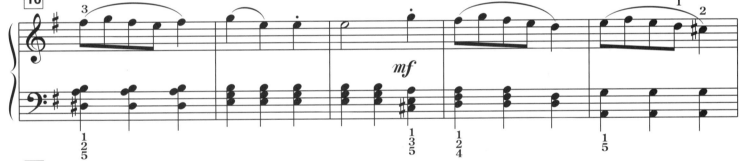

Before playing:
- Practice hands separately, observing the suggested fingering.
- Find places where the LH imitates the RH.

While playing:
- Play the RH a little louder than the LH in measures 10–13.
- In measures 3–4 and 16–17, bring out the LH as it begins.

MENUET IN D MINOR

🔊 14-11

Jean-Baptiste Lully
(1632–1687)

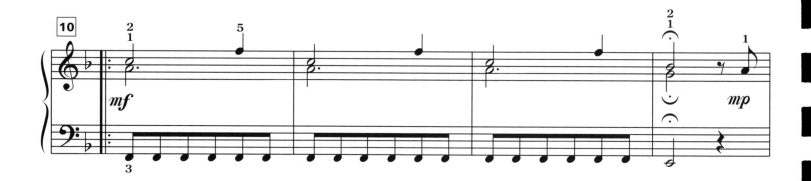

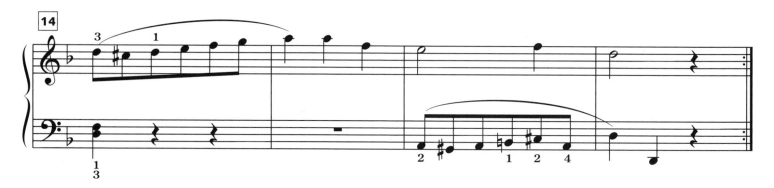

Before playing:
- Block the octaves in the LH.
- Practice the RH alone, observing the suggested fingering.

While playing:
- Play the RH a little louder than the LH.

BURLESKE

14-12

Leopold Mozart
(1719–1787)

LH detached

Before playing:
- Find places where the RH plays an octave higher or lower than written.
- Practice the RH alone, being aware of the contractions and expansions in the fingering.

While playing:
- Play the RH a little louder than the LH.
- Listen for crisp staccato notes and strong accents, always being aware of the dynamic level.

IN THE HALL OF THE MOUNTAIN KING
(PEER GYNT SUITE)

🔊)) 14-13

Edvard Grieg (1843–1907)
arr. E. L. Lancaster

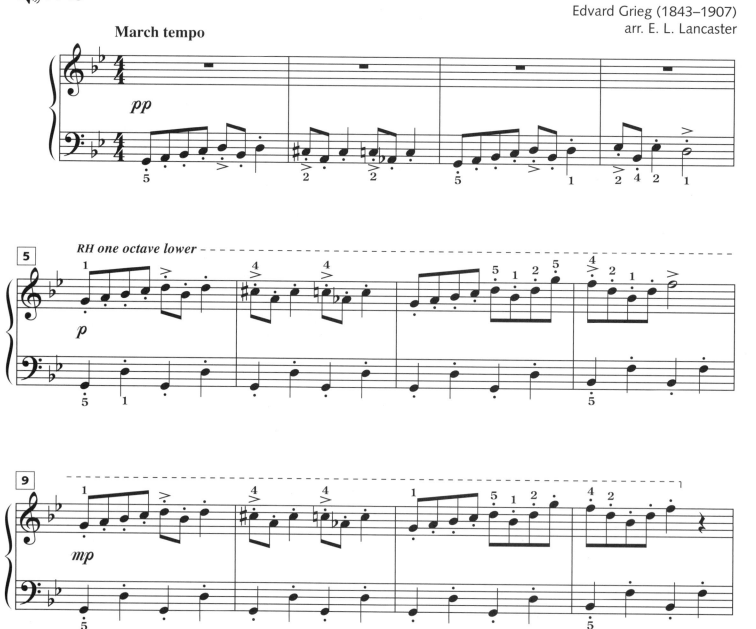

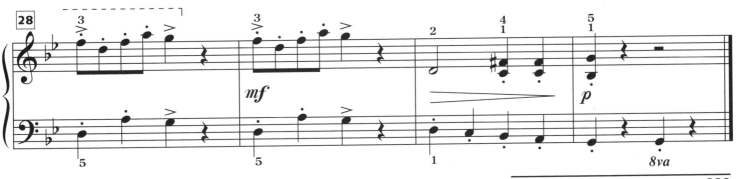

Before playing:
- Practice the RH alone, observing the contractions and expansions in the fingering.
- Label the LH chords in measures 5–8 with letter symbols.

While playing:
- Play the RH a little louder than the LH.
- Be careful not to play fast.

THE ENTERTAINER

Scott Joplin (1868–1917)
Arr. E. L. Lancaster
Kenon D. Renfrow

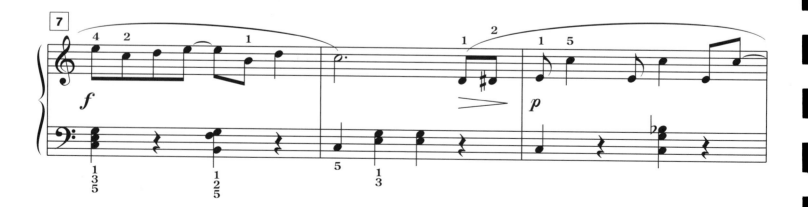

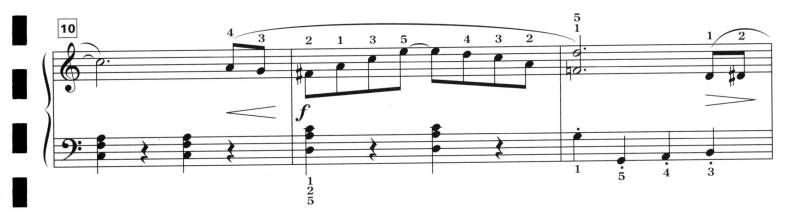

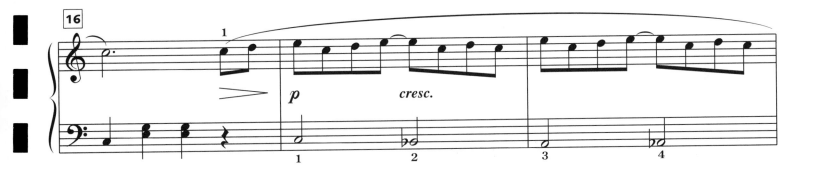

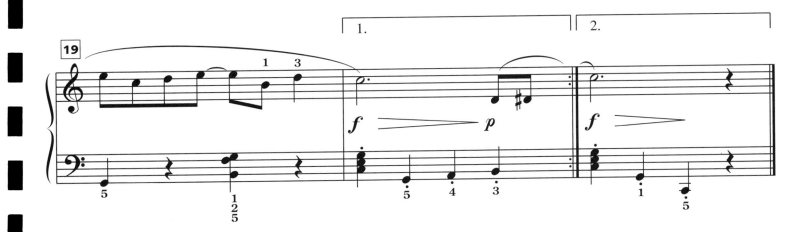

Before playing:
- Circle each LH clef change.
- Block the chords in the LH.
- Tap the rhythm hands together.

While playing:
- Play the RH a little louder than the LH.
- Listen for an even sound on each five-finger pattern and on the scale in measures 23–24.

ALLEGRETTO

🔊 14-15

Ferdinand Beyer (1803–1863)
Op. 101, No. 43

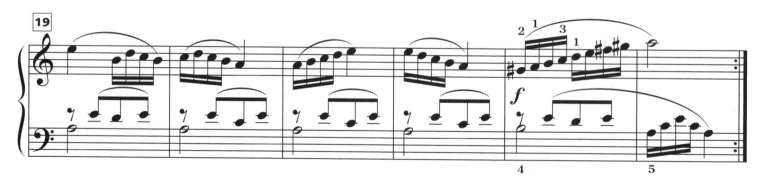

Before playing:
- Find the vi chords.
- Block the LH chords.

While playing:
- Play the RH a little louder than the LH.
- Listen for crisp staccato notes.

ETUDE IN G MAJOR

🔊 14-16

Ludwig Schytte (1843–1909)
Op. 160, No. 12

Before playing:
- Find places where the RH plays an octave lower than written.

While playing:
- Play the RH a little louder than the LH.
- Listen for crisp staccato notes and strong accents, always being aware of the dynamic level.
- Swing the eighth notes.

JUST STRUTTIN' ALONG

🔊 14-17

Martha Mier

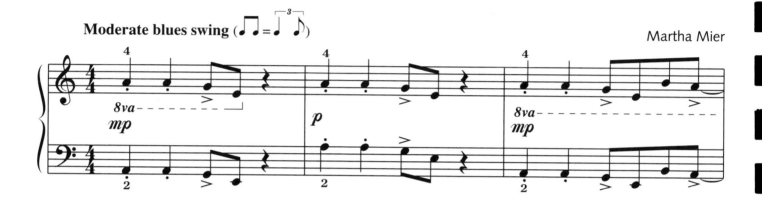

"Just Struttin' Along" from JAZZ, RAGS 'N' BLUES, Book 1, by Martha Mier
Copyright © MCMXCIII by Alfred Publishing Co., Inc.

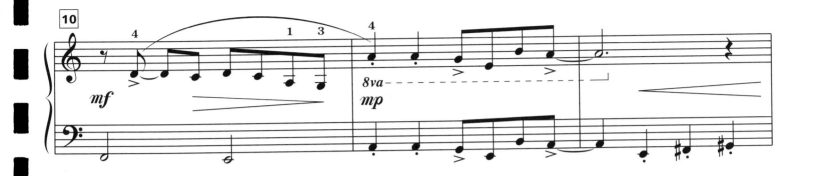

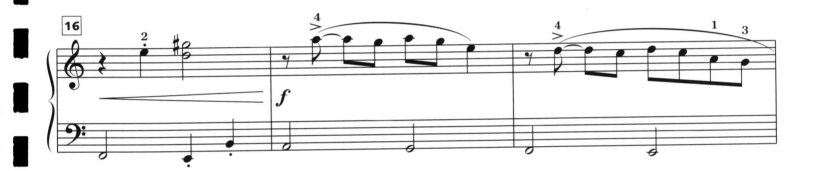

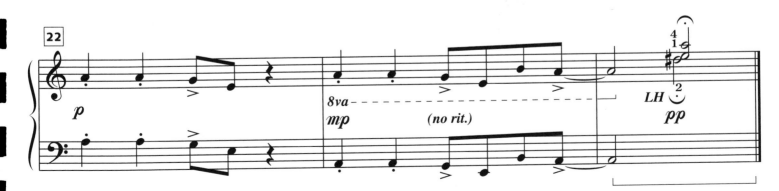

Before playing:
- Practice the RH alone, being aware of the cross-overs and cross-unders in the fingering.
- Practice the jumps in the LH in measures 17–20.

While playing:
- Shape the RH line by observing the *crescendos* and *diminuendos*.

PRELUDE NO. 1

🔊 **14-18**

Catherine Rollin

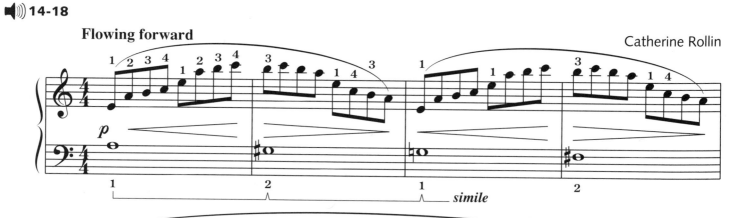

"Prelude No. 1 in A Minor" from PRELUDES FOR PIANO, Book 1, by Catherine Rollin
Copyright © MCMLXXXIX by Alfred Publishing Co., Inc.

Scale and Arpeggio Fingering Charts

Note: A dot (•) above a fingering indicates a black key.

Major Scales

Key		Fingering
C	RH:	1 2 3 1 2 3 4 1 2 3 1 2 3 4 5
	LH:	5 4 3 2 1 3 2 1 4 3 2 1 3 2 1
G	RH:	1 2 3 1 2 3 •4 1 2 3 1 2 3 •4 5
	LH:	5 4 3 2 1 3 •2 1 4 3 2 1 3 •2 1
D	RH:	1 2 •3 1 2 3 •4 1 2 •3 1 2 3 •4 5
	LH:	5 4 •3 2 1 3 •2 1 4 •3 2 1 3 •2 1
A	RH:	1 2 •3 1 2 •3 •4 1 2 •3 1 2 •3 •4 5
	LH:	5 4 •3 2 1 •3 •2 1 4 •3 2 1 •3 •2 1
E	RH:	1 •2 •3 1 2 •3 •4 1 •2 •3 1 2 •3 •4 5
	LH:	5 4 •3 2 1 •3 •2 1 4 •3 2 1 •3 •2 1
B	RH:	1 •2 •3 1 •2 •3 •4 1 •2 •3 1 •2 •3 •4 5
	LH:	4 •3 2 1 •4 •3 2 1 •3 2 1 •4 •3 2 1

(handwritten above A row: A B C D E F G A B C D E F G A)

Key		Fingering
G♭ (F♯)	RH:	•2 •3 4 1 •2 •3 1 •2 •3 4 1 •2 •3 1 •2
	LH:	•4 •3 2 1 •3 2 1 •4 •3 2 1 •3 2 1 •4
D♭ (C♯)	RH:	•2 •3 1 •2 •3 4 1 •2 •3 1 •2 •3 4 1 •2
	LH:	•3 2 1 •4 •3 2 1 •3 2 1 •4 •3 2 1 •3
A♭	RH:	•3 4 1 •2 •3 1 2 •3 4 1 •2 •3 1 2 3
	LH:	•3 2 1 •4 •3 2 1 •3 2 1 •4 •3 2 1 3
E♭	RH:	•3 1 2 •3 4 1 2 •3 1 2 •3 4 1 2 3
	LH:	•3 2 1 •4 •3 2 1 •3 2 1 •4 •3 2 1 3
B♭	RH:	•4 1 2 •3 1 2 3 •4 1 2 •3 1 2 3 •4
	LH:	•3 2 1 •4 3 2 1 •3 2 1 •4 3 2 1 3
F	RH:	1 2 3 •4 1 2 3 1 2 3 •4 1 2 3 •4
	LH:	5 4 3 2 1 3 2 1 4 3 •2 1 3 2 1

Major Arpeggios

Key		Fingering
C	RH:	1 2 3 1 2 3 5
	LH:	5 4 2 1 4 2 1
G	RH:	1 2 3 1 2 3 5
	LH:	5 4 2 1 4 2 1
D	RH:	1 •2 3 1 •2 3 5
	LH:	5 •3 2 1 •3 2 1
A	RH:	1 •2 3 1 •2 3 5
	LH:	5 •3 2 1 •3 2 1
E	RH:	1 •2 3 1 •2 3 5
	LH:	5 •3 2 1 •3 2 1
B	RH:	1 •2 •3 1 •2 •3 5
	LH:	5 •3 2 1 •3 •2 1

Key		Fingering
G♭ (F♯)	RH:	•1 •2 •3 •1 •2 •3 5
	LH:	•5 •3 •2 •1 •3 •2 1
D♭ (C♯)	RH:	•4 1 •2 •4 1 •2 •4
	LH:	•2 1 •4 •2 1 •4 •2
A♭	RH:	•4 1 •2 •4 1 •2 •4
	LH:	•2 1 •4 •2 1 •4 •2
E♭	RH:	•4 1 •2 •4 1 •2 •4
	LH:	•2 1 •4 •2 1 •4 •2
B♭	RH:	•4 1 2 •4 1 2 •4
	LH:	•3 2 1 •3 2 1 •3
F	RH:	1 2 3 1 2 3 5
	LH:	5 4 2 1 4 2 1

Harmonic Minor Scales

Key		Fingering	
a	RH:	1 2 3 1 2 3 4̇	1 2 3 1 2 3 4̇ 5
	LH:	5 4 3 2 1 3 2̇	1 4 3 2 1 3 2̇ 1
e	RH:	1 2̇ 3 1 2 3 4	1 2̇ 3 1 2 3 4 5
	LH:	5 4̇ 3 2 1 3 2̇	1 4̇ 3 2 1 3 2̇ 1
b	RH:	1 2̇ 3 1 2̇ 3 4̇	1 2̇ 3 1 2̇ 3 4 5
	LH:	4 3̇ 2 1 4̇ 3 2	1 3̇ 2 1 4̇ 3 2 1
f♯	RH:	3̇ 4̇ 1 2 3 1 2	3̇ 4̇ 1 2 3 1 2 3
	LH:	4 3 2 1 3 2 1	4 3 2 1 3 2 1 4
c♯	RH:	3̇ 4̇ 1 2̇ 3 1 2	3̇ 4̇ 1 2̇ 3 1 2 3
	LH:	3̇ 2 1 4̇ 3 2 1	3̇ 2 1 4̇ 3 2 1 3
g♯ (a♭)	RH:	3̇ 4̇ 1 2̇ 3 1 2	3̇ 4̇ 1 2̇ 3 1 2 3
	LH:	3̇ 2̇ 1 4̇ 3 2 1	3̇ 2̇ 1 4̇ 3̇ 2 1 3̇

Key		Fingering	
e♭ (d♯)	RH:	3̇ 1 2̇ 3̇ 4 1 2	3̇ 1 2̇ 3̇ 4 1 2 3̇
	LH:	2̇ 1 4̇ 3̇ 2 1 3	2̇ 1 4̇ 3̇ 2 1 3 2̇
b♭ (a♯)	RH:	4̇ 1 2̇ 3 1 2̇ 3	4̇ 1 2̇ 3 1 2̇ 3 4
	LH:	2̇ 1 3̇ 2 1 4̇ 3	2̇ 1 3̇ 2 1 4̇ 3 2
f	RH:	1 2 3̇ 4 1 2̇ 3	1 2 3̇ 4 1 2̇ 3 4
	LH:	5 4 3̇ 2 1 3̇ 2	1 4 3̇ 2 1 3̇ 2 1
c	RH:	1 2 3̇ 1 2 3 4	1 2 3̇ 1 2 3 4 5
	LH:	5 4 3̇ 2 1 3̇ 2	1 4 3̇ 2 1 3̇ 2 1
g	RH:	1 2 3̇ 1 2 3 4̇	1 2 3̇ 1 2 3 4̇ 5
	LH:	5 4 3̇ 2 1 3̇ 2̇	1 4 3̇ 2 1 3̇ 2̇ 1
d	RH:	1 2 3 1 2 3 4̇	1 2 3 1 2 3 4̇ 5
	LH:	5 4 3 2 1 3̇ 2̇	1 4 3 2 1 3̇ 2̇ 1

Minor Arpeggios

Key		Fingering	
a	RH:	1 2 3	1 2 3 5
	LH:	5 4 2	1 4 2 1
e	RH:	1 2 3	1 2 3 5
	LH:	5 4 2	1 4 2 1
b	RH:	1 2 3̇	1 2 3̇ 5
	LH:	5 4̇ 2	1 4̇ 2 1
f♯	RH:	4̇ 1 2̇	4̇ 1 2̇ 4
	LH:	2 1 4̇	2 1 4̇ 2
c♯	RH:	4̇ 1 2̇	4̇ 1 2̇ 4
	LH:	2 1 4̇	2 1 4̇ 2
g♯ (a♭)	RH:	4̇ 1 2̇	4̇ 1 2̇ 4
	LH:	2 1 4̇	2 1 4̇ 2

Key		Fingering	
e♭ (d♯)	RH:	1̇ 2̇ 3̇	1̇ 2̇ 3̇ 5̇
	LH:	5 3 2	1 3 2 1
b♭ (a♯)	RH:	2̇ 3̇ 1	2̇ 3̇ 1 2̇
	LH:	3 2 1	3 2 1 3
f	RH:	1 2̇ 3	1 2̇ 3 5
	LH:	5 4̇ 2	1 4̇ 2 1
c	RH:	1 2̇ 3	1 2̇ 3 5
	LH:	5 4̇ 2	1 4̇ 2 1
g	RH:	1 2̇ 3	1 2̇ 3 5
	LH:	5 4̇ 2	1 4̇ 2 1
d	RH:	1 2 3	1 2 3 5
	LH:	5 4 2	1 4 2 1

Appendix B

Glossary

Accent sign (>) . . . . placed over or under a note that gets special emphasis; play that note louder.

Adagio . . . . slowly.

Alla breve (¢) . . . . . cut time or $\frac{2}{2}$ time.

Alla marcia . . . . . . in march style.

Allegretto . . . . moderately fast.

Allegro . . . . quickly, happily.

Allegro non troppo . . quickly, but not too much.

Andante . . . . moving along (the word actually means "walking").

Andantino . . . . . slightly faster than andante.

Animato . . . . animated; lively.

A tempo . . . . resume original speed.

Brio . . . . vigorously.

Cantabile . . . . in a singing style.

Chromatic scale . . . made up entirely of half steps; it goes up and down, using every key, black and white.

Common time (C) . . same as $\frac{4}{4}$ time.

Comodo . . . . unhurried.

Con . . . . with.

Crescendo (<) . . . gradually louder.

Cut time (¢) . . . . . . same as $\frac{2}{2}$ time; alla breve.

D. C. al Fine . . . . . . repeat from the beginning to the word "Fine."

Decrescendo (>) . . gradually softer.

Diatonic . . . . using only notes in the given key, with no alterations.

Diminuendo (>) . . gradually softer.

Dolce . . . . sweetly.

Dominant . . . . the fifth scale degree.

Double flat (♭♭) . . . . lowers a flatted note another half step or a natural note one whole step.

Double sharp (×) . . . raises a sharped note another half step, or a natural note one whole step.

Enharmonic . . . . . . notes that are spelled (written) differently but are identical in sound.

Fermata (⌒) . . . . . hold the note under the sign longer than its full value.

Fine . . . . the end.

First ending (⌐1.___⌐) . play first time only.

Flat sign (♭) . . . . . . lowers a note one half step; play the next key to the left, whether black or white.

Forte (ƒ) . . . . loud.

Fortissimo (ƒƒ) . . . . very loud.

Giocoso . . . . humorous.

Glossary (continued)

Grand staff . . . . the bass staff and the treble staff joined together by a brace.

Grazioso . . . . gracefully.

Harmonic intervals . . distances between notes or keys that are played together.

Incomplete measure . . a measure at the beginning of a piece with fewer counts than indicated in the time signature. The missing beats are usually found in the last measure.

Intervals . . . . distances between notes or keys.

Key signature . . . . the number of sharps or flats in any key, written at the beginning of each line.

Largo . . . . very slow.

Leading tone . . . . the seventh scale degree.

Legato . . . . smoothly connected.

Ledger line . . . . used above or below the staff to extend its range.

Leggiero . . . . lightly.

Lento . . . . slow.

Maestoso . . . . majestically.

Marcato . . . . marked, stressed.

Mediant . . . . the third scale degree.

Melodic intervals . . . . distance between notes or keys that are played separately.

Mezzo forte (*mf*) . . . . . moderately loud.

Mezzo piano (*mp*) . . . . moderately soft.

Misterioso . . . . mysteriously.

Moderato . . . . moderately.

Molto . . . . much.

Moto . . . . motion.

Natural sign (♮) . . . . . . cancels a sharp or flat.

Non troppo . . . . not too much.

Octave . . . . the distance from one key on the keyboard to the next key (lower or higher) with the same letter name.

Octave sign (*8va*) . . . . . play eight scale tones (one octave) higher when the sign is above the notes; eight scale tones lower when the sign is below the notes.

Pedal mark (⌞___⌟) . . press the damper, hold it, and release it.

Pesante . . . . heavy, with emphasis.

Phrase . . . . musical thought or sentence.

Pianissimo (*pp*) . . . . . . very soft.

Piano (*p*) . . . . soft.

Più . . . . more.

Poco . . . . little.

Repeat sign (:‖) . . . . . . repeat from the beginning, or from the first repeat (‖:).

Rests . . . . signs for silence.

Ritardando
(*rit.* or *ritard.*) . . . . . gradually slowing.

Scherzando . . . . . . playful.

Second ending (⎾2.⎤) play second time only.

Sequence . . . . a short musical motive stated successively, beginning on different pitches.

Sharp sign (♯) . . . . . raises a note one half step; play the next key to the right, whether black or white.

Simile . . . . continue in the same manner.

Slur . . . . curved line over or under notes on different lines or spaces. Slurs mean to play legato.

Sostenuto . . . . . . sustained.

Staccato . . . . dots over or under notes meaning to play short, detached.

Subdominant . . . . . the fourth scale degree.

Subito (*sub.*) . . . . . suddenly.

Submediant . . . . . the sixth scale degree.

Supertonic . . . . . the second scale degree.

Syncopated notes . . . notes played between the main beats of a measure and held across the beat.

Tempo . . . . rate of speed.

Tenuto (–) . . . . . . hold the note for its full value.

Tetrachord . . . . . . a series of four notes having a pattern of whole step, whole step, half step.

Tied notes . . . . . . notes on the same line or space joined by a curved line and held for the combined values of both notes.

Time signatures . . . numbers found at the beginning of a piece or section
($\frac{2}{4}$, $\frac{3}{4}$, $\frac{4}{4}$, $\frac{6}{8}$, $\frac{3}{8}$) of a piece. The top number shows the number of beats in each measure. The bottom number shows the kind of note that gets one beat.

Tonic . . . . the first scale degree.

Tranquillo . . . . . . tranquil, calm.

Transpose . . . . . . perform in a key other than the original. Each pitch must be raised or lowered by precisely the same interval, which results in the change of key.

Triad . . . . three-note chord.

Vivace . . . . lively.

Vivo . . . . lively.

Whole step . . . . . . equal to two half steps; skip one key (black or white).

Appendix C

List of Compositions
(Alphabetical by Composer)

♪olo Repertoire

𝒟uet Repertoire

*E*nsemble Repertoire

Harmonizations (Titled)

List of Compositions (Alphabetical by Composer), continued

Reading (Titled)

Appendix D

List of Compositions
(Alphabetical by Title)

 olo Repertoire

$\mathcal{D}$uet Repertoire

List of Compositions (Alphabetical by Title), continued

Ensemble Repertoire

Harmonizations (Titled)

Reading (Titled)

Index (continued)